A Guide to Religious Thought and Practices

SPCK International Study Guide 45

A Guide to Religious Thought and Practices

Edited by
Santanu K. Patro

British Library Cataloguing-in-Publication Data
A catalogue record for this book is available from the British Library

ISBN 978–0–281–06250–8

10 9 8 7 6 5 4 3 2 1

Originated by The Manila Typesetting Company
Printed in Great Britain by Ashford Colour Press

Produced on paper from sustainable forests

Contents

Illustrations

Contributors

Santanu K. Patro is Professor and Head of the Department of Religions in Gurukul Lutheran Theological College and Research Institute, Chennai, India. His area of specialization is Hinduism and women's studies. Dr Patro has authored two books besides contributing several articles to leading academic journals and speaking in International Seminars. He is a member of the Baptist Church (CNI). In 2008–9 he served as visiting Professor in the Faculty of Theology, University of Hamburg, Germany. Currently he is the Dean of Graduate Studies and Convenor for Women, Dalit and Adivasi Concerns.

Shashi Bala is Professor of Guru Nanak Studies at Guru Nanak Dev University, Amritsar, India. She specializes in Indian philosophy, Sikh philosophy and comparative religion, and has published widely, including *The Concept of Monotheism: A Comparative Study of Major Religious Scriptures, Man: Being and Meaning – A Comparative Study* and *Sikh Metaphysics*.

Gillian Mary Bediako is currently the Acting Deputy Rector of the Akrofi-Christaller Institute of Theology, Mission and Culture, Akropong-Akuapem, Ghana, where she has served in various capacities for the past 20 years. She holds a PhD from the University of Aberdeen, Scotland. Her main field of interest is encounter between primal religion and Christian faith in its historical, phenomenological and theological dimensions. She is the editor of the *Journal of African Christian Thought*, and of Regnum Africa, the publishing house based at the Akrofi-Christaller Institute. Her own publications include *Primal Religion and the Bible: William Robertson Smith and his Heritage* and articles in journals and books.

Prabhakar Bhattacharyya is a Reader and former Head of the Department of Philosophy, Serampore College, West Bengal, India. Before joining the staff at Serampore College in 1996 he was for several years a Senior Research Fellow in the University of Burdwan. He was also associated with the postgraduate and doctoral programme of the Department of Religion in the North India Institute for Postgraduate Theological Studies. He is one of the programme officers of the National Service Scheme, government of India. His areas of interest include value orientation, environmental ethics and youth motivation. He has written many articles and books in Bengali and English, including *Value Orientation and Modern Society* and *Fanaticism*.

Roger Bowen has taught in the UK, Burma, Singapore, Kenya, Tanzania and Zambia. He was responsible for the Swahili theology textbook programme of the East African Association of Theological Colleges, and in retirement has been a chaplain to asylum seekers in the UK. He is author of ISG 11, *A Guide to Romans*, ISG 34, . . . *So I Send You: A Study Guide to Mission* and ISG 38, *A Guide to Preaching*.

Shanthikumar Hettiarachchi is a lecturer in religion and conflict, involved in cross-cultural relations and dialogue processes at the St Philip's Centre for Study and Engagement, Leicester, UK. He engages with Centre's numerous programmes of equipping all sections of the religious, cultural and ethnic communities. He obtained his PhD on majority–minority ethnic and religious conflict at the Melbourne College of Divinity, University of Melbourne, Australia. He is the founder-coordinator of the Luton Council of Faiths, Luton, UK, and his research interests are in diaspora communities, their religious affiliations in the UK, Europe and Australia and their social adjustment processes. He focuses on radicalization of religious faith, land, history and notions of chosen-ness as political tools to redress and quest for identity. He has published widely on related topics.

Priyadarshana Jain is a Lecturer in the Department of Jainology, University of Madras, Chennai, India.

Haifaa Jawad is Senior Lecturer in Islamic and Middle-Eastern Studies, Department of Theology and Religion, University of Birmingham, UK. In 2004 she was a visiting Professor in contemporary Islam at the University of Alabama, USA. From 2005 to 2008 she was a visiting lecturer at the Irish School of Ecumenics, Trinity College, Dublin, Ireland. She has specialized in the socio-political study of Islam, especially political or radical Islam; Islamic theology, women in Islam, British Islam, especially new Muslims; Islamic spirituality, Islamic ethics, Islam and the West, Europe and the Middle East and Middle-Eastern politics. Among her recent publications are: 'Islamic Spirituality and the Feminine Dimension', in *Women and the Divine* and 'Islamic Feminism: Leadership Roles and Public Representation' in *HAWWA: Journal of Women of the Middle East and the Islamic World*. She is currently working on 'The Contribution of European Converts to Islam: Britain as a Case Study' for Continuum International.

Ed Kessler is a leading thinker in contemporary Judaism and Jewish–Christian relations. He is founder-director of the Woolf Institute of Abrahamic Faiths, Cambridge, UK and Fellow of St Edmund's College, Cambridge. He teaches and writes on Jewish–Christian relations and is a prolific author. Kessler's publications include: *Bound by the Bible: Jews, Christians and the Sacrifice of Isaac*, *A Dictionary of Jewish–Christian Relations*, *What do Jews Believe?* and *An Introduction to Jewish–Christian Relations*. He writes for the printed media and broadcasts regularly on radio.

The SPCK International Study Guides

The International Study Guides (ISGs) are clear and accessible resources for the Christian Church. The series contains biblical commentaries, books on pastoral care, church history and theology. The guides are contextual and ecumenical in content and missional in direction.

The series is primarily aimed at those training for Christian ministries for whom English is an alternative language. Many other Christians will also find the ISGs useful guides. The contributors come from different countries and from a variety of religious backgrounds. Most of them are theological educators. They bring their particular perspectives to bear as they demonstrate the influence of other contexts on the subjects they address. They provide a practical emphasis alongside contemporary scholarly reflection.

For over forty years, the ISG series has aided those in ministerial formation to develop their own theology and discern God's mission in their context. Today, there is a greater awareness of plurality within the universal Christian body. This is reflected in changes to the series that draw upon the breadth of Christian experience across the globe.

Emma Wild-Wood
Editor, International Study Guides

Acknowledgements

It was a pleasant surprise to be invited by SPCK, London, to serve as editor for this book. SPCK recognized that a book of this nature must come from a context where many living religions are practised. India is the most religiously diverse country in the world. It also represents an emerging global power that tries to blend together science and technology on the one hand and religion and culture on the other. This blending of science and religion is her strength. While in Western societies religions are often thought to be traditional, devoid of modernity, Indians remain strongly religious in their symbolic and external manifestations. This book is written by people who are adherents of the faiths they write about. I have yet to see a multi-authored book such as this, written by scholars of religion who are also practitioners of their own faiths. This is a milestone in understanding world religions. In no way is this book an attempt to sermonize from one perspective or to suggest that one religion is superior to the others. Rather it is an attempt to describe religious thought and practice from the perspective of believers. In essence it shares the religious experiences of its contributors in order that readers may understand and appreciate people of different faiths.

The book is written as a textbook for those following introductory academic courses on world religions. It is also a book for anyone interested in learning about other religions. It does not claim to cover all religious traditions but introduces those that readers of the SPCK International Study Guides are most likely to encounter.

There were some roadblocks in the writing stage. One author pulled out; two others faced death and sickness in the family. All are in service in different capacities. It is their willingness and commitment that made this book possible, and I personally thank all of them for consenting to write the essays.

At SPCK my special thanks go to Dr Emma Wild-Wood, the commissioning editor, who provided real guidance and advice during the development of the book. I wish to thank my institution, the Gurukul Lutheran Theological College and Research Institute, Chennai, India for granting me permission to accept this project. I would be failing in my duty if I did not also thank my wife, Sujata, for her endurance and patience in putting up with my busy schedule, and also my children, for their cooperation. Above all I thank the almighty God who is, in fact, the centre of this book.

Santanu K. Patro

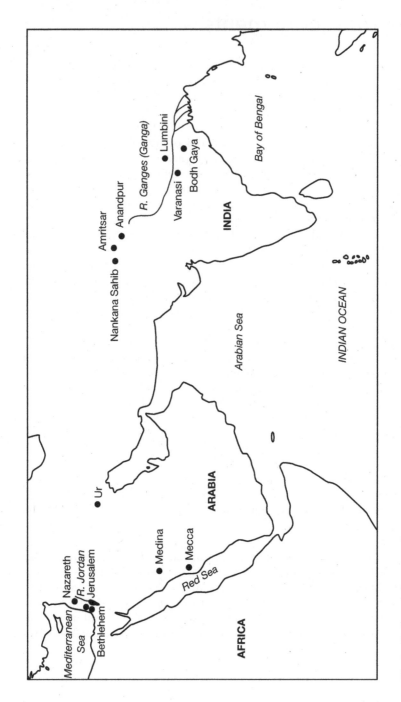

The birthplaces of major religions

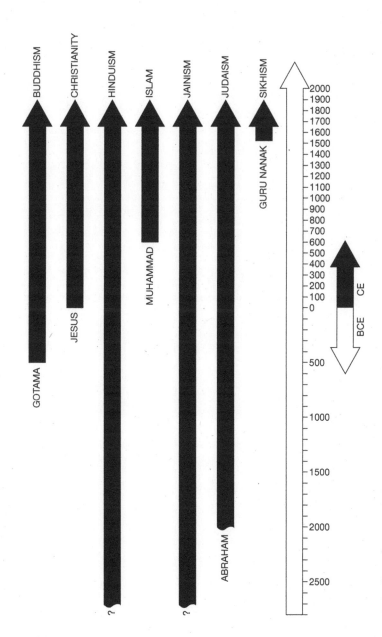

A timeline of major religions

Introduction

Santanu K. Patro

Scholars and followers of religious traditions alike take a keen interest in learning more about their own traditions and also the religious faiths and practices of their neighbours. Knowledge of other religions helps followers to understand their own faith and practice and also to appreciate the people who practise other religions. It aids understanding not only of the religious tenets but also of the religious persons. I hope that as you read this book you will learn to respect those who follow a different religious path from your own, and that you will gain insights into your own tradition.

This book is distinctive in many ways. First and foremost it is written by authors who are specialists in their fields of study. All but one are practitioners of their respective faiths, so the book is presented from the perspectives of 'insiders'. It is unapologetically written by those who consider that proper religious observance can have a vital and positive role in the contemporary world. They have endeavoured to provide an insight into their own religions that explains the historical development and the best expressions of their traditions. Second, the book therefore attempts to bring the approaches of insiders to bear on a subject that remains greatly misunderstood in academia. Written at a time when there is a global rise in interest, it challenges some of the secular assumptions of the study of religion. Third, the book is gender inclusive. As many as four of the essays are written by women, whose experiences, and those of women in general, make a significant contribution to this volume. They have remained conscious of the influence of men in the spheres of religion and, in my opinion, have sometimes been too generous to male endeavour, probably because of their reliance on the interpretations of men.

It is challenging to make the book relevant to both students of religion and the followers of religion, to comprehend the 'inside' of a religion while making the study of it as an academic discipline. The main objective is to allow both kinds of readers to gain a more authentic understanding of religions. This book does not claim to be exhaustive. The scope and size are limited, and it has not been possible to include all religious traditions. However, I hope that it will encourage you to engage in further reading and to participate in religious activities in order to gain more understanding of those professing different faiths from your own, and enable you to ask questions of each other in a spirit of mutual respect. This respect will stem from a shared acceptance of the flawed nature of our desire to understand God – for all religious traditions fall short of achieving their own high ideals. If this is achieved I think the purpose of writing a book of this nature will have been fulfilled.

The academic study of religion

The academic study of religions enables readers to gain a more objective understanding of other religions. Knowledge about religion is received not only through discourse and teaching as an insider, but also by studying a religion as an outsider in order to gain a better grasp of other people's religions. Students of religious traditions had to work hard to establish their discipline as an autonomous branch of study. They were influenced by the Enlightenment movement in the West and had to respond to students of science who pronounced that religion was dead. Academic study has attempted to provide rational world-views of religious belief and practice. It recognizes that spiritual consciousness exists in human communities. It is possible that followers of religions today may not hold the same world-view that originally evolved. However, they continue to engage in religion by reinterpreting their faith and religious practice according to the given context. Thus religion is still relevant and vibrant and continues to influence human society, although assessments about the extent of its influence may differ.

Even if some do not subscribe to any particular faith, they are guided by ethical and moral principles that have evolved from, and are defined by, religion. Many academics in the last century thought religion was dying out, but in the twenty-first century there has been greater recognition of its durability and the prominence of its role in most societies of the world. The huge progress made in science and technology has not eroded religion from society. Although secularists and fundamentalists have often portrayed science and religion as opposing forces, this view is not held by most religious people. Rather by constantly responding to new world-views, religion has manifested itself in new forms, helping believers to find a new understanding of religion.

Chapter 1 of this book examines the development of the study of religion as an autonomous discipline through the evolution of various approaches and methodologies. Since religion involves all spheres of life, its study relies on all branches of human and natural sciences. Students of religions in the last two centuries have contributed enormously to methodology by using anthropology, sociology, psychology, philosophy and theology. A variety of approaches help students of religion to deepen their understanding of a religion as an 'insider', and this in turn helps them to view other religions as understood by religious persons. I consider that religion can only be understood completely when one becomes an insider. Since we cannot become followers of all religious traditions, I recommend that religious persons must allow themselves to be exposed to other religions as much as possible and to hold back on presupposition and judgement. When we try and walk in the shoes of another we develop a different perspective that may enrich our lives and relationship with God. Walking in the shoes of another also puts us in a better position to ask questions.

> What do you understand by the phrase 'walking in the shoes of another'? How might you do this?

 ## Religion and society

No matter how secular our society appears to be, religion continues to play a significant role in public life. My own country, India, is a case in point. This young democracy is also the world's largest, and is home to many religions and ideologies. As a result, religion plays an important role in social functions. In the Christian West, religion was increasingly understood as a private affair of the individual; many assumed it would cease to exist. Yet recently Western analysts have reassessed their opinion of religion as personal and private, although many still regard it with suspicion. It is my contention that if human community is to survive along with its environment, religion has to be taken seriously in mainstream academic as well as social life. On the critical issue of climate change, for example, religions can have a key role to play in preserving and nurturing nature. If life lies at the core of every faith, then respect and protection are the fundamentals for sustaining life. Practitioners of different religious traditions understand that care and compassion for all creatures and the promotion of ethical values and human harmony lie at the heart of their religion. In some parts of the world such claims are disputed by atheists, but a careful study of religious traditions can refute their scepticism. It must be acknowledged, however, that much religious practice in history has not achieved the high ideals found among its teachings.

> How do you understand your religious tradition as promoting equality and preserving life? How well do followers carry this out? How do you see other religious traditions promoting these values?
>
> Can you give examples of religious practice within your own tradition that have fallen short of the best way of living promoted by that tradition?

Religion has much in common with the culture of a society. The non-scriptural, non-philosophical manifestations of religion are present in every culture. Within the value system of any given culture there are inbuilt religious elements. For example, the social structures – the hierarchy, values and ethics – of a society are determined by religious faith and practice. Core cultural behaviour will carry strong religious currents within it. The subtle interaction between religion and culture may mislead us into thinking that culture has replaced religion, but in a real sense religion persists through culture. The institutions and structures may take different shapes, but religion continues to influence and define culture in many societies across the globe. While Christianity is growing outside the Western world, Islam and Hinduism are also now flourishing in the West. They are re-defining religion by making their presence felt in a area that was previously almost uniquely Christian. All of them adapt to their settings and are gradually influencing the host culture. It is this ability of religion to adapt to circumstances that enables it to survive and continue in every adverse situation.

> Think of the social structures and values where you live. How are they influenced by religious traditions? What traditions have the greatest influence? Why is this?

There are many who do not want to see religion take public space. Their concerns raise questions about how religion can operate in a secular society. A distinction here should be made between the ideology of secularism, which is totally devoid of religious ideals, and secular societies, which attempted to avoid religious criteria for their governance but which are influenced by their religious history and the contemporary practice of the members of those societies. Thus secular society is not totally devoid of religious ideals, though secularism as an ideology is. Therefore secular society is not an antithesis to religious community, rather together they can help promote a single human community. Many religious communities feel that religion has the ability to contribute to the secular ethos without reducing religion to a secondary role. Yet some sections of the religious community push hard to impose ideals – their own – that are detrimental to the health of the human community, understanding religion purely as a communalist/nationalist entity, with nothing to contribute to the promotion of an inclusive and pluralistic society. Such an aggressive and violent posture has been coercive and at times counterproductive. It is impossible in today's world to hold the view that religion is territorial, since religions have moved beyond their 'home-territory'. For example, Hinduism and Judaism have, for different reasons, moved outside their territories. Both these religions have contextualized their faiths, and many of their members have downplayed any parochialism. It is often the power of the majority that makes for coercive politics. When Hindus became a majority after the partition of India and Pakistan in 1947, their faith became more exclusive.

As a student of religion, I see that at the heart of religious traditions is an endeavour to promote harmony, equality and justice. To achieve this aim we must discourage the institutionalizing of religion through the coercion of the state. For then religion becomes closely associated with the moral compromises that all states make. The credentials of some secular states equally should be questioned. Although many states constitutionally declare themselves to be secular, nevertheless they promote one particular religion and use religious symbols in public places and religious rituals in state ceremonies. The promotion of the religion of the majority threatens the rights and faiths of the minority. In a changing geopolitical structure, religious teachings on equality, justice and harmony must be highlighted. The right to human freedom and dignity are essential in order to practise one's own faith without any prejudice or threat.

Do you agree that 'religion is an endeavour to promote harmony, equality and justice'? What else might you add to that definition? Would it be true of all religions?

What do you think the relationship between religions and states should be? How does your own context influence your answer?

Historical movements of religious traditions

Primal religious traditions

Primal religions are the most misunderstood of all the religions practised today. Their traditions are the mothers of all religions, yet they have often been construed as a 'bunch of superstitions'. The author of Chapter 2 on primal religions, Dr Mary Bediako, a Christian from Ghana, has a profound experience of primal religious traditions and is deeply engaged in dialogue between these traditions and Christianity. Students of religion still struggle to find an appropriate classification for religions scattered across the globe. Although these religions have never come into contact with each other they have nevertheless evolved certain common features, such as ancestral veneration. For want of adequate description scholars use the term 'primal religious traditions', suggesting that they are the first form of religion that existed among the first human communities. This form of religious structure finds its continuity in almost all religious traditions. For example, the understanding of god, prophet, spirit, rituals, worship and so on are the continuity from primal religious traditions. The only difference is that while they are found in crude and oral forms in primal tradition, in modern religions they are made complex by elaborate scriptural traditions.

Primal religions have been denigrated because of an absence of any 'written' tradition. They have been threatened by the religions of foreign invaders, such as Christianity in most parts of the world except Asia Minor, Islam in Africa and Asia, and Hinduism and Buddhism in India and South-East Asia. Yet the world religions have often benefited from contact with primal religions by receiving extra-scriptural sources and traditions that enliven their beliefs and practices. For example, Buddhism in Korea was influenced by Shamanism, and the Aryan form of Hinduism incorporated existing faiths from the pre-Aryan period, including Dravidian traditions, thus enabling it to embrace non-Aryan people in its fold through the caste system. Christianity replaced the religions of Africa and the Amerindians, though it was not able to remove totally the primal world-views. Islam followed in the footsteps of Christianity in Africa, Central Asia and South-East Asia. Some have called these elements syncretistic and have attempted to banish them, but as Bediako shows with the example of Christianity, the faith is enriched by such influences.

If world religions were to be divided according to their features and structures, Hinduism, Buddhism, Jainism and Sikhism would represent one family, having all emerged in India. Judaism, Christianity and Islam may be grouped as another family, being strongly embedded in the culture of the Ancient Near East. There is yet another group of religions, found mostly within homogenous people groups of South-East Asia, which are interconnected with nature, geography, culture and nationality. Within this group comes Taoism, Shinto and Shamanism which, for want of space, we have not dealt with in this volume. By and large they subscribe to the features of the primal religious traditions, but their contact with modern religions, such as Buddhism, has had an impact on them. In turn, their religious practices have influenced Buddhism.

What primal religious traditions do you know? How have they influenced other religions?

From primal religious people to people of land

Alongside the primal religious traditions that existed among the tribals and Dalits – those excluded from the caste system – in my own country of India, there were four major religions of the world: Hinduism, Buddhism, Jainism and Sikhism. India is also home to almost all the other religions, Christians and Muslims making up roughly 15 per cent of the population. It has the second-largest Muslim population in the world and is significant for being the most religiously diverse of nations.

Hinduism claims to be the most accommodating and inclusive of religions. At the same time, traditionally a Hindu is Hindu by descent, and Hindus take seriously the sacredness of the land, nature and environment of the Indian subcontinent. The religion is supposed to be redundant when it crosses over the seas. It had very little allowance for 'foreigners' to own fully the Hindu religious tenets. However, as Dr Prabhakar Bhattacharyya demonstrates in Chapter 3 on Hinduism, we have seen a marked change in approach over the last century when religion as an ideology became more adaptable. Determined not to be left behind by Islam and Christianity, Hinduism has gradually become a missionary faith. The Gurus – the god-men and god-women – have in the last 50 years reinterpreted their religion and have systematized the teachings, judiciously ignoring those that promoted social and racial segregation. In particular, they denounced the age-old practice of the caste system. Today, there are more Tribal peoples and Dalits embracing Hinduism than ever before.

A religion having certain things in common with Hinduism is Judaism. It emerged at more or less the same time; the people groups of each faith moved from place to place before finally settling in their respective territories; and their religions are named after their land and people. As with the Hindus, the land is sacred to the religious life of the Jews. The difference with Judaism is that it has a strong monotheistic concept. It is the religion of the Twelve Tribes, named after the twelve sons of Jacob, and today the land is known as Israel (the name God gave to Jacob in a dream). As Ed Kessler demonstrates in Chapter 6 on Judaism, the religion has strong ethical teachings, and its political, religious and social life is very much dependent on the laws that were developed over time. In the Ancient Near East, followers of the faith were surrounded by people who engaged in other religious practices, and the Jews, or Israelites, had to fight with them to maintain the integrity of their land and religion. Although Jews now live all over the world, modern Judaism continues to be connected to this land, Israel. There are many who return to live there so that the expected messiah might return.

What is the importance of land in your own culture? How does this influence your religious tradition? How does it influence the religious traditions of others?

New religious teachers

In time, within religions with an emphasis on sacred land and on the created world, religious teachers could introduce new ideas, thus creating separate religious traditions. Judaism and Hinduism take land and creation very seriously – as much as primal religious traditions. With the coming of Buddhism we see teachers with their ideologies and philosophies leading religious movements. The first and most prominent among them is Gotama Buddha. Buddhism, Jainism, Christianity, Islam and Sikhism were all led by strong religious personalities who are accorded great status in their traditions. These personalities were responding to the particular socio-religious context of their time. For example, Christianity responded to Judaism, which was an exclusive nationalist religion found in the Ancient Near East. Jesus responded to Judaism from within it by confronting certain practices. His first followers were Jews who believed he was the leader who had been foretold and that his message was for all people. Christianity was the name given to the movement of Jesus well after his death. Similarly, both Buddhism and Jainism were revolts against Hinduism in their rejections of Vedic and Brahmanic authority, and later they founded separate religions. Islam originated as a counter-movement to Christianity and Judaism, both of which were understood to lack the fulfilment that Islam offered. The Sikh faith evolved in response to the presence of Hinduism and Islam in India. Historically all religions emerged as counter-movements that challenged and reinterpreted the religious status quo. For this reason these new movements were regarded as sectarian in their religious pursuit.

Buddhism was described by Swami Vivekananda as the 'rebellious child of Hinduism'. In many senses this is true. Though Buddhism was born in the Indian subcontinent, it flourished better in other parts of Asia. In the middle of the twentieth century it was resurrected in India in response to the struggle of the Dalits, who embraced Buddhism in protest against the Hindu caste system. Buddhism in the West is known better as an ideology than a religion. More and more people are attracted to its teachings because it provided less a structure than a spiritual ideal. Shanthikumar Hettiarachchi, in Chapter 4 on Buddhism, begins by saying, 'Buddhism is a way of life' because it prescribes a middle way with a spirituality that is socially responsible. Buddhists take seriously their ethical, social, psychological and philosophical world-view. Questions about God and revelation are not important, though they are useful concepts in inquiry. What is more important is the ultimate bliss of emancipation.

Jainism is also an ideology, as its teachings do not appear to be exclusive to the Jains. The faith emerged alongside Buddhism and brought about a revolution by challenging the existing faith, Hinduism, particularly in emphasizing 'relative pluralism' and the equality of all people. It stresses the importance of both the sacred and the secular and provides space for spirituality as well as material world-views. It maintains the importance of knowledge because this lies at the source of discrimination and the distinction between good and bad – Jainism provides a clearer understanding of dualism than other faiths offer. And it is the religion of the environment. As Priyadarshana Jain explains in Chapter 5 on Jainism, it is the relationship of the creatures that sustains the universe, and therefore their creation and destruction is unequivocally connected to *karma* theory.

In the past many books on world religions omitted Christianity because their readership was expected to be familiar with it. More recently, scholars have realized that Christianity, in all its forms, is also important for readers, both Christian and non-Christian, since there is a growing interest in other parts of the world about religions and a growing ignorance of Christianity where it has traditionally been familiar. In recent times, Christianity has grown faster in the non-Western world than in Europe. In Chapter 7 on Christianity, Roger Bowen explains that it is important that we understand Christianity also as a non-Western phenomenon.

Islam is the second-largest religion of the world and the fastest-growing faith, particularly in sub-Saharan Africa and Asia, but also in Europe and North America. The Prophet Muhammad's religion was simple and straight-forward. In Chapter 8 on Islam, Haifaa Jawad explains that the religious tenets and practices of Islam are non-discriminatory and that it has a strong community orientation. The ethics and laws that were recorded in *Hadith* (traditions) are meant for social cohesion and the delivery of justice, al-though certain interpretations and conflicts of social values have given the impression to some that Islam is an intolerant and violent religion – an understanding Jawad refutes.

Sikhism, which emerged in India in the fifteenth century, is the youngest religion examined in this book. It is the religion that was influenced both by Hinduism and Islam. Islam was already a major player in Indian religious and cultural life during the time of Guru Nanak, who wanted a religious expression that was more inclusive than that offered by the Hinduism and Islam of his day. Guru Nanak could rightly be called the precursor to all the later Guru Movement that emerged in India, particularly from the late nine-teenth century. Guru Nanak rejected the Hindu caste system and taught the formless God, a concept borrowed from Hinduism but incorporating the Islamic concept of God. In Chapter 9 on Sikhism, Shashi Bala emphasizes that scripture is central to the life and faith of the Sikh people. It was the first religion from the Indian subcontinent to carry such an emphasis, so much so that its scripture, which is personified as *Guru Granth Sahib*, is venerated as a divine being in *gurdwaras*. In a way it replaces the formless Ultimate Reality of Hinduism.

What role do religious leaders play today? Do you know leaders who are attempting to reform their tradition radically from within?

 ## Commonalities and communities

By looking at the various religions and their teachings, readers will find how unique each is in its essence and outward aspects – as well as what they have in common. All religions have the idea of the divine as their starting point. It is transcendental and beyond any human description. Nobody has fathomed it, religious teachers, prophets and messiahs attempted to define or point the way to the divine, but it remains mysterious. Studying a religion or group of religions often allows practitioners of another religion to widen their understanding of the divine as they seek to understand the comprehension of others.

But religious search does not end in God alone – it moves to human community. Though God is defined in scripture and the teachings of great seers, God is better understood in the context of believers. Each religion creates its own distinct faith community precisely because the religions have spread in particular ways, depending on the socio-cultural and geographical context. One influential factor of religion is that it gives hope of new life. Such new life may come by way of the doctrine of *moksha/nirvana* as found in the religions of the East, or that of salvation/liberation as found in Judaism, Christianity and Islam. In addressing the issues of life and death, religion also gives meaning and purpose to living and to the created order. Creation is at the core of all religions, since God is the supreme creator of the world. For many practitioners the religious experience of caring, sharing and nurturing the earth remains key to building a new society.

As we read the essays contributed by the practitioners of religion, we ask the following questions: Is religion still relevant in the scientific and modern world? Why are people still attracted to religion? Does religion offer anything substantial to life?

A second set of questions would ask: Is my faith inclusive or exclusive of other faiths? Should I attempt to make my religion more inclusive? Do I have anything to learn from others? What elements would I want to share of my own faith?

A third set of questions concerns the ethical and social attributions of society: How can we eradicate the ills of our society? Are religions able to offer something where other systems have failed? In what ways can we solve the problems that confront us from a religious perspective?

There is no straightforward answer to any of the questions. They are questions for reflection and exploration, questions to ask again and again. I have only tried to point to ways of answering them by presenting religious traditions more optimistically than they are often presented. I do so as a student of religion and as a practitioner of my own faith who experiences sanctity in everyday life.

 Further reading

Fisher, Mary Pat, *Living Religions: An Encyclopaedia of the World's Faiths* (London: Tauris, 1997).

Hinnells, John R. (ed.), *A Handbook of Living Religions* (Harmondsworth: Penguin, 1984, 1990).

1

Definitions, approaches and methodologies in the study of religions

Santanu K. Patro

 Introduction

In the recent past the study of religions has been established as an independent discipline, thanks to the development of the scientific approach. Ever since the study of religion became a discipline independent of Christian theology in Europe and North America, students have been keen to examine it from different perspectives. New theoretical approaches and definitions have developed, and methodological tools evolved in the study of religious traditions. Today, the world's religious traditions are studied as an academic discipline. This chapter will briefly explain the different disciplines engaged in the study of religion as they attempt to answer questions like: What is religion? How does a particular religion operate? It will then outline a methodological approach. In doing this, a number of prominent thinkers will briefly be mentioned. First I raise some difficulties encountered as scholars attempted to define what it was they wanted to study.

 Definitions

Ever since the study of religion became an independent discipline in universities, students of religions have been grappling with issues of definitions. Scientific study based on 'rationalism' and 'empiricism' finds religious traditions a difficult proposition. How can we define what is not 'concrete' data? This poses a serious doubt, not about the subject matter, but about the scientific base for its study. For Wilfred Cantwell Smith the very term 'religion' is 'monolithic and static'. He is not against defining an academic study of religion, but maintains that it should be about the 'living traditions', the faith components of believers. Words like 'faith' and 'traditions' convey that religions are living, vibrant and dynamic. A study need not fall within the framework of rationalism and empiricism. Definitions arise by studying the living religious communities and traditions. Such data will be fluid and changing. It can meet the objectives of serious study but will not provide an exhaustive definition.

The study of religion

Studies are made in many ways and from many perspectives. Often they are guided by the scholars' branch of specialization, such as anthropology, philosophy, sociology, theology, psychology, phenomenology and so on. Therefore it is important to see the various studies of religions from their different disciplinary perspectives.

The early phase of the scientific study of religion was primarily classified into three broad parts – history of religion, comparative religion and philosophy of religion – that often related to each other. The history of religion approach tested the authenticity of the data of religious traditions. By using comparisons, these historical materials were systematically classified. Then they were interpreted from a philosophical perspective.

One of the founders of the contemporary study of religions, Max Müller (1823–1900), used comparative mythology as a scientific tool. After establishing the historicity of other religious traditions, he rejected Christian claims that divine revelation was exclusive to Christianity. His comparative studies marked the beginning of a system of comparative philosophy, mythology and even theology. P. D. Chantepie de la Saussaye (1848–1920), another formative scholar in contemporary religious study, pursued his interest in the philosophy of religion by examining the awe towards the sacred experienced by adherents. However, he found it extremely difficult to handle such subjective data in philosophy. For him all deductive knowledge must begin by studying the manifestations of religious phenomena through historical, comparative and empirical methods.

Anthropology of religion

Anthropology of religion emphasizes that religious traditions are not just conceptual belief systems but rather a way of life in which beliefs are embedded in and formed by the practices of faith – the rituals, symbols and religious artefacts. Anthropology attempts to analyse the system of meanings that exist in religious symbols, and their relationship to society. Some anthropologists took a functionalist approach. This means that they were less interested in the origin of religion and more concerned with what these beliefs and practices do for individuals and societies.

Radcliffe-Brown's *The Andaman Islanders* (1922) was a classic example of interdisciplinary scholarship, combining sociology with psychology. Radcliffe-Brown insisted that the function of religion is to support society's cultural system.

Social anthropologists, such as E. E. Evans-Pritchard, see an awareness of the development through history as an important tool of analysis when studying language and experience. So anthropology of religion involves the observation of social life, its structures and patterns. An observation of religion helps to determine the nature of the society in question. The discipline is therefore primarily an interpretative method. It studies all aspects of culture: myths, folklores, symbols, rites, beliefs and language. Claude Lévi-Strauss analysed the complex and interrelated systems of society, understanding religious structures as the basis of social phenomena, such as kinship, marriage and language. He maintained that seemingly dissimilar belief systems had the same underlying structures. This structuralist approach has been criticized as reducing religious phenomena to mere systems of culture. It cannot fully explain religious myths, symbols, folklore and beliefs, although seeing religious traditions as part of the structure of cultures can demonstrate the ways in which religion is used to communicate knowledge and control behaviour.

Psychology of religion

The study of the psychology of religion emphasizes the varieties of religious experience. It looks at the importance of religion for the individual, and the range of religious manifestations. It is unique among the scientific approaches in that it places the upmost priority on the person's religious quests. Psychologists of religion go beyond reason and recognize that there is a force, consciousness, which tries to apprehend the infinite in a limited way. They consider that religion deals primarily with those human experiences that go beyond our understanding. In *The Varieties of Religious Experience*, William James (1842–1910) based his thesis on empirical data gained by case study. He defined religious experience as gradual, unified consciousness, through which the person grasps spiritual realities.

Experiences of the infinite recounted by religious people arise from feelings of awe, fear and fascination in the presence of the sacred, which Rudolf Otto defined as the *mysterium transcendum*. Such sacred experience suggests the idea of the holy that encounters reason and accommodates morality. Those who have had such experiences are understood to bring them into their daily lives, to infuse the ordinary, everyday with the sacred – a dialectical relationship that changes the understanding of both parts of life.

The fundamental questions that concern the psychology of religion are those that relate religious experience to social and psychological behaviour. To this end, it observes individuals' religious experiences and religious traditions. Yet experience alone cannot be the criterion of religiosity. Studies should also take into consideration other religious phenomena, such as doctrine, dogma, rites and rituals.

Sociology of religion

Early sociologists of religion regarded religion as the mainspring in the functioning of human society. The discipline emphasizes the dimension of power and social change; it also stresses the sources of social and psychological integration. Michael Hill observes that the study of religion has four main areas: religious organizations; religion and social change; religion and social cohesion; an integration of the three. Some sociologists of religion recognize religion simply as a way of maintaining social cohesion. Others recognize that it plays this role among others.

Émile Durkheim is concerned with social reality and sees religion as an agent of collectivity. For him social life is inherently religious. Rituals are the celebrations of social life, and through them a group affirms social solidarity. He also claims that religious traditions are solely the product of society and have no basis in revelation.

Max Weber, though, accepts the idea that the belief system begins with the supernatural. He finds a link between religion and such cultural institutions as economic behaviour. His case study of Protestant ethics investigated the relationship between Calvinism and early forces of capitalism. Opposing Weber, Karl Marx (1818–83) claimed that religion is only an ideological superstructure supporting the class system. To him, religion is always concerned with the self, a self that cannot fully grasp socio-economic realities and therefore does not address them adequately. It has been observed that while Marx regarded religion as a social smokescreen, and Weber saw it as a social starter-motor, Durkheim saw religion primarily as a form of social cement.

Theology of religion

The theology of religion was first developed by Christian scholars studying the religions of others in the light of Christian theology. The need for Christian theology to interact with other religious traditions has helped it to understand the myths and symbols of those traditions, as well as helping those traditions to interpret such myths and symbols from an inclusive perspective. Theology of religion today focuses on religious pluralism. Cantwell Smith insists that dialogue must become more universal in order to arrive at a global theology: a dialogue not only between Jews, Christians and Muslims but between Hindus and Christians – broadly speaking, between the Oriental and Semitic faiths. The theology of religion aims to acknowledge the claims of other religious traditions and understand them to be distinct. Tolerance is needed, not just towards other faiths but towards their theological interpretations as well. The theology of religion has often been dominated by Christian terminology and assumptions. In recent years attempts have been made to develop categories that are better shared by all religious traditions.

Philosophy of religion

Philosophy is the oldest discipline used to study religion. Immanuel Kant (1724–1804) argued that the philosophy of religion evaluates religious concepts, beliefs and practice within a framework of morality. Friedrich Schleiermacher (1768–1834) broadly agreed but refused to accept that religions could be reduced to moral life alone. Georg Hegel (1770–1831) went further and said that religious concepts and beliefs are embedded in particular traditions and can only be understood in the context of their culture. For Ludwig Feuerbach (1804–72) religion is a human product, a projection of the imagination. He and Marx felt that religious beliefs are an idealized projection of people's hopes, fear and desires. Today philosophy of religion has moved on from defining abstract ideological understandings of the ultimate reality to attempting a more classified understanding of religious life.

# Methodology

Having discussed a number of disciplines that include the study of religion, it is now appropriate to look at the systematic study of religion as an independent discipline, but one that draws on the disciplines mentioned already but employs a specific method of its own. The methodology of the study of religion is both historical and phenomenological.

A religion has meaning in a contemporary context in part because of its connections with the past. The study of the history of religions examines events in the past. This historical approach is brought to bear on other parts of the methodology, such as attention to believers' interpretations, in order to gain a broader understanding. A history of religion goes beyond articulating meanings. The task of phenomenology of religion is to classify widely divergent religious data in such a way that an overall view can be obtained about its religious content and value. It provides a method for investigating the ways in which we know reality. On its own, phenomenology of religion can be subjective, but when studied alongside history it provides a critical approach to the study. There are six methodological resources used in the study of religion, which are described here in brief.

Description

A systematic treatment of the religious traditions is gained by describing accurately the tradition and the meanings and structures as understood by believers. Description needs insight and intuition, giving due consideration to the nature of the data and to its own place of reference. Historical study does not tell the reader what is true or false, but it must evaluate the historical data in order to understand the phenomenon more critically.

Understanding

For the religious historian understanding is central to all insights. Scholars must exercise respect and tolerance for all religions and recognize where commitment to a particular faith might influence their understanding of the thoughts, feelings and actions of members of a different faith tradition. One way of doing this is to participate in the life and the rituals of the religious tradition under study. The task of deep understanding involves creative and objective participation that includes having a critical and unbiased attitude. But there are certain limitations. How can we understand fully the experience of another person through participation? Though there is no simple answer, we must avoid presuppositions if we are going to participate meaningfully.

Epoche

The literal meaning of *epoche* is 'abstraction' or 'suspension of judgement'. By suspending judgement, we try to interpret a phenomenon just as it is, and to free ourselves from our presuppositions. *Epoche* enables us to put ourselves in the position of the believer. It does not question the truth of religious tradition, but rather listens to the experiences of truth that the believer describes. This is an important step to take because religious people are as important as religious doctrine. It is through believers that beliefs, doctrine and rituals have survived through history. In taking this approach we are aiming to avoid judging the value of a religious tradition. For the convinced believers of a different tradition this can appear difficult and even dangerous. However, the suspension of judgement can better equip students to engage in comparative theological debate about relative values at a later stage, because they have honestly tried to understand a different tradition.

Eidetic vision and intention

The term 'eidetic vision' is derived from a Greek noun, *to eidòs*, meaning 'that which is seen', and hence also means 'form', 'shape' or 'essence'. In phenomenological parlance, eidetic vision is the observer's capacity to see the essentials of a situation. Having suspended prior judgements in the *epoche* stage, eidetic intuition investigates the meaning of a religious phenomenon and its relevance to believers. Its ultimate objective is to gain insight into the essence of the forms and structures of religious traditions.

Anti-reductionism

Anti-reductionism is a strategy aimed at avoiding reducing religious content to a mere academic category during investigations. Though any amount of description might not be capable of fully explaining a religious phenomenon, one must exercise restraint when interpreting the description of the believers. Anti-reductionism demands that a religious tradition be understood in its own context of reference.

Personal dimensions and experience

The study of religion must have a 'personal' approach. We will never be able to describe the essence of religious traditions unless we give due consideration to the experiences of individual believers. Their experiences provide a continuity of religious traditions from the past to the present. Personal faith is the core of truth. Therefore it is essential that investigations lead us to understand the religious person. The search for objective truth and personal dimensions of a religious faith must go hand in hand in the study of the history of religion.

 Conclusion

The study of religion, its historical development and methodological issues, should help not only to understand one's own religion, but also those of others. Students should not assume that they are capable of discovering everything about a religious tradition if they do not belong to the religious tradition they are studying. At the same time, they should not shy away from such work, as long as the methodological tools are employed with sincerity and integrity. This helps to understand and strengthen scholarship.

It is my conviction that the careful and thorough study of religions is of great practical benefit in a multi-faith world. A greater understanding of each other can encourage not simply an empty tolerance of difference but also a peaceful and harmonious life together. Gaining a respectful appreciation of another's religion enables us to develop an understanding of those also created in the image of God, and thus broaden our experience of the divine. Serious scholarship can bring a positive perspective to bear, demonstrate the contributions religious traditions bring to the world and further enhance those contributions.

 QUESTIONS

1 What religious tradition would you like to understand? How might you apply the methodology mentioned here to its study?

2 Some people think that studying another religious tradition following this methodology might be seen as a betrayal of their own faith. How would you answer this concern?

Further reading

Kitagawa, Joseph M. and Eliade, Mircea (eds), *The History of Religions: Essays in Methodology* (Chicago: University of Chicago Press, 1959).

Whaling, Frank (ed.), *Contemporary Approaches to the Study of Religion*, 2 vols (The Hague: Mouton, 1984).

2

Primal religious thought and practice

Gillian Mary Bediako

 ## Introduction: a brief account of misunderstanding

From the fifteenth century onwards, when Europeans became increasingly aware of other peoples, their religions and their cultures, the primal religious traditions of the world have been the most misunderstood and underestimated of all the religious traditions that they encountered. For a long time it was a common view in the West that the primal religions of the world reflected the presumed backward and primitive nature of the people who practised them. Primal religion was held to be the very opposite of Christian faith.

While there were many derogatory terms used to describe these religious traditions, including 'primitive', 'savage', 'heathen darkness' and 'superstition', it was the term 'Animism' that became dominant. This term was invented by the nineteenth-century British anthropologist, E. B. Tylor, to describe the religious systems of traditional societies, which he presumed to be lacking in the morality and ethics that educated persons of his time considered the heart of practical religion. Of course, for Tylor, modern persons needed to progress beyond religion altogether. For him Christianity, with its belief in spiritual reality, was also animistic!

At the World Missionary Conference held in Edinburgh in 1910, Tylor's term was used by Western missionaries to describe the religious beliefs of the 'more or less backward and degraded' peoples all over the world. Animism was described as 'the humblest of all possible teachers . . . and the least sublime of all the five great creeds' – by which was meant Chinese religions, religions of Japan, Islam, Hinduism and Animism. Animism was held by many missionary participants to provide no preparation for the Christian gospel and even to have 'no religious content'.

While one would no longer speak in such negative terms about the primal religions of the world, Animism continues as the preferred term for primal religion in some circles, and primal religions continue to be misunderstood, underestimated and misrepresented. The sense of hierarchy of religions still exists, hence greater respect is given to the religions of so-called higher civilizations – Hinduism and Buddhism, for example, or to the so-called monotheistic faiths of Islam, Judaism and Christianity – and especially those that have written scriptures. Even where the perspective on the world's religions is one that considers all to be of value, there is still a perception of contrast, such that primal religions are seen as belonging to archaic modes of existence. Among the outcomes of this are a lesser interest in dialogue with the primal religions and the small amount of space devoted to them in general studies of the world's religions. A further outcome is that it has been rare until quite recently for educated persons from a primal background to believe that those traditions have much to contribute to the modern world.

Yet all this obscures the reality, which has been well expressed by one of the most perceptive modern Western scholars of primal religion, Andrew Walls: 'All believers, and for that matter, non-believers, are primalists underneath.' This implies, for him, not only 'their historical anteriority and their basic, elemental status in human experience', but also that 'all other faiths are subsequent and represent, as it were, second thoughts'. In other words, primal religion constitutes the fundamental substratum to all subsequent religious experience. It provides universal, basic elements of human understanding of the transcendent or divine realm and the world, essential and valid religious insights that may be built upon or suppressed, but that cannot be superseded.

This chapter defines primal religions and demonstrates their vitality in the contemporary world. It provides a framework that will be helpful in appreciating their place across the globe, and suggests some commonalties between different expressions. The focus towards the end of the chapter is on African primal religions and their interface with Christianity, particularly in Ghana. However, much that is said in these specific examples is true of primal religions elsewhere in the non-Western world.

Issues in defining and naming

But what is meant by 'primal', and why has it been selected over other terms? It should be stated from the outset that primal does not mean primitive, nor does it suggest evolutionary development. Primal means more than primeval or archetypal or archaic, for it gives account of an enduring consciousness of the spiritual nature of the universe, which translates into coherent religious beliefs and ways of living religiously that retain their essential validity today.

The dominant view in the academic disciplines of anthropology and religious studies has tended to deny the existence of an overarching primal religious consciousness and to insist that one should think in terms of autonomous indigenous traditional religions as the only way to take them seriously in their own right. Yet this more recent Western view treats as of no account the history of dynamic interaction with other religious traditions, in which the primal has been an active contributor rather than a passive absorber. For it is this history, as well as the desire to convey something of the enduring nature of the primal consciousness, that form part of the rationale for the term.

For some the term 'indigenous religion' is more helpful because it does justice to the common experience of continuity of peoples and places, the common centrality of elders and ancestors as custodians of tradition, and the common veneration of particular lands. It also gives account of the wide-spread colonial experience of genocide and expulsion faced by indigenous people. While this accurately identifies important common perspectives within the primal world-view, as well as common tragic experiences, the term gives no account of the wide-ranging and enduring religious consciousness that has survived the vicissitudes of history, nor does it adequately convey the contribution that primal religion and world-view make within subsequent religious traditions.

In the Asian context, where the primal religions have often been overlaid with later religious traditions such as Hinduism and Buddhism, they have been called 'cosmic religions', in which the highest good is sought among the transcendent and sacramental mysteries of life. They are understood as the inherent and essential basis of 'metacosmic religions', in which salvation is located in the 'beyond'. These distinctions are not absolute, and many primal religions in Africa, for example, do have the concept of a more perfect afterlife. The point to note here is that metacosmic religion, far from being 'superior', cannot exist without the religiousness of cosmic religion, whereas cosmic religion can and does exist without the metacosmic. The terms cosmic and metacosmic are English renderings of Buddhist categories, which are captured in indigenous languages such as Sinhalese. The availability of such terminology indicates that the process of defining and naming primal religion may be enhanced as persons outside the West enter the debate, drawing on their own religious experience and reflection.

Although the use of the term primal has been criticized at several points, it is still the best available at present for describing these varied, yet common, religious traditions around the world. As Andrew Walls asks, 'How else are we to bring together the religions of the circumpolar peoples, of various peoples of Africa, the Indian subcontinent, South-East Asia, Inner Asia, North and South America, Australia and the Pacific?'

Primal is thus intended as a positive term that does justice to the fact that these religions are prior to all other religious traditions and underlie them all. The term also bears witness to the undeniable family likeness among the varied indigenous religious traditions around the world and down through the centuries, a likeness that cuts across all the differences. Designating these religions by the term primal helps to situate them as a truly significant phenomenon in their own right. It also recognizes the fact of religious history that they have provided the fundamental substructure of all subsequent religious experience, and that they continue, to varying degrees, in all later religious traditions.

The scope of primal religions

I have already noted Andrew Walls' listing of contemporary primal religions as comprising the religions of:

> circumpolar [Arctic] peoples, of various peoples of Africa, the Indian subcontinent [the so-called 'tribals'], South East Asia, Inner Asia [such as Siberia and Mongolia], North and South America [the 'first nation' peoples], Australia [the Aborigines] and the Pacific [Maori of New Zealand, as well as the Micronesian, Melanesian and Polynesian island groups].

To take fuller measure of the scope of primal religions, we should look back in history and add to this list the Semitic religions of the Old Testament period, the religions of Greece and Rome in the early Christian era, as well as the pre-Christian religions of the tribes-people of northern and western Europe, such as the Celts, Franks, Saxons and Nordic peoples.

Primal religion is a complex reality, defying the stereotype that it belongs to only pre-literate and technologically unsophisticated cultures. For Greek primal culture was highly literate; Egyptian, Incan and Mayan cultures were highly technological. Primal religion is also an enduring reality, some traditions, such as those of the first-nation peoples in the Americas, having endured for millennia before they were decimated by European contact. Remarkably, many still persist and are enjoying a revival in recent times.

An indication of the scope of primal religions would not be complete without mentioning the vast array of new religious movements that have emerged within primal societies as a result of contact with other religions and in particular with Christianity. These new religious movements owe something both to their own indigenous traditions and to the new incoming religions, but they are not completely identified with either. It is important to note here that by far the majority of new religious movements have arisen in interaction with Christianity. These movements display a variety of responses, which may be classified along a scale ranging from neo-primal to synthetist to Hebraist to independent church, depending on the extent to which they have adopted Christian beliefs and practices.

The fact that it was the primal encounter with Christian faith that produced the greatest number of these movements, as well as the greatest number of converts to Christianity, has led to the suggestion of affinities between the Christian and the primal traditions. The historical fact that the primal religions have been the religious background of the majority of Christians of all ages and places in the 20 centuries of Christian history, including

Christians of European ancestry, also points to such an affinity and indicates that the primal traditions are closer to Christianity than any other religious tradition.

Indeed, it is possible to suggest that the scope of primal religion includes the religion of Israel in the Old Testament and the faith of the earliest Christian communities as expressed in the New Testament. One reason why the Christian Scriptures, and particularly the Old Testament, appeal to persons of a primal background is the similarity of world-view recognized there. As John Mbiti has commented, when Africans enter the world of the Bible, 'they do not have very far to go before they realize they are walking on familiar ground'. This is not merely an African Christian experience. It is true of persons from primal societies all around the world, who read or hear the Christian Scriptures in their mother tongues. They recognize immediately an affinity of world-view and religious expression.

The epistles of the apostle Paul in the New Testament make sense as an engagement with the religious issues of the primal Gentile peoples of the Mediterranean basin (the Galatians, for example, were a Celtic people, as their name indicates), presenting Jesus as Lord within that world. The Epistle to the Hebrews has been called 'Africa's Epistle' because it shows clearly lines of continuity from the essentially primal religion of the Old Testament into its fulfilment in Jesus Christ, who is presented as supreme mediator, priest and sacrifice, these roles and functions having had a prominent place in African primal religion. This ready identification with the presentation of Jesus Christ in Hebrews is not exclusive to Africa, for these roles and functions are immediately understood within primal religion wherever it is found around the world. The definition of faith given in Hebrews 11 as the capacity to discern the unseen world of God's activity and make it the basis of one's way of living is fundamentally primal, common to primal religions around the world.

Thus it is possible to consider the way of Jesus as presented in the Christian Scriptures as the universal face of primal religion. Indeed, the teaching of Jesus on the Kingdom of God as the inbreaking of the eternal transcendent realm into human life in an unprecedented way through his life and ministry, but which finds its fulfilment beyond this life, would suggest that Christian faith qualifies as a synthesis of cosmic and metacosmic religion, fulfilling the aspirations of both perspectives.

Features of primal religion and world-view

How may we set about determining and describing the features of primal religion and world-view, given the fact that the phenomenon is so extensive and wide ranging? In order to discern the underlying commonalities, an important approach to take is to make a distinction between the particular local religious structures and arrangements that give each primal religion its distinctive shape and form, and the elements that feature in all primal religions.

Taking this into account, the first common feature to note is that primal religion engages the whole of life and is intimately bound up with the structures, functioning and livelihood of a particular community, whether it be a family, a clan, an ethnic group functioning as a nation or as an empire with subject peoples. Life is spiritual and religious, and nothing happens in the family, community, nation or empire without the spiritual realm being involved, or without religious rites being performed. This means that religious events occur as much in homes as in shrines, and that 'ordinary' people perform religious rites just as much as the religious specialists. Similarly, all the events in the human life cycle – birth, naming, coming of age, marriage, death – are attended with rites of passage involving the whole community, seen and unseen, namely, the living, the dead (understood as the 'living dead') and those as yet unborn, as well as God and the host of spirits that derive from him and act as intermediaries. Community events, such as festivals, are at one and the same time social, political and religious occasions. Many persons and families within the community, and not just the rulers and elders, have clearly designated roles and functions, being custodians of specific aspects of the celebration. These include various sacrifices of cleansing and purification, the performance of cosmic music and dance (music and dance that have symbolic spiritual meaning and spiritual efficacy), the offering of prayer and libation – all of which belong within the complex of events that make up the festival.

The spiritual realm is a complex reality, its configurations vary from community to community, but generally speaking its elements include the Supreme Being, who often has a personal name and indeed may have several names describing different aspects of his nature. He is the creator of the universe, whose abode is the heavens, but who is also always close by and shows his creatures what they should do. This is the case in most African primal religions. Looking beyond Africa, in the cases where no single deity stands out as the Supreme Being, as in ancient northern Europe, there may be ultimate forces, such as fate and time, that are perceived as higher than the gods. In ancient Celtic religions, groups of three deities would represent a concentration of power.

Often another important element of the spiritual realm is the earth, considered as a personified spiritual entity as well as a physical entity, the 'Earth Mother' who cares for the living and to whom often a day may be dedicated when no work is to be done. There will often be also a range of lesser spirits or divinities who are understood as ministering spirits of the Supreme Being, owing their existence to him, and who may be localized or manifest in particular natural entities, such as rivers, groves and mountains. Trees are especially sacred in many primal traditions as the abode of spirits or ancestors, and rites would be performed and sacrifices offered close to them. There is also often an awareness of more minor spiritual forces associated with particular creatures, as well as more impersonal spiritual power, sometimes called *mana* (in many of the languages of Oceania), that is held to reside in specific natural objects by virtue of the essentially spiritual nature of the universe; this power can be manipulated to achieve certain ends.

Whereas the Supreme Being always looms large in individual and community consciousness, being mentioned at the beginning of prayers and prior to sacrifice, and the Earth Mother sometimes also, no formal worship is instituted for them in terms of temples or shrines. The lesser spirits do have shrines for the purpose of worship and consultation, with religious specialists attached to them who act as mediums of the divinity.

The ancestors of the community constitute a further significant element. Not all the dead become ancestors, only those – men and women – who meet the criteria of ancestor (having lived a good and honourable life, having had children and having died at a venerable age). Having now passed on into the spiritual realm, they also serve as intermediaries with the Supreme Being. They constitute a different category as being essentially human spirits and part of the community – the living dead. So they are not worshipped, but they remain involved in the life of the community and are invited as participants and intermediaries in spiritual activity, being named in prayer and invited more specifically through libation. An indication that libation is invitation in some African traditions is the fact that it is performed facing an open door with a clear exit, as if making a way for the ancestors to come in, and that liquid is poured on the ground, symbolizing the hospitable act of washing the feet of visitors. This original meaning has been somewhat obscured as, through European contact, alcoholic beverage (Schnapps) has replaced the dew water that was originally used. Yet the distinction between worship of God and the religious activities associated with ancestors is still clearly indicated in the indigenous terms used for each.

Ancestors may sometimes be present with the living community to the extent of manifesting themselves through the spirit of living persons performing specific roles. At the Odwira (Purification) Festival of the Akuapem people of Ghana, for example, the custodian of the ancestral stool (throne) of the king who bears this ancestral name comes visibly under the influence of the ancestral spirit at appropriate moments when carrying the stool during the ceremony. Similarly, the young girls chosen from different family houses to carry food to the ancestors come under the influence of a family ancestral spirit while they are performing their role. These numinous manifestations are welcomed as evidence of ancestral presence and participation in the rites and rituals of the living, and are transient phenomena specific to the event. Rulers are usually sacral, in that they represent or embody ancestral power in a special way, and also act as intermediaries with the ancestral and spirit realm.

In relating to the spiritual realm, people are 'only a heartbeat away from prayer'. Prayer is a way of life. Life is spiritual because it is prayerful. Sacrifices and offerings also have an important place in rituals and ceremonies of

25

purification, atonement and appeasement. There may be blood sacrifice – of an animal such as a sheep or a chicken – or various other offerings. In times past, human sacrifices may have been called for in some communities to deal with specific, usually calamitous, circumstances.

The religious specialists, however they may be termed, would be the ones to divine and oversee whatever sacrifices or offerings are needed. Observation of heavenly bodies and their varying configurations may be one means of discerning the divine will in such matters. Indeed, religious specialists have often been experts in reading the stars and in drawing up the calendar year by which the community functions, determining when festivals and other ritual events of the year are to be held. Religious specialists are usually men and women identified in the community as gifted in speaking with God or as having a close relationship with the spiritual realm. Sometimes they are 'chosen' by spirits through possession and set apart for divine service. They may be ordinary individuals within the community in general, or within designated families, where the spiritual gift is 'passed on' from one generation to the next.

The spiritual universe of primal religion also has its 'dark side'. There is an intense awareness of evil forces, ranged against human beings and the community, protection against which is sought from the Supreme Being, the divinities and the ancestors, in particular, as well as the more minor spiritual forces. Again, it is the religious specialists who serve as 'diviners', or 'witchdoctors', diagnosing the spiritual causes of problems and misfortunes within the community and the natural world, and prescribing remedies. Evil may also incarnate itself in human beings, such persons being identified as witches or wizards, against whose machinations protection is also sought. These machinations include magic, sorcery and witchcraft, which has been defined as 'ill will let loose in the community'. This English terminology, deriving from the European primal context, may be inadequate to convey the nuances that come with the terms for the human channels of evil used in other primal religious contexts, but the principle is similar.

 ## Enduring insights of the primal religious consciousness

As indicated earlier, primal religions are often contrasted with the so-called world or historical religions, as if their localized nature and their orality set them apart and make them 'other', so that their enduring insights and perspectives become obscured. This is where the terms cosmic and meta-cosmic are helpful in conveying differences in religious perspective, while acknowledging their interrelationship. It is important therefore to understand the world-view that informs the structures and rituals of primal religion, the themes and perspectives of religious consciousness that have endured through the centuries and live on through religious change. As primal religions themselves decline, the religious consciousness that lives on becomes increasingly important.

The mystery of the Holy or the Sacred at the heart of life

Perhaps the most fundamental primal intuition of what lies at the heart of religious experience is the mystery of 'the Holy', the awareness of 'the Sacred' at the heart of life. It is difficult for modern sensibilities affected by the European Enlightenment to capture the entirely religious sense in which the transcendent realm is perceived in the primal world-view. Numen and numinous – terms for divinity drawn from the primal Roman religion of antiquity, when the term holy had greater depth of religious meaning – are perhaps helpful in conveying the sense that the transcendent reality to which primal religions refer is 'wholly other' and beyond human comprehension, just as religious experience is fundamental and unique and cannot be reduced to, or contained by, any other type of experience. Yet this experience is not located outside or beyond the world of everyday existence. Rather it lies at the heart of life.

The numinous realm has been defined as the transcendent mystery that fills human beings with awe and dread, and yet attracts in its compelling fascination. A direct outflow of this experience of the numinous realm is a sense of human weakness, of the finiteness, impurity and sinfulness of humanity and the need for a power beyond one's own, a transcendent power that is sensed and can be experienced.

It is this perspective of transcendence at the heart of life that accounts for vital elements of the primal religious experience – such as the sense of total devotion, of being cut to the heart, of deep symbolism or of participation of the whole person in worship. Among the Aborigines of Australia, the 'Dreaming' is an intense participation in the eternal realm of archetypal figures, where life and its activities originated. Another contemporary primal example of this outlook may be found in the Sun Dance of first-nation peoples of America, where the dancers undergo much physical suffering for the sake of increasing their sincerity in prayer.

A personal and spiritual universe, requiring responsible participation

In the primal world-view, therefore, there is the sense that what is primarily real is spiritual. As well as the transcendent mystery that governs all creation, all existence has an intrinsic spiritual dimension. There is thus a religious and spiritual sense of kinship with nature, in which the environment is used with respect and reverence, as also belonging to the transcendent realm. The activity of rainmaking is just one manifestation of the mysterious connection with the forces of the natural world that derives from this

Figure 2.1 A North American totem pole illustrating the relationship between a people group, its ancestor, and birds and animals

sense of kinship with nature. Totem relationships, or the kinship of ethnic groups and clans with specific animals, are another example. Primal religion thus demonstrates a religious attitude to the natural setting of human beings in the world, an attitude that affects every aspect of daily life.

There is the sense that the world is personal because the transcendent realm is personal, especially where it is held to derive from a personal Supreme Being, and it owes its dynamism to personal will. Human beings are participants in that universe as a responsible presence, affecting, and being affected by, the environment, society and the cosmos. In holding to the spiritual unity of the cosmos, primal religion allows for no dichotomy between the sacred and the secular. Human beings live in a sacramental universe where there is no sharp dichotomy between the physical and the spiritual. The physical world is understood as being patterned on the spiritual. Human life is a microcosm of the macrocosm. This might be considered a monistic view but it is generally qualified by a clear ethical dualism in respect of good and evil. This sense of the personal totality of all being becomes sharply defined and directly experienced in the life of the extended family, the clan and the ethnic group. Persons from a primal context would say, 'I am, because I participate', and beyond the immediate group would identify all humanity as a family. Yet there is also an inherent sense of ambivalence regarding the place of God and the role of the spirits in primal religion. One African theologian has described the primal universe as one of distributed or fragmented powers, in other words, a world of spiritual powers or beings more powerful and ultimate, where the relationship between them is not always clear. These transcendent powers may be benevolent or malevolent, but the benevolent powers are believed to be ultimately stronger and to provide a means of escape from the terrors of evil forces. It is thus believed possible to enter into a relationship with the benevolent spirit world, to share in its power and blessings and receive protection from evil forces. Out of this relationship arises the primal intuition of the need for sacrifice in order to maintain right relationships with the spirit world or repair the relationship when things have gone wrong.

Figure 2.2 A drawing of a picture cloth from Dahomey (Republic of Benin), depicting rituals for expelling evil spirits, including the use of gongs and ram's-head axes with lightning coming from their mouths (the latter are emblems of Shang, the storm god). The devil in the centre shows European influence.
Source: Geoffrey Parrinder, *African Mythology* (London: Paul Hamlyn, 1967)

A corollary of this is that persons of evil intent may also seek to draw on the power of malevolent forces to carry out their evil designs, practices known in English by the terms witchcraft, magic or sorcery. Each indigenous language has its own terminology to convey precisely what this entails in the context.

In addition, the belief that the source of true life is located in the transcendent realm leads to a longing for that true life not yet achieved. Once again, the primal intuition is that sacrifice is needed as the way into that quality of life.

A further outflow of the spiritual unity of all things in the primal worldview is an intense belief in the afterlife, a belief that one will share spiritual life and power beyond death. Ancestors, as the 'living dead', figure prominently as united in affection and obligation with the 'living living', and as having a mediatorial role. Life can be hopeful because of this sense of continuation beyond this life.

Fundamental outcomes of living in a sacramental universe

Some practical consequences of what it means to live in a sacramental universe are common to primal religions around the world. Religion is inseparable from, and integral to, culture. It pervades all areas of life. Words have a special potency. Often this is integral to their specific sounds. In West Africa, drum language played out on the sacred talking drums in ritual activities is an application of this sense of potency. Words are therefore sacred and must be used with care and responsibility. Other primal societies have had sacred writing, such as the 'ogham' script among ancient Celtic peoples.

This understanding of the sacredness of words is extended to the sacredness of arts and crafts, where the natural materials used, as well as the finished objects, such as drums or masks, manifest sacred powers. Primal art forms, including music and dance, can therefore only be understood as an experience and an expression of the sacred realm.

Another practical consequence is the experience of time and process – the seasons of nature and the span of life – as not linear but cyclical and reciprocal, an experience that may then be expressed in ritual – with seasonal festivals and rites of passage – and in architecture, ranging from such simple, homely structures as the *tipi* among American Indian peoples, to the spectacular feats of engineering in the pyramids and temples of the ancient Egyptians, Aztecs, Incas and Mayas.

A further consequence is a metaphysic of nature in which an accumulated practical knowledge regarding the natural environment is interrelated with a sacred knowledge. Thus hunting and fishing, the practice of agriculture and other economic activities become sacred activities to which a 'detailed cosmological lore' is attached. The Australian Aborigines are a good example here, as are also the first-nation peoples of the Americas. Healing concerns and practices demonstrate this blend of the sacred with the practical, as the knowledge and application of herbal treatments are often the outflow of spiritual discernment of causes and remedies. Such indigenous knowledge is now being re-evaluated as containing much wisdom with respect to the nurture of the environment, healing processes and many other areas of life.

A further practical consequence of the sacramental world-view is that the highest good is sought among the transcendent and sacramental mysteries of life, hence the perennial search for well-being, wholeness and harmony in personal life and the life of the community. This contrasts with 'metacosmic' religions, where salvation is located in the beyond, that is, beyond or apart from this earthly life.

In this section on the features of primal religions, I have chosen to focus on elements of general understanding and interpretation by which to approach the specifics of primal religions in different parts of the world. I consider it important to offer a framework for understanding the particulars, which can be found in compendia of religions and in more specialized studies.

 # Primal religions in contact with a wider world: discerning dynamics of change

Over the past six hundred years or so, and with rapidly gathering momentum, the wider world and its associated religious and philosophical traditions have impinged upon primal societies and imposed change, sometimes with brutal force. As land was appropriated by force and the basis of livelihood undermined, so the primal religious expressions bound up with them were undermined, put under stress and sometimes obliterated. Modernity and secularity, as fruits of the Enlightenment, have also waged an onslaught upon the primal religious consciousness and indeed upon the religious consciousness in general, and have co-opted science and technology as exclusively their fruits. What may now be seen to be remarkable is that primal spirituality has not died out and that it is able to hold its own in new forms, in particular in non-Western Christianity, which I shall consider shortly in more detail. These new forms of non-Western Christianity may now be seen to be achieving a recovery of the integration of scientific and technological knowledge within a religious outlook, a feature of some earlier primal societies.

Close attention to the responses of primal religions to their rapidly changing environment within the modern world suggests at least eight different processes, which may be defined as recession, absorption, restatement, reduction, invention, adjustment, revitalization and appropriation.

- Recession is the most common, where the disturbances caused by the pressures of modernization alongside the presence of faiths that are more universal in range have resulted in mass movements towards these religions.

- Yet one outcome of recession is the absorption of major elements of primal religions into Christian and Islamic communities so that the primal world-view may be seen to have a continued life within the new faith, while the old religious practices die out.
- Restatement describes a process whereby the primal religions respond to the presence of new religions by taking on some of their religious language and themes.
- Reduction is the process whereby a primal religion becomes reduced or confined in its scope, or where ritual persists in isolation from its original setting or is disconnected from its new environment. As an example, sacrificial practices may be kept, only now carried out in token form.
- Invention describes responses of creativity, where primal religions evolve in new settings, absorbing and adopting elements from other cultures. This may include devising a new religious system altogether in an attempt to produce a 'universal' primal religious alternative to Christianity or Islam.
- Adjustment refers to attempts to adjust and expand world-views to take account of new phenomena. Cargo cults in Melanesia are probably among the most well-known adjustment movements, where new phenomena, such as the arrival of aeroplanes, were interpreted according to ancient myths.
- Revitalization is a further response, as traditional cultural identities are asserted over against Western norms. This response is most striking among first-nation peoples of America and Australian Aborigines. This response is also accompanied by an expansion of consciousness.
- Appropriation is a response whereby primal religions are being adopted or advocated by those who historically belong to another tradition, such as, for example, a new appreciation of the primal holistic world-view in relation to a growing concern for the environment. Some 'New Age' movements that seek to recover the ancient primal religions of Europe are examples of this. Such a response may be accompanied by a new self-criticism within cultures that formerly took for granted their own superiority.

 ## Significance of primal religion within the history of religions

It has been a recurring theme within this chapter that the primal religions are in no sense a spent or outmoded force. They have found a variety of ways to survive under the impact of invasive forces, religious and secular, and may now be seen to underlie all subsequent religions to varying degrees.

In particular, they can be shown to be the substructure of Christianity, manifest most clearly in the diverse contemporary forms of non-Western Christianity. Indeed, they help to explain what makes them distinctive and can be shown to have much to do with their vitality.

The study of religious change in primal contexts reveals the dynamics at work that have reshaped the primal world-view within Christianity, so that the primal world-view has come to underlie in significant ways the new forms of Christianity that have emerged in recent decades. Much of the study has focused particularly on Africa, but the dynamics are applicable elsewhere in the non-Western world where primal religion and Christianity meet.

The most important point to note in the dynamics of change is that the elements of the Christian tradition are applied to already existing primal maps of the universe. The components of those maps – God, local divinities, ancestors, objects of power – remain in one form or another as means to understand the world and society, but the relationships between them change radically as a result of the Christian impact. Thus certain features of the primal spirit world gain prominence and take on fuller meaning, such as the apprehension of the Supreme God, with the Trinity and angelic hosts taking the place of the benevolent spiritual manifestations of personality, such as the Earth Mother and some of the lesser spirits. Other aspects of the multiplicity of divinity change in character – perhaps by being demonized – in encounter with Christian faith.

The impact of Christianity is more ambiguous with respect to the ancestors, with some tension or conflict between theory and practice. It is clear, though, that in the new emerging forms of Christianity the ancestors have not disappeared, and Christianity has to take account of them one way or another, especially their significance for cultural identity. One way in which the ancestors find a connection with Christian tradition is through the communion of saints, which now takes on a new immediacy.

The objects of power have been readily drawn into the Christian framework through the sacramental use of bread, wine and water, in particular; only the source of the power is now the God of the Scriptures, the power of Christ or of the Holy Spirit. We may say that the Christianity that is emerging in Africa and the rest of the non-Western world has become African or non-Western religion, with a continuity of world-view and inheriting the old primal goals, such as the search for protection through spiritual power. But there is also a reordering of world-view and the introduction of new symbols and sources under the impact of the Christian Scriptures. New elements in African and non-Western religion are: the person of Christ and the immediacy of the presence of God that he brings through the Holy Spirit, sometimes through dreams and visions and other gifts of the Spirit, such as prophecy and healing; the search for the will of God in place of divination, supremely through the Christian Scriptures; new models of church; the emergence of the devil and the new category of the demonic, under which are subsumed all the malevolent spiritual manifestations of personality.

Primal religion lives on, therefore, in the living forms of non-Western Christianity. What may we identify as some of the distinctive features of non-Western Christianity that derive from the primal substructure and are thus the primal contributions to the revitalization of Christianity? While this section focuses mainly on the living forms of African Christianity, the features identified may be seen to be true of the forms of Christianity in Latin America, Oceania and the parts of Asia where primal religions have been dominant.

We may note, first, a *recovery of religious experience and fervent spirituality* at the heart of Christian faith. There is a 'rending of the veil' that had been drawn by the European Enlightenment over Christian experience of the transcendent, so that the whole universe is revealed as being full of divine presence, and the divine destiny of humanity as an abiding relationship with God. The call and careers of Africa's independent prophets and the whole range of independent churches across the continent and around the world bear witness to this phenomenon. The experience of trance-visitations, the 'rending of the veil' by which William Wade Harris met with Moses, the Angel Gabriel, Elijah and Jesus, and was launched into his itinerant evangelistic ministry in the early twentieth century in West Africa, was no isolated event. It also has a biblical paradigm in the conversion of Paul.

The so-called 'mainline' Churches are responding to the hunger for vitality in spiritual experience and for the immediacy of God's presence. This began with the emergence of renewal movements within the mainline denominations. Increasingly, whole congregations are incorporating prayer vigils, healing and deliverance services into the mainstream of their activities, as well as introducing elements of spontaneity, such as times for 'praise and worship' led by a 'praise team' (not the church choir), into the regular liturgy. Where music and dance had cosmic significance in the primal world, this continues in Christian worship. Music is the language of the transcendent, expressed through singing and dancing, and these become the means by which the worshipper is transported into the spiritual realm. In the 'trance' of song and where dance movements are spiritually symbolic, 'all is spirit'.

None of these manifestations is 'exotic'. They constitute merely a recovery of the spiritual fervour of the Church in New Testament times and in succeeding centuries, only now in a non-Western manifestation, the route to them being the primal world-view. Indeed, the wholehearted group participation, the ardent fervour and deep spiritual involvement of the community in prayer, the overwhelming sense of God's presence and guidance, the certainty of his protection, the healing power of prayer, that characterize much of African and non-Western Christian worship may be associated with the profound and fundamental search for the spiritual experience necessary for a more personal and more universal discovery of the 'wholeness' of human life.

This leads to a second outcome in *the recovery of holism and of the transcendent at the heart of life*. The presence of God in the community of believers makes it into a 'transcendent' community, in which human beings experience and share in the life of God. The evidence for this takes many forms. Perhaps the most visible examples of the acknowledgement of the presence of God in the daily lives of Christians in Ghana come in the Scripture verses or proverbs expressing a religious outlook on life, written on lorries and public transport, in English or in Ghanaian mother tongues – '*Nyame ye*' (God is good), '*Nyame bekyerε*' (God will guide). A similar acknowledgement of God may also come in the names given to small enterprises, such as 'Jesus my Saviour Enterprise' (the name of a small retail grocery outlet) or 'All to Jesus [I surrender] Communication Centre'. 'Blood of the Lamb Carpet Cleaners' must be an attractive name to prospective Ghanaian customers who have confidence in the cleansing power of the blood of Jesus Christ! All these statements have, in fact, a story to tell of God's intervention in the life of the person or persons concerned. Some inscriptions may appear enigmatic to an outsider. 'No weapon' refers to Isaiah 54.17: 'No weapon fashioned against you shall prosper.' This is taken as a direct promise from God, which then becomes a statement of faith in Jesus in a world where the presence of evil working through spiritual and human agents is very real.

We might be tempted to think that such perceptions are confined to the less well-educated sectors of African society. This is in fact not the case. Christian professionals now make to Jesus Christ requests that would formerly have been addressed to spiritual powers and their human agents in a primal religious setting. Prayer for fertility, the dedication of a baby, success in an examination, the blessing of a newly built or occupied house or a new car, to ensure protection – all these are common requests and are considered entirely appropriate by educated people. The sense of reality as essentially spiritual, which was a feature of the traditional universe, has a continuing life in the African Christian universe of thought and action. Because this is a comprehensive, all-embracing understanding of reality, such preoccupations do not belong exclusively to the private or personal realm; they can be shown to be operative in social, political, economic and scientific spheres as well. In other words, educated Christians from a primal background have no difficulty in integrating science and technology into their religious and cultural universe. Once again, the primal intuition that there is no inherent dichotomy predominates.

A third feature is the *recovery of community in Christian worship*. What makes Christian worship in Africa authentically African has been identified as a strong sense of collectivity and community, characterized by much participation in virtually all aspects of the worship service – singing, clapping and dancing in worship, as in the traditional setting, with the same energy, passion and total involvement. Worship services are indeed community celebrations. Other features that testify to the communal nature of Christian worship are the increase in the use of corporate prayer, the fact that in many churches both men and women have the same opportunities to participate, and the fact that it is a common practice to organize worship services around yearly community festivals or other activities or programmes that have to do with the development of the whole community.

Fourth, we may note *the recovery of the Bible as a contemporary living witness to the presence and activity of the living God in the world, in which persons and communities of faith may participate.* The traditional importance attached to words in the primal environment now comes to attach to the Word of God. The Scriptures become the road map for the religious journey, enabling the reshaping of the primal world and the shaping and interpretation of Christian experience. For it is possible to relate the primal religious perspective to the religious experiences described in the Christian Scriptures, showing how primal religious intuitions of the mystery of the numinous at the heart of life, far from being alien, are intrinsic to the Christian Scriptures and Christian faith. This then becomes a route to recovering aspects of Christian experience lost during its modern Western phase.

This centrality of the Bible as a feature of primal Christian spirituality is not to be understood as independent of the three earlier features outlined. The independent prophets functioned in the biblical realm because they participated in the Scriptures. Scriptural inspiration, direct and indirect, informs the popular Christian spirituality that expresses itself in the public sphere, as we noted earlier. Scripture is the integrating centre, 'the authoritative, normative deposit given to us of the divine-human encounter, that lies at the heart of our faith', as Kwame Bediako describes it. This is not simply sound doctrine, it is lived experience, deriving from the evident affinity of world-view between the Bible and Africa. The fact that there is much less difference between Africa and the Bible than between traditional Africa and the secular West could be understood as an important gain for Christian faith world-wide.

It is the vernacular Bible translations, which use the religious and cultural terms from the primal traditions, that have been responsible for bringing about a transformation in society and culture and have also unleashed this fervent response of creativity in worship, in song and prayer, drawing out of the wellsprings of primal spirituality a wholehearted adoration of Jesus that is also faithful to the biblical tradition.

 ## Primal religion and new perspectives

If primal religious intuitions and experience are so fundamental to religious life as a whole, then Christians from societies that have not lost their primal memory have the opportunity to develop new ways of thinking and acting that transcend the dichotomies and polarizations imposed by Enlightenment thinking and other aspects of the Western tradition. An indication that this is not merely a Christian concern is the evidence that Islamic scholars in Africa find themselves wrestling with the same issues of identity and meaning that derive from their primal background, and are discovering common ground with Christian scholars from the same background wrestling with the same issues. In other words, there are emerging in Africa new ways of reflecting upon religion and interfaith issues, and new ways of interfaith engagement that are enabled by the primal context and take that context seriously.

Christians from a primal background have the opportunity to restore the unity of theology and spirituality that existed in the early centuries of Christian thought, because living religiously is once again seen as an indispensable element in Christian reflection and writing. It also enables Christian thought to use religious categories for speaking about God, which are more relevant to non-Western contexts than the philosophical categories commonly used in Western theology. For example, primal religions generally see religion as a system of power, and take religious life to mean being in touch with the source and channels of power in the universe. In the West, on the other hand, the Christian gospel has been seen as a system of ideas. And yet the apostle Paul's summary of the gospel is more akin to the primal perspective: 'I have complete confidence in the gospel; it is God's power to save all who believe . . .' (Rom. 1.16).

Christians from a primal background also have the opportunity to expound and interpret the Scriptures of the Old and New Testaments in fresh ways, building on the solid foundations of religious and cultural affinities and shared experience of religious journey. The various forms of primal religion in the world can become a vital resource for a fresh appreciation of the Scriptures in the testimony they bear to shared primal perceptions of the spiritual nature of reality. These perceptions include a deep awareness of transcendence in immanence, with the physical world as a sacrament of the spiritual, a deep sense of the numinous in religious experience, of the creaturehood of humanity and of human participation in a personal universe, common processes of relating to the divine realm through sacrifice and mediation, and shared anticipation not just of afterlife but of a better existence to come.

The primal world-view can restore to the study of the Christian Scriptures the unity of the Old and New Testaments in a common religious outlook, so that the Bible becomes once again a contemporary living witness to the presence and activity of the living God in the world, in which persons and communities of faith everywhere may participate. The Old Testament, in particular, may become a paradigm, a key, for interpreting the religious journeys of peoples from a primal background, illuminating the diverse paths that have prepared them to welcome Jesus Christ as the one

Figure 2.3 A Celtic cross: the ring signifies the sun and eternity and the Celtic knot design also represents eternity. Both are primal religious symbols that survived into Celtic Christianity

who saves them within their world, or recalling them from paths that may be taking them away from Jesus. In the Hebrew Bible, the history of God's dealings in the lives of people whose faith was not perfect shows the relevance of the Old Testament to the primal traditions and opens the way for the whole Scriptures to be taken as 'their story', illuminating the past and reflecting their triumphs of dependence on God, as well as their failures in disobedience and idolatry. If the lives and careers of Adam, Eve, Noah, Enoch, Abraham, Isaac, Jacob, Moses and David, now seen as 'ancestors', have an abiding relevance for every succeeding generation, so people from a primal background must have had ancestors like the biblical ancestors who, at critical points in their lives, made choices that shaped their traditions in such a way that they became ready to be merged, in Christ, with the history of all the people of God.

There is often a sense among Westerners that the primal world is remote from their experience. Some also feel this way about the Old Testament and the biblical world in general. Yet we shall do well to remember that primal religion is the Western pre-Christian heritage too, and that its negative aspects were a lesser part of the story. For primal spirituality made an enduring impact on the development of Western Christianity. One example is the Celtic Christianity of early Ireland. So the recovery of a primal world-view does not have to mean, very narrowly, the acceptance of a world dominated by witchcraft and evil spirits, or by a prosperity gospel that equates health and wealth with faith in God, as some Westerners have tended to think. Rather there is much to learn from Christians and Christian communities that have not lost their primal world-view: the fervour of their worship and prayer, the way they read and participate in the Christian Scriptures of Old and New Testaments, the strength of community living, and the practical outworking of their Christian faith in life and witness. It should therefore be possible to discover a common humanity with others and new ways of being Christian in the contemporary environment of religious and cultural plurality.

 Conclusion

This chapter on primal religions has sought to clear away some of the misconceptions that have attached themselves to the primal religions of the world in recent centuries, and to provide a framework and some tools for better understanding. It has also sought to show the vital place that the primal religions have had in the history of religions, as well as their fundamental contribution to the religious life of all humankind. Not only have they provided the essential elements of religious intuition and expression, they have also demonstrated the capacity to endure in new forms and to revitalize other faiths. This is particularly evident in their current impact within non-Western Christianity.

If the primal religions of the world have played such a fundamental role in religious history, it becomes a matter of crucial importance that this be recognized and integrated into the way we think about religion, the way we study it, and the way we integrate it into our own lives. It is particularly important for persons from the non-Western world to take in the full weight of their primal heritage and shape it into a positive contribution to contemporary religious understanding, so that people around the world may reconnect with the eternal wellsprings of primal spirituality.

 QUESTIONS

1 Why have the primal religions of the world been so often misunderstood and underestimated?

2 What are some of the essential features of primal religion?

3 What makes the primal religions of the world so important?

4 Do you agree that the Christianity you know incorporates elements of primal religion? Do you think that this is a positive process to be encouraged? Give reasons for your answer.

5 Study some theologians who have engaged with primal religion. What is your opinion of their reflections? Christian theologians include Harry Sawyerr, John Mbiti, Kwame Bediako, Lamin Sanneh and Aloysius Pieris.

Further reading

Bediako, Kwame, *Jesus in Africa: The Christian Gospel in African History and Experience* (Akropong: Regnum Africa, 2000); re-issued as *Jesus and the Gospel in Africa: History and Experience* (New York: Orbis, 2004).

Fisher, Mary Pat, *Living Religions: An Encyclopaedia of the World's Faiths* (London: Tauris, 1997).

Hinnells, John R. (ed.), *A Handbook of Living Religions* (Harmondsworth: Penguin, 1984, 1990).

Sanneh, Lamin, *Whose Religion is Christianity? The Gospel Beyond the West* (Grand Rapids: Eerdmans, 2003).

Sullivan, Lawrence E. (ed.), *Native Religions and Cultures of North America: Anthropology of the Sacred* (New York and London: Continuum, 2000).

Sullivan, Lawrence E. (ed.), *Native Religions of Central and South America: Anthropology of the Sacred* (New York and London: Continuum, 2002).

Taylor, John V., *The Primal Vision: Christian Presence Amid African Religion* (London: SCM Press, 1963).

Walls, Andrew F., *The Missionary Movement in Christian History: Studies in the Transmission of Faith* (Edinburgh and Maryknoll, NY: T. & T. Clark/Orbis, 1996).

Walls, Andrew F. , *The Cross-Cultural Process in Christian History: Studies in the Transmission and Appropriation of Faith* (Edinburgh and Maryknoll, NY: T. & T. Clark/Orbis, 2002).

3

Hindu thought and practice

Prabhakar Bhattacharyya

 Introduction

There are about a billion Hindus in the world, comprising some 13 per cent of global population. Their major festivals are celebrated in almost every country. Hindu scriptures, especially the **Upanishads**, the *Gita*, the *Ramayana* and the *Mahabharata*, are translated into all the major languages. India is sometimes known as 'Hindustan', meaning 'the land of the Hindus', since Hindus form a sizeable population in the country. Unlike the other major religions of the world, Hinduism has no specific founder. It claims to be based on the eternal truth discovered by seers, who in turn passed it on to their disciples. Though the religious tradition is several thousand years old, it never had any central organization. Hinduism is not a particular religious faith centring on a particular name of God, based on a particular scripture. Hinduism may be considered as a harmonious federation of followers of many faiths. As a result it has no single theological system. Hindu religious tradition maintains that there is no point in converting others to its faith, since all the major faiths are potent enough to lead to God.

The divine mystery of the Hindu faith was revealed to seers (**rsis**) through ancient Vedic hymns (**mantras**). It is believed that not a single word of the revealed truths was lost because the seers had perfected a rigorous technique of memorizing and recalling the hymns verbatim. Initially the *Vedas* were not written, but circulated in oral forms and were treated as more authentic than written documents. However, about two thousand years ago all the four *Vedas* were officially written down. The authority of the *Vedas* is supreme in Hinduism, but there are also other scriptures that owe their authority to the *Vedas*. In the course of time many regional and local cults came to be included in the ritualistic practices of the Hindus. Pure Vedic rituals, in their original form, are rarely practised by Hindus today.

Pre-Hindu history

An archaeological survey of India in the 1920s unearthed ruins of the Indus Valley civilization at Harappa and Mohenjo-daro. Carbon-dating tests confirmed that the civilization had not developed earlier than 2500 BCE, and certainly pre-dated the Vedic era. There is hardly any mention of this urban civilization in the *Vedas*.

We know very little about the religious practices of the Indus Valley people from this period. No structures unearthed at Harappa or Mohenjo-daro could be identified as a temple or shrine. We can form some idea about their religion from a number of discovered clay seals, copper tablets and terracotta figures, as well as some images made of metal and stone. It seems that the Indus Valley people worshipped mother goddesses, suggesting they had a strong fertility cult. A seal from Mohenjo-daro depicts a god seated on a low throne in the yogic posture, and on either side of him is kneeling a suppliant canopied by a snake's hood. A sacrificial offering on the seal – showing a pipal (fig) tree deity with seven priestesses – has been identified, suggesting that nature worship was perhaps prevalent then.

Though Hindus regard the *Vedas* as their supreme authority, the pre-Vedic religious practices of the Indus Valley people had immense influence on later Puranic Hinduism. Various practices found in later Hinduism – image worship, nature worship and worship of the Mother-Goddess – may all have had their roots in pre-Vedic practices, albeit with modifications.

Characteristics of the Hindu religious tradition

The term 'Hindu' is derived from the word *Sindhu* (Indus), the name of a river that marked the western frontier of *Aryavarta*, the settlement of the Aryans. Ancient Persians used to pronounce '*Sindhu*' as 'Hindu', as in the Persian language there was no 's' sound, and 's' was pronounced 'h'. In using the term Hindu they referred to the people living on the east side of the Indus river.

Though the Hindu religious tradition is at least four thousand years old, its followers use the term Hindu to express their identity as they have known it only over the last few centuries. Perhaps the Muslims, who ruled India from the thirteenth century, referred to all non-Muslims as Hindus. As these non-Muslim people were scattered all over India, the entire country came to be known as Hindustan, the land of Hindus. A few scholars, however, say that 'Hindu' originated from a mix of 'Himalaya' (after the mountain range) and 'Indu Sarobara', meaning Indian Ocean – so Hindustan is the land between the Himalayas and the Indian Ocean.

Religion ordinarily means a system of faith and ritual prescribed by scripture and performed by devout men and women. Hindus themselves call their religion **dharma**, which has a wider meaning. This word is derived from the Sanskrit root *dhr*, meaning 'to hold'. So *dharma* means that which holds up the essential nature of humanity. For a Hindu all human beings are divine by nature. The task of *dharma* is to bring out our divinity by purifying the mind.

Hinduism never had any central authority to regulate the lives and activities of its followers. The formation of religious organizations is only a recent trend. Now, a global confederation of Hindu religious organizations exists. Most Hindus, however, are against any exclusivist trend propagated by narrow political and diplomatic interests. Recently the Supreme Court of India condemned exclusive political ideals of Hinduism as Hindutva (a political ideology upheld by some political parties and their socio-religious wings). Traditional Hinduism maintains that all religions are true and valid paths towards God, the Ultimate Reality.

Hindus worship God through the image of their chosen deity as it is easier to concentrate on a concrete object than on something subtle or abstract. Image worship is popular and is prescribed for devotees from the lowest strata in society. Meditation and realization are more important than ritualistic worship. For meditation any form found in the cosmos, including human beings, may be taken up by beginners. **Rama**, **Krishna**, Chaitanya and Ramakrishna are all regarded as incarnations (**avatars**) of eternal religious principles. Meditation on the life and activities of an incarnation may be the object of meditation for spiritual aspirants. **Brahman**, the Ultimate, or God, is considered identical or similar to the individual self (**atman**).

Hindus are free to choose the deity of their liking. As a result of this religious freedom there are innumerable deities. The same deity is sometimes worshipped under a different name or form. Five major deities – **Vishnu**, **Shiva**, **Shakti** (Mother Goddess), **Surya** and **Ganapati** – are universally accepted by contemporary Hindus. Worshippers of each major deity form distinct cultic practices. Each of these cults has many sects and sub-sects. Present-day Hinduism may be considered to be a harmonious confederation of enormous religious sects.

Priests take care of the ceremonial aspect of Hinduism. Besides the regular rituals to sanctify major events in life, such as marriage and childbirth, there are specific rites performed by the priests on behalf of the worshipper. A priest can marry but must maintain a rigorous discipline to earn respect from fellow worshippers. Priests come from a particular caste, called Brahmin. The standard practice is for householders to invite male priests to conduct their ceremonies, though nowhere in the Hindu scriptures are women prohibited from becoming priests. Since 1980 some women priests have begun performing religious rites.

The spiritual aspect of Hinduism is generally taken care of by monks and nuns. Some organizations are run exclusively by nuns, for example the Sarada Mission, where spiritually advanced Hindus throng at the nuns' feet seeking guidance and realization. Also, spiritual personalities are recognized among the laity, who volunteer to guide people in their spiritual lives.

Hinduism does not offer any single theology or system of morality. In the *Vedas* the eternal moral principle, **rita**, is manifested in different forms in different cultural contexts.

Hindus attach much importance to the purification of food. There are specific injunctions for students, householders, upper-caste people, widows, priests and monks. Utensils must be clean, cooking must have good hygienic habits. Foods such as cereals and vegetables must be procured honestly and washed thoroughly. Although busy urban people tend to take fast food without bothering about scriptural injunctions, it is imperative for all Hindus to avoid eating beef.

It is believed that God himself takes human, even subhuman form in order to save honest and righteous people. Incarnations of God are worshipped and their ways of living are followed by spiritual aspirants. It is interesting to note that these avatars do not preach anything that contradicts the teaching of the scriptures. They only rejuvenate the followers of *sanatana dharma* (eternal religion).

Sanatana dharma

As we have seen, Hindus claim that their religion is eternal, or *sanatana*, having no founder; and *dharma* means 'that which holds up existence'. So the essential nature of something is called its *dharma*. For example, the *dharma* of fire is to burn. Likewise, *sanatana dharma* demands that there is an essential nature of humanity, distinct from the rest of creation.

Though the essential nature of every individual is divine, divinity is not *manifested* in all. Many humans are considered little more than brutes, while others are quite elevated. In some are manifest the words and deeds of divinity.

Sanatana dharma prescribes some practices that can destroy impurities so that the divine nature may be manifested. The *Veda* says, 'knower of the Absolute becomes God Himself'. Some duties are common to all. According to Manu (the manual of Brahminical law) there are ten such duties, which should be performed by everybody irrespective of their social status. These duties are steadfastness, forgiveness, application, avoidance of theft, cleanliness, repression of sensuous appetites, wisdom, learning, veracity and restraint from anger. Some systems add a few more duties to this list: moral earnestness, seeking the good of creatures, sexual continence, purity of motive, personal cleanliness, occasional fasting, moral watchfulness and devotion to a specific deity.

Scriptural traditions (*shruti*)

The Vedas

Unlike many other religions, Hinduism has numerous scriptures. However, there is a hierarchy of authority within them. The *Vedas*, ancient scriptures of the Aryans, carry the highest authority. The *Vedas* (Sanskrit for 'knowledge') are not believed to be composed by any human hand but are collections of *mantras* heard by the seers, of whom many were female, through the process of direct revelation. Because the *Vedas* are revealed they are called shruti, and their authority is never questioned. All other Hindu scriptures derive their authority from the *Vedas*.

In Vedic times – spanning approximately from 1500 BCE to 500 BCE – there was little or no temple worship. Vedic worship more precisely means 'sacrifice', and would entail making offerings in the sacred fire and uttering appropriate hymns. The important portions of the *Vedas* that deal with spiritual or transcendental knowledge are known as the *Upanishads*. They are also called **Vedanta** (see below), which literally means the 'end part' of the *Vedas*, and contain the essence of the *Vedas*.

Other sacred Hindu scriptures (*smriti*)

Broadly speaking, **smriti** implies all Hindu scriptures except the four *Vedas*. But more specifically they are manuals of ethical codes. *Manu-smriti* (Laws of Manu) is perhaps the most famous. The codes prescribe how a Hindu should spend his or her entire life, prohibiting certain acts while prescribing others. Ceremonies and rituals connected with domestic life are also discussed. Hindus believe that if the instructions of the *smritis* are properly followed, the mind will be purified and they can advance towards the spiritual goal – liberation.

Hindu society has undergone much change, hence Hindu saints compiled new *smritis* at particular times or for particular regions. Today, Hindus living in urban areas cannot properly follow the duties. Recent scientific and technological advances mean that many of the injunctions need to be revised. Swami Vivekananda (1863–1902), an acclaimed modern prophet of Hinduism, expressed the opinion that fresh *smriti* must be compiled for contemporary Hindus.

Lesser scriptures (*Āgamas*)

The *Āgamas* are Hindu scriptures that do not derive their authority from the *Vedas*. They are religious practices more suitable for the present day. People from all castes and both sexes can undergo 'agamic' practices once they have been initiated. One *Āgama* in particular, the *Shiva Āgama*, is very much allied to the **tantras**, which prescribe courses of ritualistic worship of the Divine Mother (Devi) in various forms. The tantric texts are usually in dialogue form. In tantric dialogue, Shiva answers questions put to him by his divine consort, **Parvati**. The goddess tradition is strongest in the *Shakta Āgamas*, which eulogize the femininity of God.

Puranas: folklore of the deities

The Hindu sages of ancient times presented their teachings in inspiring stories and parables. These easier explanations are also given the status of scripture, or *shastra*, and are called **Puranas**. Glimpses of ancient Indian history are found in these numerous texts, as well as accounts of the destruction and rebirth of the world. Popular versions are the *Vishnu Purana* and *Markandeya Purana*. By far the most popular is the *Bhagavata Purana* about the life of Krishna and the legendary exploits of his youth as a cowherd. A part of the *Markandeya Purana*, called the *Chandi*, is widely read by Hindus during Durgapuja, Kalipuja and on many other auspicious occasions.

The *Ramayana* and *Mahabharata* epics

Two famous epics of India, the *Ramayana* and *Mahabharata*, are also treated as scriptures. Although they are classified as 'history' and contain records of events, they nevertheless embellish their characters so that the listeners can learn how lofty ideals of religion can be put into practice in earthly life. The *Ramayana* was composed by Valmiki, the *Mahabharata* by Krishna Daipayan Vyas. Both epics have been translated into almost every Indian language. For over two thousand years ballad singers and playwrights have adopted the themes and storylines for their own creative compositions.

Bhagavat Gita

The *Gita* is a part of the epic, *Mahabharata*, and contains the great teachings of Krishna. As such it is the most popular scripture of contemporary Hindus. It contains the essence of the *Upanishads*. Not only Hindus but spiritual members of other religions also appreciate the lessons of the *Gita*. As a result the text has been translated into more than a hundred languages.

Three main scriptures: *Prasthanatraya*

The founders of all the important sects of Hinduism have based their teachings on three basic scriptures, called *Prasthanatraya*. They consist of the *Upanishads*, the *Brahma Sutra* (**sutra** means 'aphorism') or *Vedanta Darshana*, and the *Bhagavat Gita*.

 # Hindu teachings

Brahman and *atman*

Hindus believe that Brahman (God) alone is real. Distinct objects of our experience only seem to be real as we fall under the spell of God's divine **maya** (illusion). Brahman is the supreme spirit that the human mind cannot grasp. Though the human mind is incapable of describing Brahman, some suggestions about its nature are given in the scriptures. They refer to Brahman as 'That', not as 'He' or 'She', because Brahman is Impersonal God with no attributes. The *Upanishads* say that Brahman is transcendental – beyond time, space and causation – and is one undivided whole, eternal, changeless, all-pervasive, free. Elsewhere in the *Upanishads* Brahman is described as truth, consciousness and bliss, and the light of the sun, moon and stars is only a reflection of his light.

Hindus worship God as the Formless One but use innumerable names and forms. The *Rig Veda* says that each sect, even each religion, tries to explain God's glories from different perspectives, and that no religion or sect should claim their own perspective as the only true one. Hindus are free to worship God in any form that suits them, according to their capability, taste and temperament. These forms are like different types of garments, under which God is always the same. All the gods worshipped by the devotees represent one or several of his infinite powers.

A substantial part of a living being – distinct from the mind, sense-organs or physical body – is called *atman*. This is none other than Brahman, the Great One. Its essence is consciousness. It is not subject to birth, decay or death. Immortal Brahman and *atman* are the same in essence. By knowing the *atman* through suitable spiritual practices, one can realize its identity with the Supreme Self.

Though in essence *atman* is free from all bondages, it is nevertheless confined in three bodies, that is the physical, the 'subtle' and the 'causal'. The physical body is made of gross elements of nature. The subtle body is made of subtle elements of nature. The causal body consists of tiny particles of invisible cosmic energy. This causal body contains all a person's characteristics in a seed-state. Just as the seed of a tree turns into a big tree, so the thin causal body produces the life of a creature or the individual self or soul.

According to Hinduism, the individual soul is God. The soul is nothing other than Brahman in essence. Hindus believe that the reason we cannot comprehend cosmic reality is because of the spell of ignorance that clouds our perception.

Karma and rebirth

Karmasamsara is a combination of two terms: **karma** and **samsara**. *Karma* means 'action', and Hindus use it technically to mean 'fruits or effects of action'. *Samsara* means 'passing', so *karmasamsara* means 'the passing of an individual soul from birth to birth due to the effects of one's actions'. This view is popularly known as the doctrine of *karma* and rebirth.

Hindus believe that each deed is bound to produce its effect sooner or later. A good or meritorious deed brings pleasure while an evil deed brings pain. All the effects of action are not exhausted in one lifetime. Only a portion of it is to be exhausted in the present lifespan. The remaining part is stored to give fruit in the next birth. The fruits of our present deeds are 'being stored up'.

What we call fate, or luck, is nothing but the fruit of our own past deeds. We cannot change fate or brighten our luck by any means, as the evil and good actions of our past life are bound to bear fruits in the present life. However, we can make our future lives happy by continuously doing good or meritorious deeds and abstaining from evil ones.

At each birth we get a fresh 'gross body', made out of materials taken as food. Hence the gross body, our outermost cover, is called 'covering made of food'. This gross body has been compared to a garment that is thrown out after use. Likewise, when the gross body becomes useless the soul throws it out and reappears in another fresh gross body. In Hindu terminology, death and subsequent rebirth means 'changing worn out bodies for fresh ones'.

There is a finer and stronger body inside each gross body that is not affected by disease, old age or death. Through countless births and deaths the same 'fine body', the active part of our being, is the companion of the soul. It consists of intellect, the mind, five types of vital energy and the finer counterparts of five organs of perception and five organs of action. This fine body is, however, not active by itself. It is animated by *atman* (the self or soul), source of all life, activity and consciousness.

Four stages of life

The lifespan of a Hindu should be divided into four stages, known as **asramas** (see Figure 3.1). These four stages are a student (Brahmacarya), married householder (Grihasta), recluse or retired person (Vanaprastha) and finally one in renunciation (**Sannyasa**). A specific list of duties (*dharmas*) are prescribed for each of these stages. A student has to maintain his teacher's comforts, collect fuel, offer oblations or incense to the sacrificial fire and collect alms. However, the foremost duty is to practise strict sexual abstinence.

A married person living with his family is obliged to perform five sacrificial ceremonies. These include offering food to animals, serving guests and neighbours; offering oblations to the sacred fire; paying respects to fathers and forefathers, even to their departed souls; and lastly reading the scriptures. Besides performing the five sacrificial ceremonies, the married person must have children by living with a spouse. The Hindu scriptures

---

1. **Student (Brahmacarya)**
   learns roles within religion, politics or trades

2. **Married householder (Grihasta)**
   works and brings up a family

3. **Recluse or retired person (Vanaprastha)**
   focuses on spiritual matters and helps with grandchildren

4. **Renouncer (Sannyasa)**
   renounces ties to family and property, focuses on liberation

---

Figure 3.1 The four stages of life: these stages of life are for Hindus who choose to follow the Vedic way. They are not considered necessary for labourers.

then prescribe periods of abstinence after this cohabitation and procreation of a child.

Having completed his prescribed duties, the householder is supposed to move into the third stage of life (though very few in contemporary Hinduism do this), that of the recluse, in which he should become celibate. Some of his duties now include dining on the leftovers of a meal had with guests; living on the roots and fruits of the forest; and no longer caring about physical beauty or fashion.

By performing the duties prescribed for the first three stages of life, a man attains mental serenity and equanimity. Then he enters the fourth stage of life, in which he renounces the world. As a *sannyasin*, or *yati*, he is supposed to be gentle to all sentient creatures. He embodies harmlessness, truthfulness, restraint from theft, sexual abstinence, cleanliness, contentment, rigorous spiritual practice, recitation of Vedic texts and meditation on God.

Unmarried Hindu women are supposed to maintain sexual abstinence just like their male counterparts. Once married, she becomes a partner with her husband in performing all duties, social and religious. Although remarriage is permissible by law, a Hindu widow usually prefers to live the life of a devotee. There are many spiritually elevated women in Hindu families who guide spiritual disciples. Hindu girls, after completing their education, may opt for the life of renunciation. Hindu nuns are a modern phenomenon. They successfully run schools, colleges, hospitals and other charitable organizations.

The caste system

During the Vedic period the entire population of India was classified into four social categories (**varnas**), better known as 'castes' (see Figure 3.2 overleaf). These castes are, in descending order, priests or professionals (*brahmana*); rulers, administrators, soldiers (**kshatriya**); peasant farmers, self-employed artisans and merchants (*vaishya*); and lastly servants and skilled and unskilled labourers (*shudra*). The criterion of classification, according to the *Bhagavad Gita*, is intelligence and *karma*. However, in time castes became hereditary and each one gave birth to many more sub-castes, or occupational groups, in Hindu society.

The top three castes are obliged to do sacrificial ceremonies, study and charity. The *brahmana* teach and lead the ceremonial sacrifices. The *kshatriya* act as an armed force to protect people from external aggression and internal disturbances, and chastise wrong-doers. Duties that *only* the peasant farmers and merchants may do include buying and selling, farming and rearing animals. The *shudra* have to be subservient to all three other groups.

Contemporary Hindus living in India and other countries of the world can hardly practise all the duties prescribed for the castes. *Shudras* are stationed at the bottom of the caste hierarchy and from a social point of view their status is derogatory. The government of India is trying to elevate their status by legislative measures.

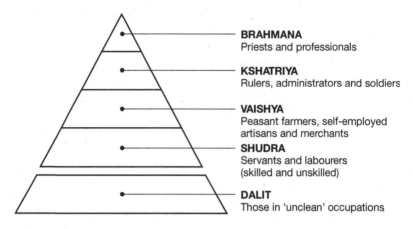

Figure 3.2 Hindu castes

One category of the population, commonly known as *dalit*, falls outside the constitution of the caste system. Literally meaning 'oppressed, discriminated against, trampled under', *dalit* refers to all those involved in unclean occupations (leather-workers, carcass-handlers, night-soil scavengers, washer-men), who are stigmatized as 'untouchables' by upper-caste Hindus. These people were compelled to live outside towns and villages. Social interaction with these people, traditionally called *chandals*, was strictly prohibited. They are isolated from the rest of society and denied access to Hindu temples, Brahmin priests and the *Vedas*, but they have developed their own folk religion instead (see 'Folk traditions' below).

Paths of liberation

Broadly speaking there are two paths of liberation: the Path of Desire and the Path of Renunciation. Householders generally follow the Path of Desire, whereas monks and spiritual aspirants follow the harder Path of Renunciation. A devout Hindu who follows the Path of Desire must strictly obey the injunctions and prohibitions prescribed in the scriptures. Desire for enjoyment may extend beyond this earthly world. The scriptures describe some 'Fine Worlds' that the soul can enter after death in its subtle body. It is believed that in these Fine Worlds happiness is multiplied many times over and lasts longer, depending on the meritorious deeds performed in this earthly life. However, as soon as the fruits of meritorious deeds are exhausted, the soul has to take birth again in this earthly world of 'action' in order to store up more good *karma*. Hindus believe that there are four 'needs of life': **kama**, *artha*, *dharma* and **moksha**. The first three are goals related to personal satisfaction, social status and high morality. The supreme goal of human life is liberation (*moksha*). *Kama* means any pleasure derived through the senses, including enjoyments of art, literature and sexual activity. *Artha*, or wealth, is a value implying economic and political needs, which must be fulfilled if the personality is to develop properly. *Dharma* is the total world-view of Hindus, which would include a scheme of right conduct to be followed in various circumstances. *Kama* and *artha*, when guided by *dharma*, can elevate a person to a higher plane on the Path of Desire, and then the urge for liberation comes to mind.

For those who aspire to liberation of the soul the Hindu scriptures prescribe the harder Path of Renunciation. To follow this path the most important quality is aversion to the objects of enjoyment. Depending on one's nature and temperament, one chooses certain paths, known as **yogas**. Four main paths to liberation have been identified: *karma yoga*, or way of action; *bhakti yoga*, or way of devotion; *jnana yoga*, or way of knowledge; and *raja yoga*, the Classical method.

Some *yogas* require the participant to renounce the worldly life; others require a mental detachment from the cares of everyday life. Those who practise *karma yoga* (the *yoga* of action) endeavour to negate their *karma* by emptying themselves of the desire to earn rewards for their actions. When going about their lives, they must treat every daily duty with an even calmness of mind, absolving lethargy and restlessness and creating a clear vision. Once this purity of mind is fully achieved and ignorance is banished, the self (*atman*) becomes obvious. Lord Buddha, ninth incarnation of Hinduism, is treated as a living embodiment of the *karma yoga* ideal.

Similar to *karma yoga* in its aim is **bhakti** (devotion). *Bhakti* is defined as unflinching devotion to one's own chosen ideal. To aid devotion and minimize self-awareness, a **guru** (spiritual teacher) chooses the aspect of God most suitable for the devotee in the form of a *mantra* (specific sound symbol). The guru confides the appropriate *mantra* at the time of initiation and explains how to worship through symbol or image. The devotee must try to establish a strong personal relationship with the divine – perhaps in serving God as their master or caring for God like a child; others try to establish a friendship with God; some even fall in love with God.

One of the harder *yogas* is *jnana*, which Hindus tend to undertake only when they have mastered less demanding forms. **Jnana** means 'self-knowledge', and the idea is that devotees must strive directly to understand the nature of consciousness. This comes only to those who learn to distinguish between ordinary awareness in one's bodily condition and the unchanging self, or pure consciousness. In the process of grasping this subtle distinction, one must possess a high degree of mental control – to be content in any circumstance, tolerate afflictions without bearing grudges, and above all be able to concentrate the mind. When this concentration is mature the disciple will become one with the eternal spirit, or Brahman, and become liberated while still alive.

The Classical School of *yoga*, known as *raja*, aims to achieve this state through a series of physical exercises. The devotee has to adopt particular postures in which the spinal cord is kept erect, and the head, neck and chest held in a straight line. Rhythmic breathing helps to concentrate the mind. Aspirants must then endeavour to detach the inner sense organs from the outer limbs, thus keeping them relaxed. Regular practice steadies the mind and soothes the nerves, resulting in greater powers of observation, reasoning and memory. After much practice the mind becomes ready to concentrate on a single object or idea.

The final stage of any *yoga* is known as **samadhi**, or concentration par excellence. Even on reaching this level, there is a risk of falling back because at this stage a **yogi** has immense power at his disposal. If he or she starts using this power, there will be no liberation. But if the yogi regularly practises *samadhi* on his own mind, eventually it will become perfectly still. At this stage the real self, *atman*, is manifested in divine glory and is liberated. Coming back from the high plane of this state, a yogi seems to be a person filled with divine love, whose heart is full of peace with no desire, fear or grief. Through yogic practice all sorts of physical ailments, nervous disorders – even insanity – may be cured.

Schools of Vedanta

The *Vedas* gave birth to various systems of Indian philosophy, known as **darshanas** (doctrines). The most important of these was known as Vedanta. Its main themes are contained in the *Upanishads*. Within this stream of salvation philosophy there were three important schools, named after their founders: Samkara (or Shankara), Ramanuja and Madhva. All the schools maintain that there is only one Ultimate Reality, Brahman. Their differences are mainly due to varied conceptions of the soul, the world and their relation to Brahman. Samkara (*c.* 788–*c.* 820 CE) interpreted the *Upanishads* and *Brahma Sutra*, and founded the Advaita Vedanta, or School of Unqualified Monism. Commentaries on the same texts by Ramanuja (*c.* 1017–1137) inaugurated the Visistadvaita Vedanta, or School of Qualified Monism. And Madhva (1197–1280) introduced a new way of thinking called *Dvaitavada*, or Dualism.

Samkara held that there is only one Reality and that the world around us is not a real creation, rather a projection by *maya* (illusion), the magical power that is indistinguishable from God. The real Brahman is concealed from us because of our ignorance (*avidya*). Samkara, however, maintained that from the practical perspective of unenlightened ordinary people, the world appears to be real and God is conceived as having attributes. From the empirical perspective the self appears to be limited by the body and behaves like a finite ego. From the transcendental perspective, God is indeterminate and devoid of character, unable to be worshipped, but can be reached by the appropriate practice of *jnana yoga*. After such attainment the soul is free from the illusory ideas that separated it from God and is now free from all miseries. Indeed, he or she becomes God-self.

In his School of Qualified Monism, Ramanuja also maintained that God is the only Reality. But unlike Samkara he believed that the everyday world was not an illusion, but as real as God. He also taught that *atman* was distinguishable from, not identical with, Brahman. He taught that Brahman is made up of two parts: matter, which has no consciousness, and souls, which do have consciousness. God is possessed of all supremely good qualities. Matter eternally exists in him. Souls are conceived as infinitely small substances that also have eternal existence. Every soul is endowed with a material body in accordance with its *karma*, and is so confined until completely dissociated from the body.

The School of Duality, founded by Madhva, outlined two kinds of reality: the independent and the dependent. Only the Supreme Being (God) is independent. Dependent reality consists of positives and negatives: conscious souls are positive, while unconscious matter is negative. Although the soul and the world are real eternal entities, they are dependent on God.

Madhva identified Brahman with Vishnu as the Creator, Sustainer and Destroyer of the world. Vishnu is endowed with a supernatural body and rules our souls: so God is both transcendent (beyond us) and immanent (within us). God is manifest in various forms, appearing and reappearing as incarnations (*avatars*), and is mystically present in sacred images. According to dualistic thinking, matter originates from cosmic energy found in nature and gradually returns to it. In creating forms out of this energy God partakes in it himself. But ignorance obscures our spiritual power and screens off the Supreme Being. Liberation, which is fellowship with God, can only become a spiritual reality once 'unessential' forms are cast off.

 One God, many gods

Though Hindus believe that the Ultimate Reality, or Brahman, is one, as creator of the universe he has innumerable attributes that human languages are insufficient to describe. Devotees find it spiritually uplifting to worship Brahman through these different aspects that are seen as deities. The worshipper chooses certain attributes and forms a mental image of his or her chosen deity. Theoretically there can be as many gods and goddesses as there are devotees.

In ancient Vedic times there was no temple of gods. Hymns described their attributes, which included associations with nature, such as fire, water, wind, earth, the moon, light, dawn and so on. The chief deity was Indra, symbol of royal power. In later post-Vedic times the aspects of God became more concisely defined as a trinity: Brahma creates the world, Vishnu sustains it and Shiva destroys it. The process of creation, preservation and destruction continues in a perpetual cycle. In balancing preservation with destruction, Brahma symbolizes the possibility of existence that results from the union of opposites. All the many gods and goddesses worshipped by contemporary Hindus are somehow related to these three major deities of the trinity. For example, the Divine Mother is worshipped as Durga, **Kali**, Jagaddhatri, but all are the different images of Shakti (consort of Shiva).

Lord Vishnu is popularly worshipped in the form of human incarnations: Rama and Krishna. Rama is depicted holding a bow in one hand and giving blessings with the other, while Lord Krishna is worshipped holding a flute to his mouth as if blowing. Hanuman, the monkey-god, is also associated with Vishnu. *Ramayana* pictures Hanuman as a rare combination, having extraordinary physical strength and wisdom. In Indian temples specially erected for Hanuman, we find the image in a heroic pose, usually with a club in his left hand and a mountain in his right hand, symbolizing his physical strength.

Shiva is worshipped in both human form and as the *linga* (phallus). He is depicted as a handsome young man with strong limbs. He has four arms, two holding a trident and drum, the other two in poses suggesting assurance of protection and encouragement. His crown has long matted hair from which the river Ganges is said to flow. Various 'strings' are about his person to signify the sacred thread of *atman*: a necklace, arm-bracelets, serpents swarming over his body and a garland of skulls round his neck.

Worship of the divine mother, or Shakti, is very popular in India. When Shakti, or 'energy', is in a static condition before evolution, when the universe is yet to be created, that state is called Brahman. When it starts evolving into creation it becomes Shakti. Just as fire and its burning power are inseparable, so Brahma and Shakti also cannot be separated. Each member of the Hindu trinity has his consort, or Shakti: Sarasvati is the Shakti of Brahma, Lakshmi is the Shakti of Vishnu, and Parvati is the Shakti of Shiva. Sarasvati is the personification of all knowledge: the sciences, arts, crafts and skills. Lakshmi, goddess of fortune, is worshipped in almost all Hindu households. She is enchantingly beautiful, stands on a lotus and holds lotuses in her hands.

An overwhelming majority of the goddesses of Hinduism are variations of Parvati, the consort of Shiva. Durga is the most widely worshipped aspect of Shakti. Literally meaning 'one who is difficult to approach', she personifies the total powers of the gods and is naturally difficult to know. The worship of Kali is also common among devotees of the Divine Mother, Devi. Kali's name, 'the Black One', with its typical depiction of angry red face and protruding tongue, indicate the painful, suffering side of mother nature. Together with the light and bountiful side, the twin aspects of nature as pain and pleasure, life and death are presented.

All worship of the Hindus starts with honouring **Ganesh** (or Ganapati), who is the god of prudence; successful ventures and will keep his devotees on the path of righteousness. He has a human body with an elephant's head, always with one tusk broken. His big belly is decorated with a snake to symbolize divine wisdom, yet he rides on a chariot borne by a mouse, traditionally the one creature the elephant is said to fear.

Modern history

Though Hinduism is a religion of pre-historic origin it has undergone many changes during the course of recorded history. Lord Buddha, the founder of Buddhism, is considered by the Hindus to be an incarnation of God. Historical personalities such as Sankara, Ramanuja, Srichaityanya, Nanak and many others have contributed a lot in moulding the Hindu mind.

Islamic rule in India for several centuries made Hindus conservative and orthodox, even superstitious. European invasion from the seventeenth century onwards brought the message of renaissance. European missionaries tried to convert Hindus and Muslims to Christianity, and as a reaction to this and also as a mark of self-assertion, Hindu revivalist movements started up.

The first reform movement in modern India was launched by Raja Rammohan Roy (1772–1831). His writings and advocacy pressured the government into banning the custom, known as **sati**, of burning widows on the funeral pyre of their husbands. He also tried to stop child marriage and domestic harassment of women by opening girls' schools. His mission was later carried on by the members of Brahma Samaj, who ultimately formed a separate sect. Brahmas are worshippers of God in absolute form and their method of worship is almost similar to that of Christians.

Dayanand Swarasati founded Arya Samaj to rejuvenate Hinduism in the light of the *Vedas* and *Upanishads*. He was against cast privilege and promoted the re-conversion of former Hindus from other religions. Members of Arya Samaj contributed a lot in teaching nationalism throughout undivided India. Many martyrs in the struggle to free India from colonial rule came from Arya Samaj.

Swami Vivekananda (1863–1902), disciple of Sri Ramakrishna (1836–86), founded the Ramakrishna Mission in 1897 for the liberation of the self and welfare of humanity. Sri Ramakrishna taught that all religions are true and the right path to God. The Ramakrishna movement has had a tremendous influence on people's minds for more than a hundred years, with thousands of organizations founded throughout the world promoting his liberal message.

Nineteenth-century India witnessed the emergence of hundreds of luminaries – Rishi Bankim Chandra, Sri Aurobinda, Bal Gangadhar Tilak, Mahatma Gandhi – who contributed to the reinterpretation of Hindu scriptures, combating superstition and establishing welfare programmes to raise the standard of living for fellow Hindus.

It is interesting to note that so often in the wake of reform comes an orthodox reaction. The abolition of *sati*, child marriage, widow re-marriage and other reforms were strongly protested by orthodox Hindus. When Indian nationalism developed, these reactionaries started consolidating the Hindu line on orthodox beliefs and practices. In 1925 Rastriya Sayangsevak Sangha was established to work for the cause of Hindu nationalism (Hindutva) which, as noted above, is a political ideology upheld by some political parties and their socio-religious wings.

In the twentieth century we find the emergence of some religious personalities, such as Yogananda Paramhansa, A. C. Dey Bhaktivedanta, Sai Baba, Ravisankar, Anandamurti, Osho Rajnish and many others, who became very popular outside India. Subsequently they established organizations for the propagation of certain aspects of Hinduism, and as a result there are Hindu temples built in different countries of the world. Though the main teachings of these religious leaders hardly contradict traditional Hinduism, many of them have imported some elements, even magic and miracles, to attract disaffected young people. Some modern gurus even claim to be God incarnated, and there is no church of Hinduism to contradict their tall claims. However, they are often exposed by the media.

Today elite Hindus are mostly liberal and respectful towards other faiths. Motivated use of religion for narrow political gain is disliked by the majority of Hindus. Nevertheless, Hindus have to bear this stigma because of the few fanatics.

Contemporary traditions and movements

The *Bhakti* movement

The word *bhakti* means devotion, and implies faith, love, loving surrender, devotional attachment and piety. It is closely related to **puja**, meaning adoration, reverence, worship, and represents supreme attachment to God. The *Bhakti* movement began in the Tamil region of south India in the third century, when the Shiva saint Tirumoolar and his disciples started a tradition of offering self-surrendering prayers based on ancient Vedic rituals.

But *Bhakti* turned into a movement in the medieval period, when it was influenced by indigenous forms of worship as well as Semitic religions such as Islam. Two distinct but complementary traditions developed in the movement. The Saintly tradition was characterized by rapture, moral enthusiasm, divine intoxication and deep spiritual experience. Working against this trend was the Acharya tradition, which tried to prevent *Bhakti* from degenerating into a purely subjective emotion by formulating a new conceptual framework.

By the second half of the first millennium, religious poets dominated the movement. The impassioned hymns of such poets as the Nayanars (devotees of Shiva), Alvars (those immersed in God's love) and the **Vaishnava** (devotees of Vishnu) conveyed a powerful sense of devotion to God. The popular *Bhakti* movement spread to all parts of India. However, the religious ideas of Caitanya (1486–1533) came into conflict with the orthodox Hindu social system, especially the priestcraft. Cutting across the entrenched caste system of India, he preached not only that no ritual was essential to achieve union with God but also that the passionate chanting of God's glory with love was alone enough to liberate even a degenerate soul.

Kabir (1398–1518) was hostile towards caste discrimination, idolatry, pilgrimage, vows and the external paraphernalia of religious life. He rejected the doctrine of incarnations and also the authority of the scriptures. Instead he preached – to both Hindus and Muslims – that they should endeavour to conquer hatred and extend their love to all human beings, as God resides in all.

Guru Nanak (1469–1538) also rejected rituals, pilgrimage and fasting. He argued against discrimination and intolerance. Both Hindus and Muslims were attracted by his pleasant personality and teachings. In him began a long line of ten Gurus that culminated in the formation of a new faith called Sikhism.

Guru movements

The guru, or spiritual guide, has drawn immense respect from disciples throughout the Hindu religious tradition. But 'guru movement' is a new coinage by non-Hindu scholars to explain certain recent trends in popular Hinduism. 'Guru' is the living embodiment of God on earth. So by serving and worshipping a guru, a disciple is said actually worship God. Any contribution to fulfilling a guru's mission is considered a meritorious deed. Unlike traditional Hinduism, the guru movement is characterized by organization. After initiation, disciples become members of the organization and have to follow its rules. There are, of course, separate rules for monks and householders. Besides conducting spiritual training, contemporary Hindu organizations take up educational, cultural and social works as regular activities.

A number of living Hindu religious teachers are regarded as gurus even by people from other faiths. The initiation given to an individual does not require his or her conversion to Hinduism. Pluralistic toleration has made contemporary 'gurus' acceptable to many people throughout the world. Hindu temples are now seen almost everywhere as a result of the guru movement.

 # Worship and festivals

Hindu worship is very simple. Devotees choose a deity and offer anything they like to it. After initiation, he or she worships the deity, as advised by the guru. This advice would include details of the holy *mantra*, a personal utterance that should be performed as much as possible during the auspicious hours of dawn, noon and dusk.

Besides daily worship, there are ceremonies to attend on special occasions. During advents of the solar and lunar calendar, priests are invited to perform rituals on behalf of the worshipper. Some Hindus maintain a shrine in their own home, where daily worship is performed either by the devotee or by a professional priest. The procedure for formal worship requires great punctiliousness about the details concerning offerings, utensils, decoration, posture and movement, along with a perfect enunciation of the Vedic and Puranic *mantras*. There are volumes of books written by experts on such ritual observances. But whatever the worship – daily or festive – a follower of any cult has to offer *puja* to at least the five deities of the major cults: Vishnu, Shiva, Devi (or Shakti, Mother Goddess), Surya and Ganapati/Ganesh. Some deities are more dominant in some regions than others. For example, Bengal is dominated by devotees of Vishnu and Devi, while the south Indian provinces are inhabited mostly by devotees of Shiva as well as Vishnu.

Of the innumerable deities worshipped, each has at least one festival every year for ceremonial worship. Some festivals are popular in particular regions, such as Ganesh Chaturthi, Sripancami, Kojagari Puja. Other, bigger festivals may be observed by Hindus everywhere. Some major festivals – Durgapuja, Kalipuja, Diwali, Holi, Janmastami – are celebrated not only throughout India but in other countries where Hindus live.

Each linguistic group and sect of Hinduism has its own calendar of festivals. An ephemeris is published every year listing dates and moments of auspicious importance. New Year's Day, full moons and new moons, solar and lunar eclipses, are all prescribed for special festivals, including ritualistic baths in holy rivers, such as the Ganges.

Folk traditions

Some Hindu rituals and festivals cannot be traced to Vedic or Puranic origins. We may call these 'popular folk traditions'. Though there is no scriptural injunction to follow, there is no prohibition either against performing these rituals. The traditions are mostly oral.

Women's involvement is significant, and some *bratas* (ceremonies) are prescribed for women only. Some are prescribed for unmarried girls, others for housewives and a few others for widows. Through the performance of these ceremonies Hindu women become pious. They learn to sacrifice their own personal interest for the greater benefit of their husbands, children and relatives, even the community at large. The stability of a traditional Hindu family is greatly influenced by these folk ceremonies.

The major turning events of a Hindu's life are called *samskaras* (sacraments). There are ten in all, though some are now virtually obsolete. Marriage, birth rites, Vedic initiation, naming a child, taking solid food all belong to classical Hinduism and are still relevant today. Around each *samskara* folk traditions have developed, which vary according to local culture. The priests perform the Vedic and Puranic aspects of the ceremony on behalf of the worshipper, and the rest of the activities are carried out by the family, relatives and neighbours. Popular folk tradition is important to all sectors of Hindu society.

Because the *dalit* ('Untouchables') were prohibited from participating in any mainstream worship, their ancestors developed a special kind of folk religion within local communities in direct response to local conditions. The *Ramayana*, *Mahabharata* and the *Puranas*, however, did play a major role in creating their ethos. Though each *dalit* community has its own distinctive deities, ceremonies and saints, there is also a more superstitious level of belief manifested in ghosts, demons and spirit possession.

Village tradition

The village tradition of Hinduism is deeply rooted in the soil of India's grazing lands, ploughed fields and other features of agrarian society. Every old village has a presiding deity, usually a goddess, who draws reverence from all the villagers. A big tree, a few rocks or the earthly remains of some departed souls are often treated by the people as representing divine power.

Formal worship in the temples is performed by priests, who utter mystic *mantras* that are hardly understood by the ordinary person. In the evenings, scripture-reading sessions happen regularly, religious lessons are imparted through stories and parables spoken in popular vernacular, and devotional songs are sung.

After reaping the harvests, the villagers celebrate their festivals with grandeur. Fairs are often organized to add to their enjoyment. Telecommunication facilities have enabled popular festivals to be celebrated in virtually every village. Village traditions, though fading near the bigger towns, still continue in remote villages.

The dichotomy in the caste system means that Hindu villagers are divided into two constituent groups. Although the members of each caste are organically linked throughout the whole region, the caste system divides each village into compacted groups of families.

Conclusion

Hinduism, though a very old religion, is still a dynamic one. Several Hindu organizations are active in, and outside, India and play a major role in moulding the religious psyche of modern Hindus. However, the orthodox Hindus living in villages are still guided in the main by their own traditional family priests. The liberation of women is being appreciated in all sections of Hindu society. Meanwhile the spread of scientific and secular education adopted by the majority of Hindus is gradually reducing religious superstition to a minimum.

? QUESTIONS

1 What are the distinctive features of Hinduism?

2 Give an account of contemporary traditions and movements within Hinduism.

3 What are the scriptures of Hinduism? What are the major festivals of Hinduism and when do they occur?

4 What is the relation between God and individual self? Explain the relation between God and the world.

5 Explain the Hindu view on Karma and rebirth.

Glossary

asrama one of the four stages of life of a Hindu
atman the self; soul
avatar incarnation of God (i.e. descent of the Universal Spirit)
bhakti devotion; intense love for God
Brahman literally, the Great One; Impersonal God; Absolute Reality
darshana any system of Hindu philosophy
dharma essential quality underlying the cosmos; code of ethics; duty
Ganapati/Ganesh Hindu elephant-like deity
guru spiritual guide
jnana knowledge
Kali name of God as the Divine Mother
kama lust; desire
karma action; deed; work
Krishna incarnation of God as Vishnu (the Preserver)
kshatriya primary social group responsible for protection of society from external aggression
mantra sacred formula uttered in connection with rituals; mystic syllable
maya illusion
moksha liberation of the soul from all kinds of bondage
Parvati incarnation of the Divine Mother
puja worship
Purana(s) class of popular scriptural texts
Rama incarnation of God as Vishnu
rita Vedic principle of rhythm in the universe
rsis ancient seers
samadhi high concentration; trance; super-conscious state
samsara cycle of life through repeated births and deaths; worldly life
Sannyasa renunciation of social ties; final stage of Hindu life

sati widow's self-immolation on her husband's funeral pyre
Shakti Divine Power; name of God as the Divine Mother
Shiva one of the Hindu trinity representing God as the Destroyer
shruti that which is heard; revealed knowledge
smriti that which is remembered; any scripture other than the *Vedas*
Surya Hindu deity of the Sun
sutra aphorism; terse saying embodying a lesson
tantra class of scriptural texts presenting God as the Divine Mother
Upanishad(s) Hindu scriptures included in the *Vedas* mainly about the eternal verities of life
Vaishnava Hindu sect, or member of it, worshipping God as Vishnu
varna any of four primary social categories in ancient India; caste
Vedanta the end of the *Vedas*; school of Hindu thought based on the *Upanishads*
Vishnu God as the Preserver; one of the Hindu trinity
yoga union with God; course of spiritual discipline making for such union
yogi one who strives earnestly for union with God, especially through *raja yoga*

 # Further reading

Altekar, A. S., *The Position of Women in Hindu Civilization* (Delhi: Motilal Banarsidas, 1983).

Anand, Subhash, *Major Hindu Festivals: A Christian Appreciation* (Bandra: St Paul Publications, 1991).

Basham, A. L., *The Origins and Development of Classical Hinduism* (Oxford: Oxford University Press, 1990).

Bhargava, P. L., *Vedic Religion and Culture: An Exposition of Distinct Facts* (New Delhi: D. K. Printworld (P) Ltd, 1994).

Chatterjee, Satischandra, *The Fundamentals of Hinduism: A Philosophical Study* (Calcutta: University of Calcutta, 1970).

Klostermaier, K., *A Survey of Hinduism* (New Delhi: Munshiram Manoharlal, 1990).

Mahadevan, T. M. P., *Outlines of Hinduism* (Bombay: Chetana, 1977).

4
Buddhist thought and practice

Shanthikumar Hettiarachchi

 ## Introduction

Buddhism is a way of life. In order to appreciate this way of life we need to study the life and teaching of the Buddha, and the development of Buddhism, its modern manifestations and its responses to contemporary issues. We need to recognize that Buddhism adapts to changes in society. Buddhist thought should not be seen solely as a historical sequence. Following in the Buddha's footsteps, Buddhism focuses on the *here and now*. In presenting the faith as a contemporary, lived religion, I aim to bring Buddhism closer to our readers and their lives, issues of everyday loss and gain, despair and happiness. Together we will look at human structures while also focusing on the internal transformation that acts as a catalyst for moral change. For according to Buddhism, moral change is basic to societal change.

 ## Gotama the Buddha

In approximately 560 BCE, Siddhartha **Gotama** was born in Lumbini in northern India (modern Nepal), where his father, Suddhodana, was the ruler. Suddhodana sheltered his son from the outside world and surrounded him with pleasures and wealth. Despite his father's efforts at keeping away the unpleasant realities of life outside the court, Gotama had four life-changing encounters. First he saw an older person walking frail and tired, then a sick person in pain, third a dead person being carried for cremation, and finally an ascetic wandering peacefully. Profoundly affected by the suffering and pain he witnessed, Gotama decided to leave the luxury of life in the palace and began a quest through austerity to find the answer to the problem of pain and human suffering (**dukkha**), more correctly translated as unsatisfactoriness.

Soon after the birth of his son Rahula, Gotama, aged 29, left his palace to seek a solution to his question of human suffering through the traditional methods of observing extremes of both luxury and austerity. While deep in

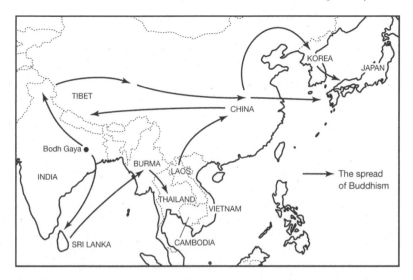

Figure 4.1 The spread of Buddhism

meditation under a Bo (or Bodhi) tree, Gotama at the age of 35 attained 'enlightenment' in Bodh Gaya (modern Bihar, India). He preached for 45 years and taught all kinds of people: men and women, kings and peasants, priests and outcasts, bankers and beggars, holy men and thieves. He passed away at the age of 80 in Kushinagara (modern Uttara Pradesh, India). Buddha never wanted a chief disciple after he passed away; instead he wished his disciples to rely upon his teaching, the *dhamma*. After his death his disciples spread his teachings to other parts of India, where they were adapted to local cultures. Even though his chief disciples happened to be men, at the request of Ananda and his stepmother, Gotama the Buddha seems to have given his consent to establish a female order of monks as practitioners and teachers. He set women on an equal footing with men in religious vocation and social responsibility, and accepted that they possessed all the qualities required to achieve high levels of religious experience and discipline, just like their male counterparts.

🪷 Early Buddhist schools of thought

Buddhism in Asia can be classified geographically or in terms of tradition; that is, according to the different schools (*yanas*) that developed (see Figure 4.2 overleaf). The two main schools are Theravada and Mahayana. The East Asian countries of China, Korea, Japan and Vietnam all belong to the Mahayana tradition. Literally this means 'Greater vehicle' but is best described as a movement encompassing a variety of views and expositions of the fundamentals of the Buddhist world-view. A great emphasis is placed on the values of compassion (**karuna**) and insight or wisdom (*prajna* or **panna**). The *Bodhisattvas* (embodiments of the spiritual ideal) devote their ultimate service to others and become a new model for religious practice and life. Tibet, Mongolia and parts of the former Soviet Union follow the Vajarayana tradition that grew out of Mahayana. The school is best translated as 'Diamond vehicle', a term designating the path of 'tantric' Buddhism. This tradition emphasizes the imperishable nature of the enlightenment (*bodhi*), the invisibility of appearances, emptiness (*sunyata*), compassion and insight, or wisdom.

The South and South-East Asian countries, such as Sri Lanka, Burma, Laos, Cambodia and Thailand, all follow the Theravada tradition. This tradition, which is more ascetic than the Mahayana, is regarded as orthodox and is sometimes referred to as Pali Buddhism because its canon of scriptures is written in the ancient Indic language, Pali (whereas Mahayana scripture is written in Sanskrit). Theravada is also known as Hinayana and Savakayana. However, the term Hinayana has derogatory overtones, hence is less used to identify this specific school of thought, which is more popularly known as Theravada. The term Savakayana (Vehicle of the Hearers) was given its name by the Mahayana groups to refer to the early disciples who had 'heard' the teachings of the Buddha, and by putting them into practice sought to become *arahants* (those who have attained the goal of enlightenment or awakening).

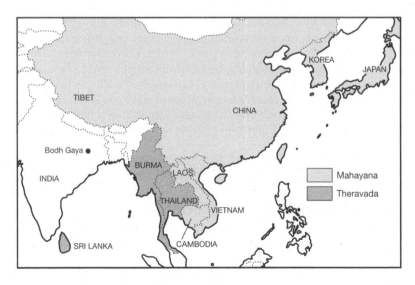

Figure 4.2 Schools of Buddhism

The Buddhist style of teaching

It must be specifically noted that what the Buddha found was not necessarily a 'god-experience', as was the case with many other spiritually enlightened persons in history. Buddha never claimed to be a deity – someone to be followed – but rather considered himself a 'pointer' to a higher reality. He was not called a **guru**, which was quite usual among his contemporary Hindu mendicants, but instead was called a **Sattha**, an all-knowing teacher and leader. His style of teaching was a skilful adaptation of a spiritual culture to the level and concerns of his hearers. His dialogic method, which invoked responses from his varied audiences, moved them to seek his vision and the truth he was communicating, but without feeling any imposition. He allowed his audience to question him and he gave responses in return. A classic example was when the Buddha was once asked by the **Brahmins** (the priestly group) about how one can attain union with the **Brahman**, creator God in Hinduism. In his usual response, the Buddha did not deny the possibility of such union, but proposed that it could be attained through developing a spiritual regime where one engages in meditation, through loving kindness and compassion, instead of through the traditional Vedic method of animal sacrifices.

He responded to questions in an analytical and logical fashion. Some he did not answer; for some he posed a counter-question in order to expose the concealed presuppositions in the question. For others he first clarified the nature of the question and encouraged his listeners to seek answers for themselves as a way of building character and self-worth. An example of the Buddha's intervention appears in one of the greatest texts in the Pali canon, the *Kalamasutta*. In this, Buddha admonished the inhabitants of a village for listening to a group of visiting teachers who were boasting about their own teachings and criticizing those of others. When the Buddha too visited the village, he also was approached by the inhabitants and asked several questions. His response was that it was natural to be uncertain and disillusioned as to what is true and false in the teaching they had heard so far. Buddha taught them that they should not accept anything simply on the grounds of revelation, tradition or report. He went on to list other grounds: that they should not accept something because it is a product of pure reasoning, or because it might be true from a particular standpoint, or because of a superficial assessment of the facts, or because it conforms to one's preconceived notions, or because it is authoritative, or because of the prestige of their teacher. Buddha emphasized self-reliance, investigative knowledge and experiential testing of what is heard before making a sound judgement on matters of crucial concern. He was neither satisfied with purely rational speculation nor authoritative tradition that underestimated the human potential for inquiry and logical thinking. He also warned his hearers and disciples not to react emotionally to what they heard. Instead he encouraged them to assess patiently the degree of truth or falseness in what was said.

Three marks of reality in Buddhist thought

Understanding the three signs of nature or phenomena is useful in grasping the central Buddhist teachings on human reality and its predicament. Once again three Pali words are used to describe it. The first is **anicca**, meaning that everything is subject to change; second, *dukkha*, meaning that there is an all-pervasive unsatisfactoriness; and third, **anatta**, meaning that nothing has a separate self, better described as 'no-soul theory'.

The phenomenon of change (*anicca*) is what is experienced in every moment of existence. Nothing in the world is permanently fixed. It is a fact that if we were to sit on the bank of a flowing river and close our eyes for a moment and open them again, then what we see is the same river but a different volume of water. It is obvious that we are not the same person now physically, emotionally and mentally that we were ten years ago. Our being is in a state of flux, and this is true of everything and everywhere in nature.

The concept of *dukkha* is best translated as 'unsatisfactoriness', which means that even a moment of happiness, rapture or satisfaction would again revert to the moments of despair and loss previously felt, which causes even more craving and further entangles our selves in a web of craving that ends in 'unsatisfactoriness'.

The notion of soul (*atta* or **atman**) is a key philosophical reality in Hinduism, out of which Buddhism historically emerged. Buddhism proposed a radical alternative way of life. Unlike Hinduism, it does not teach that there is a permanent entity called 'soul'. Instead, Buddhism begins with a no-soul basis. It presents itself as a stream of thought that considers 'here and now' and existential concerns rather than issues and questions for which there are only inadequate explanations, which in turn are likely to lead to more confusion, perhaps even conflict.

Who are the Buddhists?

A Buddhist is someone who understands the Buddha's teaching, who is convinced that his teaching will lead to emancipation and who is willing to follow the path. This process is what the Buddhists consider to be the path to blissfulness. Traditionally Buddhists see themselves as taking refuge in the *Buddha* (the Enlightened one), the *dhamma* (the teaching) and the *sangha* (community of monks). These elements are called the Triple Gem (*thisarana*), the refuges. Adherence to the Triple Gem is the first step towards a fuller observance of the Five Precepts (**panchasila**) of Buddhism.

The Five Precepts

The Buddha's teaching is ethical in all its aspects. It presents a basic moral code for virtuous and wholesome living, well summed up in five precepts:

1 I undertake to abstain from killing any form of life.

2 I undertake to abstain from taking what is not given.

3 I undertake to abstain from misbehaviour including adultery.

4 I undertake to abstain from lying.

5 I undertake to abstain from taking any kind of intoxicants that cause loss of mindfulness.

The Buddha's approach is neither pessimistic in viewing the whole of life as negative nor optimistic in considering that life is perfect. Buddha looked at the nature of reality as it is. He was a realist. His primary concern was to respond positively to our present predicament, which he identified as human unsatisfactoriness. However, his lifetime teaching was based on observable categories of living that human beings should strive to manage if they wish to tread the path. He was of the opinion that his teaching (*dhamma*) must be used like a raft to cross over a river rather than it being the end of the pursuit. The Buddhist view is that to be born human is a rare opportunity; therefore it must be lived virtuously to attain ultimate freedom.

The Four Noble Truths

The Buddha's proposal for his listeners was to understand things 'as they are'. Faith and belief might be important but were seen as only a means to achieving the fundamental goal of ultimate freedom. He expounded that the nature of reality was that human beings are entangled in a rollercoaster of unsatisfactoriness. His insight into this reality was gained through his own realization and the discovery of the Four Noble Truths. This scheme of thought is founded on the reality of the human predicament of unsatisfactoriness, its cause, cessation and the path to its cessation. One may recognize these four states simply for what they are, as they are experienced, and then act appropriately for each one. First comprehend the predicament of unsatisfactoriness, then abandon its cause. In bringing about its cessation on a single occasion, we move further along the path to its final cessation. The scheme is a very pragmatic way to approach the phenomenon of unsatisfactoriness. Let us see how it is outlined in the four Buddhist categories of truth:

1 **There is unsatisfactoriness**. The Buddha realized that pain and unsatisfactoriness are everywhere in nature and human life. The reality of existence means that all will encounter unsatisfactoriness. Birth is painful and so is death. Sickness and old age are painful. Throughout life, all living things encounter unsatisfactoriness. It is the most existential predicament in human interaction.

2 **There is a cause of this unsatisfactoriness**. The Gotama believed that the root cause of this unsatisfactoriness is desire (**tanha**). This is unchecked satisfaction, wealth, and other forms of selfish enjoyment that cause

unsatisfactoriness. These cravings can never be satisfied as long as they are rooted in ignorance.

3 **Unsatisfactoriness can cease.** Pain, futility and vanity will cease when all desires are transformed through a process of disciplined ethical and spiritual training.

4 **There is a way that leads to the cessation of this unsatisfactoriness.** Buddha further expounds the fourth truth and calls it the Noble Eightfold Path.

The Noble Eightfold Path

The Buddhist proposition to follow the Eightfold Path helps to extinguish all craving, which is a stumbling block to true joy and bliss. The Eightfold Path is a system of therapy designed to develop a disciplined conduct that will release people from the lurking tendencies caused by ignorance and craving. The eight factors are:

1 right understanding

2 right thought

3 right speech

4 right action

5 right livelihood

6 right effort

7 right mindfulness

8 right concentration.

Of the Eightfold Path, 1 and 2 are in pursuit of wisdom (*panna*); 3, 4 and 5 are in pursuit of an ethical path (**sila**); 6, 7 and 8 are in pursuit of mental discipline (**samadhi**). The three aspects – ethical path, mental discipline and wisdom – are fundamental to Buddhist training and discipline.

Training in the two latter aspects leads to the realization of Ultimate Reality, with complete freedom, happiness and peace, through moral, spiritual and intellectual perfection. The Buddhist ideal is to opt for a life of middle ground, avoiding all extreme ideas, because they eventually lead to anxiety and disappointment.

✿ Three core concepts in Buddhism

Three important concepts in understanding Buddhism are **karma**, **samsara** and **nirvana**. They have been the most debated and misinterpreted of concepts ever since they were first discussed in Buddhist history, especially when encountering other world-views. Buddha's approach to each of these realities was different from both contemporary Hindu and Jaina views as his teachings primarily contained ethical and pragmatic moorings from which to view life and reality.

What is *karma*?

The notion of *karma* is not unique to Buddhism. It has its roots in Vedic Hinduism and also shares with the Jain spiritual path, but each of those traditions carries a slightly different understanding, even though some fundamental nuances remain the same. *Karma* means the law of cause and effect in a person's life: reaping what one has sown. Buddhists accept that every person must go through a process of birth and rebirth until the person reaches the state of *nirvana* in which one breaks this cycle of births (*samsara*). The simplest explanation of *karma* would be to state, 'You are what you are, and do what you do, as a result of what you were and did in a previous birth.' For a Buddhist what you will be in the next life depends on your actions in this present life – the cycle of life (*samsara*) is unstoppable unless you attain final freedom (*nirvana*) from being born. Hence Buddhists consider human life to be paramount. It is central to seeking a solution to the human predicament of unsatisfactoriness that they must attempt while in human form. The Buddha said that human life was a noble state. In his own words, it is as rare as a one-eyed turtle that sees the full moon through the eye of a yoke floating in the ocean. Thus life should not be wasted on wanton distractions that may divert one's focus from meaning, fulfilment, happiness and bliss.

What is *samsara*?

The law of *samsara* is one of the most perplexing and difficult concepts in Buddhism to understand. It holds that everything is in a cycle of birth and rebirth. Buddha taught that people do not have individual souls. The existence of an individual self or ego is an illusion (**maya**). There is no eternal substance of a person that goes through the rebirth cycle. The Buddha differs here substantially from all Hindu thought on *samsara*. The three words in the Indic traditions that dissect the meaning of life and life-after-death – *karma, samsara* and *nirvana* – together embrace the concept of reincarnation. This is the notion of rebirth that refers to a different set of meanings and circumstances in a different situation of life and life-after-death. According to the Buddhist scholar, **Bhikkhu** Nyanatiloka, some commentaries do not attach any ethical significance to the theory of rebirth but maintain that belief in *karma* and rebirth are a sufficient inducement to moral behaviour here and now. When we understand that our good and bad actions can rebound upon ourselves and determine our future lives, bringing either happiness or unsatisfactoriness, this gives us a decisive reason to avoid unwholesome conduct and pursue the good and well-being of all. Accordingly, if the Buddhist model is to be accepted, what is it that goes through the cycle of births if not the individual soul? The Buddhist response is that what goes through the rebirth cycle is only a set of feelings, impressions, present moments, and the *karma* that is passed on. In other words, one process leads to another, and a personality in one existence is the direct cause of the type of individuality that appears in the next existence. The new individual in the next life will not be exactly the same person. However, the Buddhist world-view does not aspire to existence, even though it occurs. Hence the emphasis it places on the next life is difficult to understand because in the Buddhist scheme of thought the goal is *nirvana*.

What is *nirvana*?

Nirvana literally means 'the blowing out' of existence. *Nirvana* is very different from the Christian concept of heaven, the Islamic idea of paradise or the Hindu or Jaina notion of *moksa*. *Nirvana* is not a 'place' like heaven or paradise but rather a state of being. What exactly it is Buddha never really articulated. *Nirvana* is a perennial state of being. It is the state in which the law of *karma* and the rebirth cycle come to an end. It is the end of all feelings of unsatisfactoriness and unwholesome clinging and attachments, a state in which there are no desires and the individual consciousness comes to an end. It is a condition where there is neither earth nor water, neither air nor light, neither limitless space nor limitless time. There is no kind of being, neither this world nor that world. There is no arising or passing away, no dying, no cause or effect, no change or standing still. Even though *nirvana* is expressed in negative terms, the reality of *nirvana* itself is not negative. If *nirvana* does indicate any negative nuance, then it is the annihilation of illusion and of the false idea of the self. *Nirvana* is neither negative nor positive, as these ideas are relative and fall within the phenomenal world in which each thing exists along with its opposite: for example, joy and sorrow. The negation of negative value does not result in a negative. The Buddha's most comprehensive description of *nirvana* was the well-known synonym, freedom (*mutti*). No one would say freedom is negative, yet the term may have a negative aspect: freedom is always a liberation from something destructive, which is evil and negative. But freedom is not negative in itself. So *nirvana*, or *vimutti*, absolute freedom, is freedom from all defilements, craving or greed, hatred, delusion and ignorance. It also includes freedom from all terms of duality, relativity, time and space. Some popular and ill-informed expressions, such as that the Buddha 'entered into *Nirvana*' after his death, have given rise to speculation that *nirvana* is a state, a position or a realm in which there is some sort of pleasurable existence. *Nirvana* in Buddhist understanding is fully passed away, fully blown or fully extinct because neither the Buddha nor others who have attained the ultimate goal have re-existence after death. It is not a state of existence with celestial beings, paradise, heaven or any other reality. However, some scholars argue that 'nirvana can be realized in their very life: it is not necessary to wait till you die to attain it.' Samyutta Nikaya confirms this position:

> He who has realized the Truth, Nirvana, is the happiest being in the world. He is free from all complexes and obsessions, the worries and troubles that torment others. He does not repent the past nor does he brood over the future. He lives fully in the present.

God and Buddhism

The notion of God and Buddhism has always been a central discussion within theistic traditions as the concept of a personal or creator God does not fit into the Buddhist world-view. It would be mistaken to identify the Buddha as a 'mere human being'. When the Buddha was asked whether he was a human being, **Brahma** (God) or **Mara** (the Evil One), he denied that he was any one of them and claimed that he was Buddha, that is, an Enlightened being who had attained the transcendent. This does not make the Buddha unique as it is a status to which any human being can aspire. Therefore God and revelation are not at the core of the Buddhist inquiry into the nature of reality, even though such inquiry may be helpful in the pursuit of the ultimate bliss of emancipation, *nirvana*.

Today there are many schools of thought within Buddhism, and some of them differ in their concept of the divine and the place of the Buddha. The Theravada school of thought (school of the Elders) maintains that Buddhism is a non-theistic ethical discipline, a system of self-training, anthropocentric, stressing ethics and mind-culture and therefore must be treated differently from the theistic traditions with their creeds, confessions, decrees and theologies. Even though this austere position is popular among the Theravadins, the 'god talk' is very much part of the discourse in some of the Mahayana traditions. It is unfair to say, as some have claimed, that Buddhism promotes atheism. Rather it is one of the major traditions that is non-theistic, with a focus that has shifted from god-centred discourse within 'religion' to the nature of reality here and now.

The theological rigour of the concept of God, with its own very valid contribution to the development of thought and institutions in communities, is a formidable critical tool. The concept of God, according to Buddhism, is useful in helping those who emphasize the centrality of faith to take steps towards achieving higher spiritual goals. It helps them to reach out to a valid source of knowledge and to be fully aware of the present human predicament of unsatisfactoriness. Therefore the Buddhist option for a middle way means opting for a spiritual life led through wholesome, uncomplicated living and behaviour in society. The human predicament of unsatisfactoriness and the search for a solution to this central question in the Buddhist world-view takes serious ethical, moral, psychological, social and philo-sophical dimensions. It draws the attention of ordinary people, monks, scholars and all those who are interested in what the Buddha has taught. It continues to capture peoples' imagination and attempts to quench the thirst people have for meaning and purpose in life, just as it is important for believers in God to examine the theological implications of what it means for them to believe and to belong. These approaches continue to interest people in all walks of life in their pursuit of happiness, joy and meaning.

Buddhist devotion and prayers

An observation of Buddhist practice the world over would indicate that dev-otees from every Buddhist school of thought are mostly ordinary people. And they have their devotional practices just like the devotees of other faith traditions. The Hindus call it the way of devotion, which is one of the ways of attaining the highest goal within the Hindu tradition. Buddhists too observe certain devotional practices, such as offering flowers, or light and incense at the Buddha's statue or site of his relics. Even though the Buddha distanced himself as an object of undue homage, nevertheless he has become an icon in the Buddhist world. His relics are venerated in vari-ous shrines, and such places have become celebrated places of pilgrimages. Some shrines are now located at sites historically associated with the Bud-dha – his place of birth (Lumbini); the place where he preached his famous Sermon in the Deer Park (Benares); the very spot where he received his Enlightenment (Bodh Gaya); and his place of death (Kusinara). All are located in India or present Nepal. There is also the site of the famous tooth relic of the Buddha, located in Kandy, Sri Lanka. Magnificent statues, pago-das, stupas (relic monuments) and temples have become perennial objects of homage and veneration. However, most Buddhists are aware that what-ever devotional activity they are engaged in would be of merit to themselves and others, even non-Buddhists, involved in the activity. The Buddha would become the focus of such merits but is not considered to be a giver of merits or grace to the devotees. The Buddha remains a graceful invocation for the devotee so that the person in the act of devotion attunes himself or herself to higher pursuits. Hence devotion becomes a means of subscribing oneself to a discipline of spiritual culture. Unlike their Christian, Jewish or Muslim counterparts, Buddhists do not offer prayers, supplication or thanksgiving, but instead invoke the name of the Buddha and reflect on his teaching, con-stantly making efforts to make their thoughts and actions meritorious and wholesome. Buddhists would not ask the Buddha for mercy or compassion or for any other favour, but would engage in prayerful activities, similar to those of their co-religionists, in an attempt to be associated with the teach-ings of the Buddha.

In this sense Buddhism falls within the parameters of a religious persuasion, even though it stands out more specifically as a philosophical school of thought whose aim is to make 'being' better. However, historically it has grown into a tradition that has absorbed previously held cultural identities, whether Hindu or other primal religious traditions. In its development Buddhism has neither compromised its core claims nor intentionally flushed out what already existed – an approach to life that is typically Buddhist.

Zen

A form of Buddhism that has been adopted all over the world for its powerful simplicity is Zen. The essential element of Zen Buddhism is found in its name, for Zen means 'meditation'. It teaches that enlightenment is achieved through the profound realization that one is already an enlightened being. One of the central points of Zen is obtaining understanding through *intuition*. Words and sentences are thought to have no fixed meaning. They have meaning only in relation to who is using them, who they are talking to and the situation in which they are being used. Logic is usually considered irrelevant.

There is some doubt as to who officially began Zen. Many Zen thinkers believe that it began when Buddha achieved enlightenment. Other Zen masters think that the founder was a south-Indian Pallava prince who became a monk, called Bodhidharma. He travelled to China to teach a special mode of transmission without the use of words.

Zen emerged as a distinct school of Buddhism in China in the seventh century CE. It is thought to have developed alongside various revivals in Mahayana Buddhism, among them the Yogacara and Madhyamaka philosophies and the Prajnaparamita literature (a core text in Mahayana thought), and among local traditions in China, particularly Taoism. From China Zen spread southwards to Vietnam and eastwards to Korea and Japan.

Zen developed a way of Buddhist practice that concentrated on direct experience rather than on rational creeds or revealed scriptures. Wisdom was passed not through words but through a lineage of direct transmission of thought from teacher to student. Meditation is not confined to the lotus position but can be done while performing everyday tasks, such as sweeping leaves. Zen arts are widely known as a means of helping the practitioner to attain a state of understanding. Examples include the tea ceremony (*chado*), flower arranging, calligraphy, painting and certain military arts such as fencing and archery.

Buddhism and other religions

Buddhism accepts that it is one of many human pursuits for meaning and happiness. According to the Brahmajalasutta of the Dhiga Nikaya, there were already 62 different views in circulation when the Buddha began to preach. Two major schools of thought predominated: that of materialism or annihilation (that all life is dissolved at death) and the view of permanence or eternalism (the unchanging immutable soul that is not destroyed). The Buddha never intended to establish yet another view, adding one more to the famous 62. Rather he strove to establish what is called truth – something ever present in society but concealed by the dust of ignorance and craving. Buddha considered many views to be too dogmatic, carrying implicit judgements on those who believe otherwise. He maintained that it was unwholesome to campaign that 'this is indeed the truth, all else is falsehood'.

Buddha speaks of a cycle of misery – an attachment to ideology – that leads to unwholesome activity causing injury both to oneself and to others. If a religious persuasion or ideological thinking is bent on imposing itself on a community, then it certainly leads to conflict and the disintegration of societies. Religions and their teachings are devised to make people and their social behaviour right and acceptable, and for the good of all. If religions became competitors rather than complementary, then each religious tradition becomes the 'sole truth claimer', not only to 'stamp the truth' but also to become the 'dispenser of that truth'. Dysfunctional religious behaviour, the Buddha says, is untenable for the building of a good society. Hence even the Buddhist approach to itself is self-critical.

Developments in Buddhism

Over the past 150 years Buddhism has undergone considerable change. It has had to face unsympathetic and sometimes destructive forces within its land of origin, India. Moguls, communists and colonial influence all had their impacts, turning it into a minority religious tradition within India. However, since the Second World War Buddhism has provided a new religio-cultural continuity to certain Buddhist communities in South and East Asia, and has regained the ground lost, especially under colonial rule. These recoveries have been expressed in various ways. Some Buddhist institutions have even become politicized in order to assert their indigenous identity. Broadly, four contemporary changes in Buddhism can be identified as follows.

Since the 1970s traditional Buddhist countries have articulated different movements of Buddhist ethos, for example in active political engagement or campaigning for higher social status, and cultural revivals. Second, Buddhism outside Asia has found new interest groups that have spawned a multitude of different Buddhist schools of thought and practice, from the Americas to Europe and Australia. Third, a new wave of migrations since the Second World War has created diaspora Buddhist communities who have imported their various 'cultural Buddhisms'. Diaspora communities are devising ways of leading a Buddhist life in their adopted homelands around the world. The fourth influence is that of the traditional Western misunderstanding that regards Buddhism as apolitical and naval-gazing. It thinks that Buddhism proposes a negative soteriology (theory of salvation) or that it takes flight from the world. These ideas have been debunked by the higher monks and Buddhist institutions that were actively involved in the independence movements of the former French colonies of Vietnam, Cambodia and Laos, and former British colonies, such as Burma and Sri Lanka.

Radical monks from Sri Lanka, for example, have brought Buddhism into active political involvement in the nation's legislature and through both parliamentary and extra-parliamentary pressure groups. They believe that taking part in active politics is integral to the life of a monk if the cause is beneficial to humanity. Buddhist movements in the twentieth century have demonstrated an alternative approach to repression, as in the case of China's occupation of Tibet or the Vietnam conflict. They have also portrayed themselves as new schools of thoughts within the world of Buddhism. Taiwan, Hong Kong, Singapore and Korea all manifested different brands of Buddhist thought, and each adapted to the new geopolitical situation on the ground. Japan, with its state-implied Shinto tradition embedded in nationalism, was humiliated in the Second World War yet produced another manifestation of traditional Buddhism in a fresh way within. One such movement was the Soka Gakkai (Value Creation Society), a movement that began in the 1930s, based on the teaching of the medieval Buddhist monk Nichiren. Most of its thinking is based on the Lotus Sutra, a text it considers to contain the Buddha's definitive teaching. The school exists broadly within the Mahayana tradition, but places great emphasis on art, music and dance, elements that symbolize its message about protecting the environment and enhancing spiritual growth.

The Lamas of Tibet

The fourteenth Dalai Lama, Tenzin Gyatso (born 1935), is perhaps the most internationally known Buddhist figure, though other monks and lay Buddhists have also campaigned for their cause. It is clear that the Western world has been able to access the Tibetan manifestation of Buddhism through such personalities as Tenzin Gyatso and Kelsang Gyatso (born 1931). The Dalai Lama (meaning literally 'Ocean' guru, or teacher) is believed to be the incarnation of Avalokiteshvara, the heavenly *bodhisattva* ('buddha-to-be'), who embodies infinite compassion.

The beliefs of both Tenzin and Kelsang are rooted in early Buddhism but each has interpreted Buddhist thought and practice in relation to their lives and struggles in their own particular historical, cultural and political circumstances. Tenzin was forced to flee Tibet in 1959 in order to escape Chinese repression. From his base in northern India he represents not only Buddhism but also the political cause of Tibetan people, and attempts to preserve Tibet's spiritual and cultural heritage. Kelsang's westward journey was prompted at the request of his root guru, Trijang Rinpoche, and he is the resident teacher at the Manjushri Institute (now known as Manjushri Kadampa Meditation Centre) in England.

The impact of these leaders on their communities and on the world at large projects the historical Buddhist legacy into the religious discourse of the twenty-first century in a decisive way. These formidable witnesses exemplify the inner free thought and critical sense of inquiry that the Buddha himself wished his disciples to possess. He did not wish others to imitate *him* but rather the *teaching* he expounded. Having the freedom to think and thinking freely was the basis of being a Buddhist. He would opt for an ethical route in pursuit of a wholesome life and a society that appreciates freedom of thought, liberty and ethical behaviour. Tenzin and Kelsang are both thoroughly Tibetan, yet they will consider the possibility of living with Buddhists who have different approaches to life.

 A path for all

The Buddhist path is an invitation to everyone to embrace an ethical path that leads to wholesome behaviour. To become a Buddhist is to tread the path discovered and taught by the Buddha. He says that he is only 'a pointer' and that each person needs to pursue his or her own meaning, happiness and fulfilment – one is refuge unto oneself. On the one hand Buddhist teaching inspires the disciple to take life and its chores seriously, and on the other hand it establishes our potential and worldly predicament in juxtaposition. These parameters are set up within the Buddhist world-view so that those who wish to pursue the path are led to do so in freedom, for the self and for others. Freedom in Buddhism is spiritual blissfulness without the transient rapture of worldly achievements which, though imparting momentary enjoyment, does not deliver authentic happiness. This latter is secured when one is able to plunge into the inner search for meaning, blissfulness and understanding of the nature of reality of ourselves and others. It is in this sense that Buddhism can be called a path open for all willing to embrace the spiritual culture enunciated by the Buddha through his empirical knowledge and wisdom and utter compassion for humanity.

The genius of Buddhism is that its fundamentals are virtually unintrusive, yet it is ethically persuasive for those who encounter it at its core. When we are convinced of the Buddhist propositions then we are challenged to practise Buddhism, and without practice we cease to be Buddhist. Buddhism's positive aversion to belief systems and doctrine is what enables it to speak of the sublime without 'god talk', proposing itself as a non-theistic tradition.

Buddhism pursues a cognitive ethical path with a social conscience, and presents a critique both of the 'self' and the 'other'. This self-examination is essential for social transformation. It proposes an agenda both for the contemplative and the activist in society. It relentlessly campaigns to evoke compassion, though mindful that wisdom is a skill in action. One can be absorbed in solitude but must return to the human circle where life throbs and evolves. Buddha himself was a wanderer, an ascetic, but his life, especially as an itinerant teacher, was a pedagogy for authentic practice for every walk of life. He was astutely focused on the idea of preaching what one practises and practising what one preaches – a universal message that preachers have also to be practitioners if they wish to be credible.

Buddhism stands out in the family of world religions as a tradition bold and frontal about an ethical behaviour imperative for society-building and good governance. Buddhism affirms human life as it gives people the great opportunity to achieve their inner yearning for meaning and happiness, here and now and hereafter.

 ## QUESTIONS

1 In what ways does Buddhism propose to its readers and listeners to adopt a life of simplicity, of disciplined spiritual culture and compassion?

2 What lessons can be drawn from the Buddhist approach to ethical living about the present-day profit-based market with its global effects, excessive consumption patterns and the utter greed (*tanha*) that led to the present financial crisis?

3 Buddhism says that absolutism and dogmatism are futile creeds, that they are unhealthy for society-building and human character formation. Give examples of this, and discuss how such positions have been unproductive and have tended to fragment society and undermine human behaviour.

 # Glossary

anatta no-soul theory
anicca theory of impermanence
atman individual soul
Bhikkhu monk
Brahma great one, creator of the Universe in Hindu mythology
Brahman Supreme Being, universal consciousness, unborn, uncreated
Brahmin the priestly caste in Hindu social stratification
dukkha traditionally translated as 'suffering', but best understood as 'unsatisfactoriness'

Gotama (Pali), Gautama (Sanskrit) the first name of the Buddha
Guru teacher
karuna compassion
karma actions past and present
Mara personification of evil
maya illusion/mirage
nirvana cessation of all births and death: blissfulness
panchasila the five moral precepts
panna wisdom
samadhi mental discipline
samsara cycle of births and deaths
Sattha epitaph referring to Buddha as 'teacher of gods and humans'
sila ethical path
tanha craving

Further reading

Harvey, Peter, *An Introduction To Buddhism: Teachings, History and Practices* (Cambridge: Cambridge University Press, 2004).

5

Jaina thought and practice

Priyadarshana Jain

 Introduction

Jainism is one of the oldest living religions, existing before both the Aryan and Vedic civilizations. Indeed, it is not merely a religion or philosophy but a way of life. The antiquity of Jainism can be traced to the most primitive currents of thought. Although it flourished and declined at different times, it remains a way of life, primarily in India. Jainism has had a profound influence on many Indian cultures. Through its teachings, through the behaviour of its followers and through its art and architecture it has affected millions of people. The expressions of the Jaina heritage are among the great treasures that India has given to the world.

Some unique features of Jainism are that its followers consider their religion to be eternal; it is without beginning and shall continue to exist as long as mankind continues to strive for freedom from ignorance, bondage and suffering. It has no founder but is revealed from time to time by legendary teachers, called **Tirthankaras** (meaning 'ford makers', referring to their capacity as role models to enable their followers to cross the 'ocean' of transmigration). It is a religion of purely human origin, that is, it was first practised and then preached by the ones who have become pure, perfect, enlightened and omniscient, called *Jinas, Arihantas, Siddhas, Kevalins* or *Tirthankaras*.

Jains around the globe greet each other by saying *Jai Jinendra*, which means victory to the *Jinas* who have 'conquered' themselves. The word *Jina* is derived from the root word *Ji*, meaning 'to conquer'. The Jinas have not conquered external lands or people but the enemies within: attachment, aversion, anger, conceit, deceit, greed, lust, jealousy and so on. It is indeed relatively easy to conquer external foes but difficult to conquer the internal foes. Those who conquer the self – the passions and senses – move about righteously and become gods among humanity – purified, perfected and liberated, thus rising to Godhood.

Jainism does not believe in a creator God and has no creation theory. It says that the world is without beginning or end, and people are responsible for themselves. The law of *karma* works automatically; the expression 'as you sow, so you reap' sums up the law of cause and effect. The Jinas, who are the gods of the Jains, have liberated themselves from the web of *karmas* and the cycle of births and deaths, and hence they are the spiritual victors and true heroes. All living beings have the potential to manifest this Godhood, or Jinahood, that is latent in each being.

There are around 15 to 20 million Jains worldwide adhering to the path preached by Jinas, engaging in self-conquest through the art of right living, righteousness and compassion. It is a religion that promotes peace and universal harmony through non-violence and strong ethical foundations. It is an eco-friendly religion and has been a forerunner in protecting the rights of animals, plants and even micro-organisms. In this age of global warming and terrorism, when unrestrained human activities are causing environmental degradation and widespread terror, there is a need to understand the role of various religions afresh.

The history of Jainism

There is some disagreement among scholars about the origins of Jainism. Hindu and Buddhist literature both refer to it as an ancient religion. Archaeological evidence of the Indus Valley Civilization (3500 to 3000 BCE) in India suggests the worship of Jaina deities; many rulers in ancient Bihar and surrounding territories were either patrons or followers of those deities.

Tradition of the *Tirthankaras*

Jains believe that time is cyclical and measured in eons. In every descending and ascending phase of the time cycle there appear 24 *Tirthankaras*. They first work out their enlightenment through divine insight and then teach the path of happiness and perfection through the way of life popularly known as Jainism. Lord Rishabhdeva, the first *Tirthankara*, lived millions of years ago. The last of the 24 great spiritual guides of this eon was Vardhamāna Mahāvira, who lived from 599 to 527 BCE. Mahāvira did not found any new religion, as is sometimes supposed, but revived the already existing one and expounded the same religious, philosophical and ethical teachings of the previous *Tirthankaras*.

All the *Tirthankaras* were born into *kshatriya* (warrior) clans. Many important elements of Jainist social life were established by the first *Tirthankara*. Rishabhdeva devised a stable social order and became the first king. He made Vinita (modern Ayodhya) the capital of his kingdom and gave the first laws of governance. He also imparted the skills of various arts, crafts, agriculture, use of fire, the wheel and so on. Rishabhdeva is regarded as the pioneer of education and civilization. He gave equal status to women and divided society into three classes (*varnas*): warrior, merchant and labourer. The scholarly class (*brahmana*) was added later by his son Bharata.

Rishabhdeva was the first to establish a political order, laying the foundations of non-violence, mutual co-existence, universal brotherhood and sustainable development. He ruled for a long time with justice, far-sightedness and detachment. However, he longed for spiritual accomplishment and so renounced the world and became absorbed in meditation and austerities in a bid to release himself from the shackles of bondage and transmigration. He eventually became enlightened and was hailed as the first *Tirthankara*. Thereupon he established a fourfold order that characterizes Jainism today. This order makes up the righteous society and consists of monks, nuns, male and female lay followers. He travelled far and wide preaching the messages of non-violence and non-attachment that have remained the basic principles of the Jaina religion.

Some of the later *Tirthankaras* also ruled wisely, while others renounced the world in the prime of their youth. The succession of the *Tirthankaras* was not continuous, rather there were long intervals between them. The twenty-fourth and last, Mahāvira, is regarded as the saviour of mankind.

The life and teachings of Vardhamāna Mahāvira

The period from the eighth to the sixth century BCE was an age of intellectual renaissance in India and Asia. On the one side were the Vedic ritualism and animal sacrifices of early Hinduism, on the other an abundance of philosophical speculation. Mahāvira was born at such a time in Kundalpura, Bihar, to King Siddhartha and Queen Trishala around 599 BCE. He was believed to have been born with exceptional intellectual and spiritual gifts, including perfect perception, scriptural knowledge and clairvoyance. Despite being surrounded by the luxuries of the royal court, the young Mahāvira remained detached and spiritually absorbed. He showed great compassion for others and looked upon each soul as his own, knowing that it had the same potential for greatness and perfection.

At the age of 30, after the demise of his parents, Mahāvira renounced the world and led an austere life for twelve and a half years. He roamed the wild lands of northern India in order to annihilate his *karmas* and purify himself. He encountered hardships along the way, but with steady progression eventually became enlightened when, it is believed, supreme omniscience was manifested in him. Thereupon he undertook the role of a great religious teacher and reformer.

In teaching *nirvana* and a life of asceticism and non-violence, Mahāvira anticipated some of the ideals of Buddhism. Indeed, he was a senior contemporary of the Buddha but the two never met. Mahāvira's teachings are universal and relevant for all times. In Anuvrata ethics he taught knowledge management, time management, anger management, stress management, the art of right living as well as the art of dying. In mastering these areas it is believed one can release the self from spiritual crisis and also resolve crises in society and the environment. He taught compassion and reverence for all life. All living beings desire to live, none wants to die, and hence **ahimsa** (non-violence) is the crux of Jaina ethics. All other virtues are derived from this great principle. He said that inner conversion from materialism to spirituality, purity of heart and a straightforward life are the way to freedom and liberation.

Concentration and other austere practices enable the soul to annihilate the karmic influx and enjoy eternal bliss. He further said that anger destroys love, pride destroys modesty, deceit destroys friendship and greed destroys all. The soul is the doer and enjoyer of both happiness and misery; it is its own friend when it acts righteously and its own foe when it acts unrighteously.

Decline, revival and schism

Jainism has undergone many phases of growth and decline. Although north and west India remained its heartland, the south of India too was a stronghold of Jainism until about the eighth century CE. Gujarat and Rajasthan maintained their positions as strong centres of Jainism. Various factors have contributed to the growth of Jainism when circumstances favoured it. The religion is inherently tolerant as it believes in 'relative pluralism' and teaches equality for all, irrespective of caste, creed, colour or gender. Jainism can adapt to different times and environments and always has respect for other faiths. It uses vernacular languages for scripture and sermons. Jains have earned a reputation for honesty, loyalty and philanthropy; they provide food, shelter and medical care to all in need.

On the other hand, Jainism has declined periodically. In the medieval period, persecution occurred when political circumstances changed, especially when the ruling elite converted to Hinduism. A lack of infrastructure and leadership led to the fragmentation of Jainism into more sects, who together lacked a common purpose.

Almost 150 years after the *nirvana* of Lord Mahāvira there emerged two strong sects in Jainism: the Svetāmbaras and Digambaras, a division that became firmly entrenched by the first century CE. The Svetāmbaras are clad in white, the Digambaras are sky clad (that is, naked). There are no fundamental doctrinal differences between these two main Jain sects, but even with the passage of time sectarian differences persist over rituals, customs and manners. These differences are not spiritually significant. Each of the above sects is further divided into many sub-sects.

Jainism in practice

Scripture

The sacred scriptures of the Jainas are called *Āgamas*. They contain the revelations of Mahāvira. He conceptualized the content of the Jaina scriptures, which take a twelvefold form known as Dvadasanga. This occupies the most prominent place in Jaina canonical literature. As the *Āgamas* were handed down orally over 1,000 years and documented only in about the fifth century CE, the sacred religious literature was partly lost. What was available was collated by the Svetāmbaras. The Digambaras, however, consider that all the sacred canonical literature was lost and only some later religious literature is considered important by them.

The language of the Svetāmbara *Āgamas* is Prakrit, one of the oldest Indian languages, belonging to the Indo-European language family. Besides the sacred texts there are numerous commentaries on the *Āgamas* written in Prakrit and Sanskrit. The Jains never showed partiality for one language, as the Brahmanas did for Sanskrit and the Buddhists for Pali. Instead they cultivated all the languages of their time and place.

Beliefs

The promulgators of the Jaina tradition did not have the tools and technology of modern science but their intuition and reasoning were undoubtedly profound. They searched for nothing less than ultimate happiness. Hence the concepts of soul, *karma* and rebirth are indispensable in Jaina philosophy. Jaina beliefs centre on the fact that humans have a dual personality: material and spiritual. The spiritual personality is ever struggling to break the shackles of the material conditioning. According to Jainism, humans alone are responsible for all their actions. No god, nor his prophet or deputy, can interfere with the destiny of any being, with the creation of the universe or anything happening in the universe. To achieve freedom and release from bondage one has to apprehend the nature of reality as it is. Jaina epistemology, metaphysics and ethics enable us to understand this reality and achieve the ultimate goal of self-realization, self-purification and emancipation.

Epistemology

Essential to understanding Jaina philosophy is a grasp of its theory of knowledge. The Jainas have developed a system that analyses the problem of the relation of knowledge to the self. *Upayoga*, or the function of knowing and seeing, is the essential characteristic of the soul and is inherent in the self. The self cannot exist without knowledge. The self illumines itself and all others in the light of this knowledge. But this potential of the soul is also thwarted by its ignorance. As a result it is veiled by karmic layers and is subject to suffering. The Jaina texts reveal the five types of knowledge: sensory experience, scriptural knowledge, clairvoyance, telepathic knowledge and omniscience. The first two are acquired through the medium of senses and mind, while the last three are acquired directly by the soul and are called extra-sensory perception.

Omniscience is that supreme knowledge that enables the soul to apprehend the nature of all substances, along with all their modes of past, present and future simultaneously. This pure and perfect knowledge is the perfect manifestation of the pure and perfect soul. This supreme knowledge of the omniscients reveals the nature of reality as changing yet permanent. Although reality is uncreated and eternal its modes keep on changing. Just as gold has permanent physical and chemical properties yet can be found in different shapes at different times, so also the soul is endowed with the characteristics of infinite knowledge, vision, bliss and power yet at the same time is subjected to sufferings in the ephemeral body. The entire range of substances found in the universe are broadly classified into two major categories: the living and the non-living. Jaina metaphysics and ethics are based on the nature and interaction of these two substances.

Metaphysics: soul and *karma*

The concepts of soul, *karma* and rebirth are to be understood through the metaphysical foundations of Jainism. When the two categories, or *reals*, of living and non-living come into contact with each other, certain positive and negative energies are produced that condition the soul. When these energies are exhausted the soul is liberated. In Jaina philosophy the soul is living, while the body, senses, mind and *karma* are classified as non-living and corporeal in nature. When their association is auspicious it is termed as merit or virtue; when it is inauspicious it is demerit or sin.

Soul, spirit, *Jiva*, *atman*, *Brahman* and so on are all synonyms for the self. It is characterized by consciousness and is eternal but in the bondaged state it is subject to births and deaths. It is the only agent responsible for all its actions. All souls have the same capacity for development yet each grows in different ways. The bondaged souls and *karma* have co-existed since time immemorial but their association can be terminated through right attitude, rational knowledge and right action.

The concept of *karma* occupies a significant position in Jaina philosophy in particular and in Indian philosophy in general. It is the theory of cause and effect that operates automatically. It provides a rational and satisfying explanation to the apparently inexplicable phenomena of birth and death, of happiness and misery, of inequalities in mental and physical attainments and of the existence of different species of living beings. In ordinary parlance *karma* means action, deed, work or duty. In Jaina metaphysics it means that form of subtle matter that gets attracted to the soul due to the operation of attachment, hatred, delusion and passions taking place in the soul. It is so subtle that it cannot be perceived by any of our senses. It is a million times finer than the waves of sound, light or electricity and is the primary cause that keeps the universe going. Jaina ethics springs logically from this theory of *karma* as it trains the spiritual aspirants to overcome all hurdles on the battlefield of self-conquest.

Ethics

Jaina ethics is the most glorious part of Jainism, and has been defined by some authors as 'ethical realism'. Spirituality is for the person in God, ethics is for the person in society. Though humanity's conduct in society is the normal field of ethics, the Jaina thinkers have linked ethics with metaphysical ideals. Followers of Jainism are expected to pursue righteous conduct after they have cultivated an intelligent faith in right gods, right gurus and right *dharma*. To attain *nirvana* the rules of conduct must be observed and corresponding virtues must be acquired.

Jainism has prescribed different rules of conduct for ascetics and householders. Five great vows – non-violence, truthfulness, non-stealing, celibacy and non-possession – are observed by ascetics to protect against lapses of conduct and therefore karmic influx. By following a path of discipline, they endeavour to control the mind and transcend it in order to progress along the spiritual path of perfection. An ascetic maintains a pure attitude of mind, absorbing the spiritual teachings of the *Jinas*. He is houseless and penniless and walks barefoot, teaching the lessons of compassionate living to strife-torn mankind. In obedience to their doctrine of non-violence, some Jains cover their mouths so as to reduce the risk of injuring anything, thereby also preventing the impurity that comes from causing suffering.

Householders take minor vows and try to gain spiritual edification while attending to their daily responsibilities. Ascetics and lay persons alike have to observe six daily duties: equanimity, devotion to the *Tirthankaras*, reverence towards ascetics, penitential retreat, meditation and detachment, and partial renunciation of food, drink, and comfort. Studying scriptures, making donations, listening to discourses and fasting are regularly observed by Jains worldwide. Giving up the sevenfold debaucheries of consuming meat, alcohol, drugs, gambling, hunting, stealing, and visiting prostitutes and other women is a pre-requisite of treading the path of liberation. Besides following this ethical code of conduct a Jain is taught the art of dying. As death is inevitable a Jain learns the significance of embracing it with a detached spirit that is holy and peaceful.

Religious practices

Rituals

All religious practices focus on those that can bring about self-conquest. They are not mandatory and should be observed according to one's capacity. In Jainism, rituals are regarded as a part of right conduct, intended to lead people on a journey from the material to the spiritual realm. Rituals consist in reciting the sacred **sutras**, veneration of the *Jinas* and spiritual masters, and scriptural study. The purpose of worship and prayers in Jainism is not objective but subjective, and is undertaken for personal spiritual accomplishment.

Though unnecessary for the spiritually advanced, rituals can, in the earlier stages of spiritual development, aid devotion and worship. Group rituals help to keep the community together and provide a sense of common identity. There is no uniformity of observance of rituals and no priesthood in Jainism. Consecration ceremonies and purificatory rites are supervised by expert guides. Social rituals performed at the time of birth, marriage and death show the influence of the Hindu community over the Jaina community.

Festivals and pilgrimage

The festivals of the Jains follow either the traditional Indian calendar or the *Vira samvat* era marking the *nirvana* day of Lord Mahāvira in 527 BCE. The most popular sacred festivals are the Paryusana Parva celebrated for eight days as a period of confession, atonement and expiation, and Diwali, marking the *nirvana* day of Lord Mahāvira. Besides these there are many occasions on which the Jains gather throughout the year and celebrate festivals in a spirit of renunciation and devotion. Barefoot pilgrimages are also undertaken to the sites of Jaina saints. About every 12 years thousands of Jaina pilgrims descend on the southern Indian town of Shravana Belgola, the oldest Jaina centre of pilgrimage. Here they anoint the gigantic statue of the saint Lord Bahubali that towers over the town.

Jainism in the modern world

Jainism is as relevant today as it was at the beginning of the world. Its values of pluralism, peaceful co-existence, reverence for all life – voiced through environmental concern, animal welfare and vegetarianism – and its holistic and rational approach to life have influenced civilized minds all over the globe. The Jain community worldwide continues to provide solutions to the many challenges posed to modern society through its principles of non-violence, relative pluralism and, above all, non-possession. Until the middle of the twentieth century the West had not encountered Jainism, and even today most people have not heard of it. Yet with the adherence to the above principles by around 14,000 monks and nuns as well as ardent lay followers, the Jains are very much ahead of their time. In comparison with the small size of the minority that they form, the varied philanthropic activities they undertake and the influence they generate in the promotion of fundamental universal values are proportionately large.

Jainism has never gone out of its way to convert people from one faith to another, but profoundly asserts that conversion from materialism to spirituality is the highest ideal. Its policies of 'live and let live' and 'help ever and hurt never' need to be systematically presented in the modern context. The Jaina community needs to do more to promote peace and harmony through interfaith dialogue. Knowledge management and human-resource management, taught centuries ago by the legendary *Tirthankaras*, need to be translated into action before it is too late.

At first impression the Jaina community might seem to be affluent, having many of its members in business and the professions. But there are also families below the poverty line requiring housing, welfare and training. Unlike their Brahmanic counterparts in India, the community rejects the caste system and opposes any social division based on birth. Jainism asserts that each individual has a capacity for higher spiritual development, and his or her status in society depends upon each individual's karmic pattern. Thus members of its community come from various backgrounds. The Indian government accepts Jains as a distinct group with its own religious identity.

The Jains have contributed richly to the development of the arts and architecture. Their beautifully intricate designs of temples in different states of India are famous. Jains believe that their sacred images should be housed in aesthetically pleasing buildings so that they inspire devotion among their worshippers.

Health

Health is wealth. The physical health of a person is directly or indirectly influenced by mental health. Jainism says that behind all good health is spiritual health. If the spiritual health of a person is good then the mind and physique can function smoothly. Good health is an attitude of the mind, and so Jains always think positively and are optimistic. Suicide and crime in the Jaina community is minimal. The most devout of the Jains do not eat after sunset or before sunrise because in the absence of the sun's rays microbes are highly active and liable to cause indigestion and other health hazards. The devout undertake rigorous fasts throughout the year, especially during the four months of the rainy season when vegetation is active and thus violence to it becomes inevitable. Jains follow a life of simple living and high thinking. They lead a life of contentment and self-restraint, thereby finding ample time to carry out philanthropic and spiritual activities.

The Jaina emblem

The emblem (see Figure 5.1, overleaf) indicates the fourfold existence of hell, heaven, human kingdom, and lower plant and animal kingdom. If those who inhabit these realms follow true religion of right faith, right knowledge and right conduct, they will reach the abode of the perfected souls, signified by the curve at the top of the emblem.

In a second form (see Figure 5.2, overleaf) the emblem includes a **swastika**, indicating the fourfold existence, a hand signifying *ahimsa* and a mantra underneath the emblem in Sanskrit, to denote that all life forms are mutually interdependent.

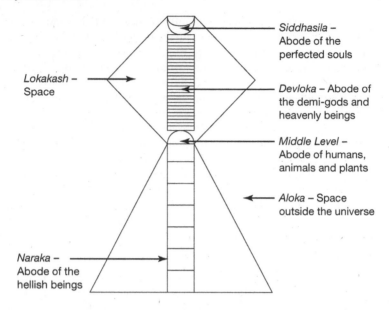

Figure 5.1 The Jaina emblem (1): the four abodes
Source: Adopted from www.ejainism.com

परस्परोपग्रहो जीवानाम्

Figure 5.2 The Jaina emblem (2): the swastika, hand and mantra. The Sanskrit mantra at the bottom of the emblem says *Parsparograho jivanam* – 'Live and let live'
Source: Adopted from www.faithresource.org

Glossary

ahimsa doctrine of non-violence
nirvana final liberation
sutra a religious text
swastika ancient Indian auspicious symbol
Tirthankara one of 24 spiritual teachers of Jainism

Further reading

Sangave, Vilas A., *Aspects of Jaina Religion* (New Delhi: Bharatiya Jnanpith, 1990).

Shah, Natubhai, *Jainism – The World of Conquerors* (Brighton: Sussex Academic Press, 1998).

Shastri, Devendramuni, *A Source-Book in Jaina Philosophy* (Udaipur: Sri Tarak Guru Jain Granthalaya, 1983).

Tukol, T. K., *Compendium of Jainism* (Dharwad: Prasaranga, Karnatak University, 1980).

6

Jewish thought and practice

Ed Kessler

 Introduction

Judaism is full of different opinions and there is no single definition of Judaism that is acceptable to all Jews. Some maintain that Judaism is solely a religion; others that it is a culture; still others emphasize nationhood and attachment to the Land of Israel. And just as there is disagreement about the definition of Judaism so there is rarely a single agreed Jewish view of any topic. It is, however, possible to outline a picture of Judaism that gives some sense of the wide variety of views held by Jews. Think of a large family, filled with plenty of humour, tension and disagreement, but a family whose members also love and support one another.

Judaism provides its families with many ways to live and is aptly described as a way of life. This chapter will examine the Jewish way of life, the expectations of being part of the Jewish family and the tensions that arise, which include disagreements between secular Jews who emphasize culture and ignore religious practice, and religious Jews for whom a godless life is meaningless. We will look at the differences between Reform Jews, who emphasize religious innovation, and Orthodox Jews, for whom tradition is central. And there are the disagreements between Israeli Jews, who emphasize the need to live in the Land of Israel, and diaspora Jews, who remain spiritually attached to the Land but are content living their lives outside.

Consequently Judaism is best understood as consisting of a religion and a culture and a people. This is illustrated by the story of a couple with marital problems who visit the Rabbi to seek his help. The Rabbi asks each of them to see him individually. The husband enters the Rabbi's study and explains his predicament. The Rabbi listens sympathetically and says to him 'You are right.' The husband leaves. His wife enters the study and explains the problems in their relationship. The Rabbi listens carefully, nods his head, and when she finishes says to her, 'You are right.' When the Rabbi returns home that evening he tells his wife what happened. She turns round to him and asks, 'How can they both be right?' The Rabbi thinks for a moment and then responds, 'You are right.'

Of course, it is possible to have more than one right answer to a question, but in Judaism this approach is commonplace. The **Talmud**, for example, one of the most important collections of Jewish writings from the fifth century CE, sometimes concludes a discussion with the word *teyku* ('let the problem stand'). Because the Rabbis were unable to choose one from a number of answers to a problem, they decided it was better to accept that there could be more than one possible answer than to choose the wrong one. The ability to allow for conflicting positions is a feature of Judaism. It is generally posited that the opposite of truth is falsehood: a Jew might suggest that the opposite of one truth may well be another, more profound truth.

The word 'Jew' comes from the name Judah, a tribe of Israel, whose capital was Jerusalem. After the ten tribes of Israel were taken into exile by the Assyrians in 721 BCE and were forever lost, Jews were identified as belonging principally to the area known as Judea. Today the Jewish people number approximately 15 million, which is very small in comparison with other religions (for example, for approximately every 100 Christians there is one Jew). Yet for a small people whose origins go back some 4,000 years, Judaism has not only survived but also flourished. It has made a significant contribution to the religious experience of humanity, being a major influence on the creation and development of at least two of the world's religions – Christianity and Islam.

Being a minority profoundly affects the ways Jews lead their lives. From biblical times to the modern day, Jews have been aware that they represent but a small percentage of humankind. In the **Mishnah**, a second-century CE text, the Rabbis ask why the Bible begins with Adam and not with Abraham, who is viewed as the Father of the Jewish people. The Rabbis suggest that the reason is to teach that everyone is descended from the same person. 'A single human being was first created for the sake of peace among humanity, so no person can say to another, "my father was greater than yours."' In other words, the emphasis is on a common humanity. Indeed, the Bible makes it clear that even the biblical peoples who oppressed the Children of Israel – the people of Assyria, who took the ten tribes of Israel into exile, and of Egypt, who forced the Children of Israel to work in slavery – are both to be viewed as having, like Israel, their own special relationship with God. As the prophet Isaiah puts it, 'Blessed be My people Egypt, My handiwork, Assyria, and My very own Israel' (Isa. 19.25).

Being a small minority also means that even in Israel, where the majority of citizens are Jewish, there is a strong sense of being surrounded by non-Jews. Often the non-Jewish world has caused much suffering, culminating in the murder of six million Jews in the Second World War, known as the **Holocaust**. The existence of antisemitism and the horrors of the Holocaust have made a deep impression on Judaism that continues to this day. Indeed, the Holocaust has had a significant impact on Christianity as well.

For Christians it resulted in an awareness of the immensity of the burden of guilt that the Church carried, not only because of its general silence, with some noble exceptions, from 1933 to 1945, but also because of its 'teaching of contempt' towards Jews and Judaism over so many centuries. It was this attitude that sowed the seeds of hatred and made it so easy for Hitler to use antisemitism as a political weapon. Although Nazism was opposed to Christianity, Hitler often justified his antisemitic policies with reference to the Church's historical attitudes towards Judaism. For Jews, therefore, one consequence of being a small minority has been the growing sense that the outside world is a threat.

One positive consequence, however, has been a high level of sensitivity to other peoples, and especially a concern for the vulnerable in society. A command in Leviticus is to 'love your neighbour as yourself'. The Five Books of Moses (also called the **Pentateuch**) further commands Jews on 36 separate occasions to 'love the stranger' because 'you were strangers in the land of Egypt'. The extent to which all peoples address themselves to the needy and vulnerable demonstrates, according to the Jewish way of thinking, the extent to which they are godly.

The Bible and monotheism

Judaism begins with the affirmation of one God. 'Hear O Israel, the LORD is our God, the LORD alone' (Deut. 6.4), which is the first line of the most famous Jewish prayer, the **Shema**. The prayer begins with recognition of God's oneness and uniqueness and moves on to the obligations that arise from this new knowledge:

> *You shall love the LORD your God with all your heart, and with all your soul, and with all your might. Take to heart these instructions with which I charge you this day. Impress them upon your children.* (Deut. 6.5–7)

Jews experience revelation in a personal encounter with God. The Bible does not ask whether God exists but rather, What does God say to me? What is my function in the world? The Bible portrays an encounter with a God who cares passionately and who addresses humanity in the quiet moments of its existence. For many Jews, myself included, the encounter with God is more than an acceptance of an intellectual proposition. When the seventeenth-century scientist and philosopher Blaise Pascal died, a note was discovered sewn into his overcoat. It read, 'Not the God of the Philosophers but the God of Abraham, Isaac and Jacob.' Pascal had come to realize that although 'proofs' of God's existence can be approached rationally and by philosophical means, it is only the exceptional mind that follows an intellectual pathway to an encounter with the Divine. More often than not, it is personal encounter that is decisive.

The truth of this is demonstrated by the question Moses asked God:

'When they [the Children of Israel] say to me: "What is His name?" What shall I say to them?' And God said to Moses: 'Eh'yeh asher eh'yeh [I AM THAT I AM]'; He continued, 'Thus you shall say to the Israelites: Eh'yeh [I AM] sent me to you.'   (Exod. 3.13–14)

God's reply is understood on one level as, 'He for whom no word or name is sufficient.' But Martin Buber, a twentieth-century Jewish philosopher, taught that it means, 'I am where I shall be encountered,' for God who is

Figure 6.1   The Shema in Hebrew and English
Source: Adopted from www.hebrew4christians.net

truly God cannot be expressed but only addressed. Buber developed this idea further in his book, *I and Thou*. He maintained that a personal relationship with God is only truly personal when we feel not only awe and respect on the human side but also not overwhelmed in our relationship with God.

 The Torah

The foundation of all Jewish writings is the **Torah** which, in its narrowest sense, refers solely to the Five Books of Moses. But it is the object of continual study and interpretation. 'Turn [the Torah] over and over again, for everything is in it. Contemplate it and grow old and grey over it.' (*Ethics of the Fathers* 5.25). This is exemplified by **Midrash** (meaning 'search' or 'enquiry') in which the Rabbis expounded the text, word by word, deriving ethical precepts and messianic expectations from the biblical stories.

Hebrew is the language of the Torah and almost the entire Bible. Towards the end of the biblical period, Jews in the Land of Israel spoke Aramaic but prayed in Hebrew. Hebrew remained solely a language for prayer and study for all Jews until, in recent times, it was revived as a spoken language in Israel, recreated from a language of history and religion into a language of everyday life.

Today Midrash has the nuance of 'exposition', illustrating the elucidation of Scripture where its meaning seems to be ambiguous. The purpose of the interpretations is to uncover what has always been there but was previously unseen or undiscovered. There are, in Midrash, no wrong interpretations. Yet on some questions it is possible to detect a general thrust sufficient for certain conclusions to be drawn as broad principles – always provided that a confident assertion is tempered by a healthy degree of scepticism.

Side by side with the development of Midrash, teaching academies created another type of literature: the Talmud (literally meaning 'learning' or 'study'). The Talmud consists primarily of legal and ethical debates about God's laws. Any attempt to lead a life in accordance with biblical precepts faces certain difficulties caused by gaps in the biblical narrative or uncertainty over the meaning of particular terms. For example, the Bible states that 'no manner of work' should be done on the Sabbath – but what exactly is meant by work? The Talmud tries to answer this question and other similar ones.

Two of the most famous Rabbis mentioned in the Talmud are Hillel and Shammai. They lived during the reign of King Herod (37–4 BCE), an oppressive period in Jewish history because of the Roman occupation of Palestine. Hillel was more liberal than Shammai in his views, being more lenient, for example, in his acceptance of converts to Judaism. The Talmud records:

> Once there was a Gentile who came to Rabbi Shammai, and said: 'Convert me on the condition that you teach me the whole Torah while I stand on one foot.' Shammai rejected him. The man then came to Rabbi Hillel, who converted him, saying: 'Do not do unto others as you would not wish to be done to yourself; this is the whole Torah. The rest is commentary, go and learn it.'
> (*Babylonian Talmud, Shabbat 31a*)

The similarity to the 'Golden Rule' of Jesus (Luke 6.31) is striking but, interestingly, Judaism has never exhibited proselytizing tendencies, unlike Christianity (and Islam). This may have been the result of its minority status in Christian (and Muslim) countries, but may also have resulted from Judaism's emphasis on right action rather than right belief.

Generally, Jews have not understood their mission to include converting others to Judaism, but rather as to act as witness to the One God and to be faithful to the Torah and its covenantal obligations. Non-Jews are not targets for conversion because the righteous people of all nations will have a share in the world to come. Scholars disagree about whether Jews actively sought converts in the early centuries, but when Christianity became the official religion of the Roman Empire in the late fourth century, missionary activity was made illegal for Jews.

An oral tradition was needed to accompany the Written Torah because, even with its 613 commandments, it is an insufficient guide to Jewish life. For example, the Fourth of the Ten Commandments states, 'Remember the Sabbath day and keep it holy' (Exod. 20.8). As the Sabbath is included in the Ten Commandments it is clearly regarded as important. Yet when one looks for the specific biblical laws on how the day should be observed, one finds only injunctions against lighting a fire, leaving one's home, cutting down a tree, ploughing and harvesting. Would merely refraining from these few activities fulfil the biblical command to make the Sabbath holy? Indeed, the rituals that are most commonly associated with the Sabbath – lighting candles, blessing bread and wine, the weekly reading of the Torah – are found not in the Written but in the Oral Torah.

Orthodox Jews believe that the Torah today is no different from that which Moses received from God. This does not imply that the text of the Torah should be understood literally, for God conveyed not only the words of the Torah but also its meaning. God gave rules as to how the laws were to be understood and implemented, and these laws were passed down as an oral tradition. This tradition was eventually written down as the Mishnah and the Talmud, which Orthodox Jews continue to use in their practice of Judaism.

Progressive Jews – a term that includes Liberal, Reform, Conservative and other non-orthodox religious groups – generally accept that, though divinely revealed, the Torah was written down by human hand and therefore contains error as well as truth. They maintain that today's Written Torah has been edited together from several documents. They maintain that the laws of Moses are no longer binding in their literal interpretation, and it is today's generation that must assess what God wants of them.

For their part secular and humanist Jews, though they reject the divine elements, still view the Torah as central to maintaining the Jewishness of life. Although their focus is on Judaism as a culture rather than as a religion, they value the Torah for what it teaches in order to live an ethical Jewish life. Secular Jews are often criticized by religious Jews for their rather tenuous 'bagel connection' with Judaism, but it is interesting that the Torah, and Jewish observance, remain central to Jewish practice, whatever the depth of belief.

Rabbinic Judaism

It is unclear when the so-called 'Rabbinic period' in Jewish history began. Perhaps it started as early as the fifth century BCE with the return to Jerusalem of Nehemiah and Ezra, or as late as the second century BCE. What is certain is that the rabbinic way of life represented a new stage in the development of Judaism. And it enabled Jews to survive without a homeland or a Temple, which was destroyed by the Romans in 70 CE.

There were many different Jewish groups around in the first century: Pharisees, Sadducees, Essenes, Hellenizers, Zealots and the followers of Jesus. In contrast with the Zealots, who concentrated on removing foreigners from Jewish soil, the Pharisees (later known as the Rabbis) emphasized study of the Torah and its application in **Halakhah** (Jewish law). The Pharisees also maintained a belief in the afterlife, described a messiah whose arrival would herald an era of world peace and stressed the importance of individual and communal prayer. They were the forerunners of Rabbinic Judaism.

The Sadducees were a Temple-centred aristocracy who wanted to maintain the priestly caste. Like the Hellenizers they were also willing to incorporate Greek culture into their lives, something that the Pharisees opposed. A third group, the Essenes, consisted of desert-based monastic orders that believed that other Jewish groups had corrupted the Temple. They were ascetics who adopted strict dietary laws and maintained a celibate life. One group of Essenes lived near the Dead Sea where, in 1947, a Bedouin shepherd discovered manuscripts that came to be known as the Dead Sea Scrolls.

The Jewish followers of Jesus were the only other Jewish sect who survived the destruction of the Temple. Jesus was a Jew who followed Jewish customs, such as the dietary laws; he prayed in the Temple and was called a Rabbi. Christians rivalled the Rabbis in their search for adherents to their teachings. The date of the split between Judaism and Christianity has been the subject of much debate. Some suggest it began as early as Paul of Tarsus (around 60 CE), others as late as the emperor

Constantine (around 300 CE) or even later. One scholar, James Dunn, has sensibly described the separation in terms of a *series* of 'partings of the ways'.

The Rabbis replaced the religious obligation of pilgrimage to the Temple with prayer, study of Scripture and works of piety. In so doing, the need for a sanctuary in Jerusalem was eliminated and Judaism became a religion capable of being fulfilled anywhere. Contemporary Judaism is ultimately derived from the rabbinic movement of the first centuries. As a result of their endeavours, Jews (alongside Christians) have been called by Muslims *Ahl al-Kitab* ('the people of the book'), although a more accurate description might be 'people of the books', for there are many sacred books. Constant study is one of the prime obligations of religious Jews. Even secular Jews acknowledge the centrality of Jewish literary tradition.

Covenant

God initiated a covenant with a community – the Jewish people – and that community accepts certain obligations and responsibilities as his partner. The English word 'covenant' is the standard translation of the Hebrew *berit*, generally understood as agreement. *Berit* was translated into Greek as 'decree' (*diathèkè*) and into Latin as 'testament' (*testamentum*), which became the Christian designation for both parts of the Christian Bible – the Old and the New Testaments.

For Jews the Bible describes how the Children of Israel entered into a relationship with God through God's election. 'You are the children of the LORD your God . . . You are a people consecrated to the LORD your God: the LORD chose you among all other peoples on earth to be His treasured [*segulah*] people' (Deut. 14.1–2). The word *segulah* refers to a special possession, implying that although all peoples belong to the Lord, the Children of Israel are particularly cherished and its people are to become known as a holy people.

God's covenant with Israel is associated especially with the Land of Israel. In Genesis 17.8 God states: 'I assign the land you sojourn in to you and your offspring to come, all the land of Canaan as an everlasting holding. I will be their God.' Jews understand the Promised Land as an integral part of the covenant.

Another aspect of covenant is that Israel is not chosen out of arbitrary preference for a particular people but in order that God's name be blessed. God and the people of God are described as partners. A two-way relationship is emphasized. The Jewish people are expected to respond to God by being faithful to the Torah and by keeping the covenant. Thus covenant assumes mutuality, for the two parties – divine and human – make an agreement.

A tradition of arguing with God is part of this covenantal relationship. Abraham, for example, famously argued with God when the cities of Sodom and Gomorrah were about to be destroyed. The willingness to enter into a personal conversation, captured in Isaiah's comment, 'come now let us reason together' (Isa. 1.12), demonstrates the close relationship between the Jewish people and God. For Jews the Bible is not simply what happened in the distant past to someone else; it is my story, what happened to my ancestors and, therefore, insofar as I carry on their story, to me.

But what happens should God fail to fulfil his part of the covenant? A fundamental challenge to the covenant between God and Israel occurred during the years 1933 to 1945. The horrors of the Holocaust have, for many Jews, shaken to the core their relationship with God.

Antisemitism and the Holocaust

From slavery in Egypt through to the concentration camps and the Holocaust, there has never been a time when Jews have not had to think deeply about the problem of suffering as they encountered it in their own lives. Each generation of Jews has a story to tell about facing anti-Judaism and, in more recent centuries, antisemitism. Anti-Judaism refers to anti-Jewish theology in the pre-Enlightenment period, whereas antisemitism refers to hatred of Jews since the Enlightenment, rooted in theories of 'scientific racism' and cultural mistrust. Recent forms of antisemitism have appeared in the guise of extreme anti-Zionism and neo-Nazism.

Anti-Judaism became incorporated into mainstream Christian theology from early on. The Church Fathers, for example, taught that Jews had been replaced by Christians as God's people. This is the beginning of the Christian theology of supersessionism (that Christianity superseded Judaism), which regarded Judaism as a religious wasteland. From the fourth century especially, Christian preachers began to turn upon Judaism with great vehemence. Such teaching and preaching sowed the seeds for anti-Jewish attitudes that came to dominate Christian thinking from the fourth to the twentieth centuries: Jewish suffering was deemed a divine punishment for the death of Jesus and the rejection of Christianity.

The position of Jews under Islam was quite different. Despite a subordinate status in Muslim society, Jews (and Christians) were granted security, freedom of worship and a large measure of self-government. They were called *Ahl dhimma* or 'People of the Covenant', and were categorized as non-Muslim subjects living in Muslim territories who, in return for paying a tax, were guaranteed protection and safety. For these reasons Judaism flourished more under Muslim than under Christian rule.

In Christendom, during the medieval period in particular, Jews were viewed as satanic figures, and Christians felt free to attack them with a divine seal of approval. Despite the many bleak centuries, there were periods of tolerance, such as the Golden Age in medieval Spain around 1000 CE. At that time a relatively peaceful co-existence between Jews, Christians and

Muslims prevailed, and Jews developed a flourishing culture of science and literature. But this was the exception. Intense anti-Judaism was the norm, demonstrated by the Crusaders who, on their way to liberating the Holy Land from the Muslims, attacked Jewish communities en route in areas such as the German Rhineland. In the fifteenth century Jews were persecuted during the Spanish Inquisition, and in 1492 expelled from Spain. In Germany in the 1520s, Martin Luther initially expressed sympathy for Jewish suffering, but once he realized that they would not convert to his branch of Christianity, preached viciously against them, particularly in the final years of his life.

The coming of the modern era, and a measure of social liberation, did result in political freedom for individual Jews in certain countries, but not for the Jewish people as a community. It also led to a revival of antisemitism. In Russia the situation was particularly difficult, and Jewish communities faced frequent pogroms and attacks.

The Church viewed Jews and Judaism as a threat to the Christian culture of Europe and propounded a 'teaching of contempt'. It was this that sowed the seeds of hatred and made it so easy for Hitler to use antisemitism as a political weapon. With some noble exceptions the Church was silent during the horrors of 1933 to 1945. Although no one would deny that Nazism was opposed to Christianity, Hitler justified antisemitism with reference to Christian attitudes towards Judaism, and found much in Christian teaching that the Nazis could use. During this period six million Jews perished alongside five million non-Jews (including Gypsies, Serbs, members of the Polish intelligentsia, resistance fighters from all the nations, German opponents of Nazism, homosexuals, Jehovah's Witnesses, habitual criminals and those considered generally 'anti-social'). The Holocaust was a carefully planned act of genocide. By the end of the Second World War, one-third of the world Jewish population had been murdered in the Holocaust. (Some Jews do not like to use the term 'Holocaust' because etymologically it has sacrificial overtones, meaning a 'burnt offering' to appease God. **Shoah**, which has connotations of destruction, rupture and doubt, is more often used.)

The Shoah shattered Victorian optimism and confidence in human progress that had existed at the turn of the twentieth century. For me it also epitomizes the inadequacy of secular human values. The question for many is not 'Where was God at Auschwitz?' but rather 'Where was humanity?' Yet I am aware that the Holocaust represents a huge challenge to religion not only because of the failure of people – particularly religious people – to act in the face of evil but also through its challenge to theology: how could God allow the Shoah to happen?

It is a profound challenge to all religious people, and there are no easy answers that can evade the terror of the Shoah. Indeed, after the Shoah, theology can never be the same again.

Elie Wiesel, a well-known Holocaust survivor, recounts how three great Jewish scholars created a rabbinic court of law during their incarceration in

Auschwitz. Their purpose was to indict God. The trial lasted several nights. Witnesses were heard, evidence was gathered, conclusions were drawn, all of which finally issued in a unanimous verdict: the Lord God Almighty, Creator of Heaven and earth, was found guilty of crimes against humanity and of breaking his covenant with the Children of Israel. What happened next was astonishing. After what Wiesel described as an 'infinity of silence', one of the Talmudic scholars looked at the sky and said, 'It's time for evening prayers', and the members of the tribunal proceeded to recite Ma-ariv, the evening service.

There are many religious responses to the Holocaust. Some ultra-Orthodox Jews speak of the Shoah as a punishment for Israel's unfaithfulness. Others link the horrors with the miracle of the rebirth of the State of Israel. Still others find their faith in God shattered and believe that God deserted his people or that there existed an eclipse of God. Some thinkers have spoken of a limited God who is not in total control; others have spoken of a God who suffers or who shares human suffering.

Many, like me, find themselves swinging between doubt and faith, for I struggle with the Shoah in my attempt to come to terms with it. The name Israel is particularly apt because it means, 'he who struggles with God'.

A survivor of the Holocaust, Rabbi Hugo Gryn, said, 'I believe that God was there, violated and blasphemed.' He tells how on the Day of Atonement, 'I dissolved in crying. I must have sobbed for hours . . . Then, I seemed to be granted a curious inner peace . . . I believe God was also crying . . . I found God.' But it was not the God of his childhood, the God whom he had expected miraculously to rescue the Jewish People. God was crying.

Richard Rubenstein offered another response, concluding that it was no longer possible to believe in divine election and that traditional belief in God was dead. Instead, Jews had to reinterpret their heritage and become a 'normal' nation. Rubenstein aimed to demythologize Judaism, yet keep the traditions and observances that helped maintain its distinctive identity. Within this new interpretative framework the State of Israel became central since it established a political normality, taken for granted by other nations whose states had existed for much longer.

Emil Fackenheim rejected the claim that God was dead, and defined the Shoah as a unique event that held significance not only for Jews but for all humanity. *What* happened might be explained, he suggested, but *why* was impossible to understand. Yet while the Shoah is without meaning, it issues a commandment – the six hundred and fourteenth. Fackenheim wrote that 'the authentic Jew of today is forbidden to hand Hitler yet another posthumous victory.' To this end Jews must retain their identity, resist assimilation and only marry within their faith.

Fackenheim also introduced the notion of *tikkun olam* ('mending the world'), a mystical concept to describe the human effort of relating to God. The better the relationship between Jews and God, the more 'whole' the world becomes and the less fractured the relationship between God and humanity. After the Holocaust, such mending is more difficult and, Fackenheim suggests, all the more necessary.

Irving Greenberg suggests that the Holocaust represents the beginning of a third era of the covenant between God and Israel. In the biblical age the Exodus represented redemption; in the rabbinic age the destruction of the Temple represented tragedy. In the modern age the Shoah represents redemption through destruction and the rebirth of the State of Israel. The covenant was endangered because of the potential death of the whole Jewish people, but Jews responded with a continuing commitment to remaining Jewish. For Greenberg the relationship between God and the Jewish people has been renewed, this time at the initiative of the people. The Jewish people no longer owe obedience to God (for they were not in the wrong), but voluntarily act out of renewed hope.

Israel

Jews have always had an attachment to, and a presence in, the Land of Israel. Even after the destruction of the Second Temple in 70 CE by the Romans, and the expulsion of Jews from Jerusalem, Jews looked forward to a messianic return. There seems to have been a continuous if somewhat tenuous Jewish existence in the Holy Land since biblical times. In the fourth century the Church Father Jerome, who lived near Bethlehem, reported that there were few Christians and that most of the people in the country were Jews; in the fifth and sixth centuries there were flourishing rabbinical schools in Galilee and especially in the city of Tiberias. In the medieval period Jewish communities were regularly established in cities such as Acre and Safed.

In the second half of the nineteenth century a new type of immigrant to the Holy Land began to arrive, fleeing persecution in Russia and Eastern Europe and founding collective agricultural settlements known as **kibbutzim**. The arrival of significant numbers of Jews from the 1880s onwards marked the beginning of modern Zionism, which led eventually to the creation of the modern State of Israel in 1948.

Theodore Herzl (1860–1904) is known as the founder of the Jewish State. He argued that Jews could only be safe if they had their own land, and that diaspora life would lead to catastrophe (borne out, tragically, by the Shoah). For Herzl the future Jewish state was a socialist utopia.

In 1917 the British government issued the Balfour Declaration, agreeing that a Jewish state should be established in the Palestine region, which they governed as a protectorate. Over the next few years Jewish immigration increased and important institutions were founded, such as the Hebrew University in Jerusalem in 1925. Hebrew was reborn, recreated from a language of history and religion into a language of everyday life.

In 1947 the United Nations agreed to partition the contested land between Jews and Arabs. On 14 May 1948 David ben Gurion became the first

Prime Minister of the State of Israel. Immediately, the surrounding Arab states invaded and the new state was forced to fight the first of several major wars. The War of Independence in 1949 resulted in the survival of Israel and also the beginning of a Palestinian refugee crisis – many Palestinians were placed in refugee camps, refused citizenship in Arab countries and not allowed to return to Israel. They became pawns in a political game and suffered – and continue to suffer – while the conflict between Israel and her neighbours failed to be resolved.

For most of its history Israel has had a deeply troubled relationship with the Arab states that surround it. Notable among recent conflicts were the Six-Day War in 1967, the Yom Kippur War in 1973 and the Lebanon War in 1982. The first steps towards peace came when Israel signed treaties with Egypt in 1979 and with Jordan in 1994. There have also been direct negotiations with the Palestinians, which have so far promised more than they have delivered. For Jews the recreation of a Jewish State in the Land of Israel nearly 2,000 years after the previous Jewish commonwealth is something of a miracle. It is also miraculous that Israel survived its early years, sustained by the help and support of foreign allies, such as Russia in the 1950s and the USA from the 1970s onwards.

Some 20 per cent of the population of Israel are Muslims (1.1 million) and 2 per cent are Christians (180,000), all of whom are full citizens of the Jewish state. Although the Israeli Arab population has its own press, school system and members of parliament, there are striking imbalances between Jews and Arabs, for example in terms of resource allocation. These remain to be redressed. In the West Bank there are more than 1 million Palestinians, some of whom fall under the governance of the Palestinian Authority. Most Israelis and Palestinians seek peaceful relations but this seems as far off as ever.

The territorial distances between the Palestinians and Israelis are smaller than the emotional gap between the two peoples. They do not trust each other. Israelis are angry with the Palestinians because they rejected the Camp David proposals in 2000 and returned to the use of terror. Palestinians are angry because they live in poverty, under the constant threat of violence.

Although much of Israel's history has been about winning wars in the face of great hostility, a successful future may depend on an even harder task: winning the peace. The qualities that win wars are not necessarily the same qualities that win the peace. For one thing, winning wars often results in a tendency to glorify military prowess, leading to an unhealthy self-reliance and self-belief bordering on arrogance. For another, war inevitably engenders enmity and hatred, neither of which provides a foundation upon which peace can be built. Palestinians living in the West Bank since 1967 have, for the most part, only experienced Israeli occupation and power. It is surely little wonder that the attitudes of many towards Israel are so negative.

Yet Israelis face the danger of renewed aggression from neighbours or regional superpowers. Iran's threat in 2005 to 'remove Israel from the map of the world' serves to reinforce this outlook. Israelis seek to hold on to territorial gains until wide-ranging peace is agreed. But in the end there will be no security for Israel until mutual grievance is replaced by mutual trust. To win the peace Israel needs not only to make territorial concessions – as it did by returning Sinai to Egypt in 1979 and by leaving Gaza in 2005 – but also strive to build bridges of understanding and friendship, between ordinary Israelis and Palestinians in particular, and Arabs in general.

In an anecdote that serves to illustrate the problem there were two brothers. Each owned half a field, but each wanted the half he did not have and neither would give up his half. They called in a Rabbi known for his wisdom. He lay down under a tree in the field with his ear to the ground and appeared to fall asleep. After a time the brothers grew impatient, complaining that the Rabbi was wasting their time. But he told them that he had been listening to the ground. It had told him that neither of them owned the ground. It owned them. And one day, he said, they would be inside it.

 ## Shabbat

At the end of the first chapter of Genesis, God surveys all that had been created over the first six days and finds it 'very good'. At the beginning of chapter two, God ceases (*shavat*) creating and blesses the seventh day to make it holy. The Sabbath (from the Hebrew root meaning 'to cease') is a weekly day of rest observed from sunset on Friday night until nightfall the following evening.

Judaism accords the Sabbath the status of a holy day, for it is the first holy day mentioned in the Bible and God was the first to observe it. As well as commemorating God's creation of the universe, **Shabbat** represents a taste of a future messianic world. There is a belief that the messiah will come if every Jew properly observes two consecutive Sabbaths.

The Sabbath is a day of rest and a time for prayer, both at home and in synagogue. In synagogue, reading the Torah is the central part of the Saturday morning service. According to Jewish mystical writings, the Sabbath represents both the male and female principles in the Godhead, which are united on this day like no other. Perhaps this is one reason why marital intercourse is regarded as especially meritorious on Friday night.

Some of the best-known Sabbath customs surround the Friday-night meal, which begins with a blessing over two candles followed by a prayer over wine and over the bread, or *challa*, which consists of two loaves. These serve as a reminder of the two portions of manna gathered by the Israelites in the desert on the Sabbath eve. The Sabbath ends with Saturday evening prayers, called **havdalah** ('separation'), to mark the transition from the holy day to the secular week.

The cycle of festivals

The busiest time of year in the Jewish calendar is the autumn, when four festivals take place within a month (see Table 6.1). The Jewish calendar is lunisolar, which means that while Jewish festivals occur around the same time of year, they do not occur on the same day as the solar calendar.

Rosh Hashana and Yom Kippur

The season begins with the New Year, **Rosh Hashana**, held on the first and second of the Hebrew month of Tishri. This festival has but one similarity with the celebrations that surround the end of the secular New Year on 31 December: the making of New Year's resolutions. Rosh Hashana is a time not of parties but of looking back at the mistakes of the year just ended and reflecting on the changes in lifestyle that are needed to lead a better life in the year ahead.

This reflection includes seeking reconciliation with people who have been wronged during the year. The Rabbis explain that before asking God for forgiveness of sins we must first seek to right the wrongs we have committed against others. Consequently Rosh Hashana is a solemn festival requiring self-reflection. It also marks the beginning of a ten-day period that ends with the observance of **Yom Kippur**, the Day of Atonement. The Ten Days of Awe, as they are sometimes called, are a time for *teshuva* (repentance), *tefilla* (prayer) and *tzedaka* (charity).

During the Rosh Hashana service the community hears the primitive sounds of a ram's horn (**shofar**) being blown on more than a hundred occasions. According to the great Jewish teacher of medieval Spain, Moses Maimonides, its purpose is to wake up the congregation and to prompt Jews to think about what they can do to make themselves better people.

Yom Kippur occurs ten days later and is the holiest day of the year. Traditionally all Jewish adults, defined as those over the age of 13, fast and pray. Often Jews who do not observe any other custom will fast or acknowledge the seriousness of this day, one way or another. Some friends of mine who are not at all observant – even those who are devout atheists – attend synagogue. They particularly enjoy the traditional music and feel a sense of connection with other Jews who are observing the day.

There are many additions to the regular synagogue prayers, the most important being the *Al Chet*, or *Vidui*, the confession of sins. All sins are confessed in the plural ('we are guilty'), emphasizing communal responsibility of which we are all part. Another feature of the Yom Kippur service is the reading of Jonah to teach that if people are sincere in their prayers God will always accept their *teshuva*, even from an entire city of sinners.

According to Ecclesiastes, 'There is not one good man on earth who does what is best and doesn't err' (7.20). Sin separates humanity from God but

Table 6.1 The Jewish calendar of festivals

Month	Festival	Description
1 Tishri September/October	Rosh Hashanah literally, 'head of the year'	New Year. Time of reflection
10 Tishri September/October	Yom Kippur literally, 'Day of Atonement'	Day of Atonement. Time of fasting and repentance
15 Tishri September/October	Sukkot literally, 'booths'	Autumn harvest festival. Commemorates temporary booths during Israelite wandering in desert
22 Tishri September/October	Shemini Atzeret literally, 'eighth day of gathering'	Marks end of Sukkot
23 Tishri September/October	Simchat Torah literally, 'rejoicing of the Torah'	Commemorates completion of annual reading of the Pentateuch
25 Kislev December	Chanukah literally, 'dedication'	Winter Festival of Lights
15 Shevat January	Tu-bishvat literally, '15th Shevat'	New Year for Trees
14 Adar March	Purim literally, 'lots'	Celebrates averted genocide as told in Esther
15 Nissan March/April	Pesach literally, 'sacrificial lamb' and 'passing over'	Spring festival to commem- orate exodus from Egypt
27 Nissan April	Yom ha Shoah literally, 'Day of Holocaust'	Holocaust Memorial Day
5 Iyyar April/May	Yom Ha-atzmut literally, 'Day of Independence'	Israel Independence Day
6 Sivan June	Shavuot literally, 'weeks'	Spring festival commem- orating the giving of the Torah to Moses at Sinai
9 Av August	Tisha BeAv literally, '9th Av'	Day of fasting and mourning for the destruction of both Temples and other atrocities

repentance provides a way back, for God will show compassion. The Bible has many words for regret or repent but the most common is *shuv*, 'to turn, or return', which is the basis for the word *teshuva*. Thus repentance means turning back to God, turning from the ways of evil to the ways of righteousness. As the Prophet Malachi put it, '"Turn back to me, and I will turn back to you," says the LORD of Hosts' (Mal. 3.7).

Sukkot

The third major autumn festival is **Sukkot**, meaning 'Booths'. A *sukkah* is built of branches and leaves with openings to enable the light of the sun, moon and stars to be seen. In celebration of the harvest the *sukkah* is decorated with fruits and vegetables hung from the roof and walls. The Talmud commends Jews to 'dwell in the *sukkah* as you would live in your home'. However, even most Orthodox Jews fulfil the **mitzvah** (commandments) by simply eating meals and studying in the *sukkah*.

In biblical times Sukkot was a harvest festival but later took on additional meaning, recalling the temporary shelters in which the Children of Israel lived while they wandered through the desert for 40 years. On the last day of Sukkot Jews celebrate Simchat Torah, 'rejoicing in the Torah', which marks the completion of the annual cycle of weekly Torah readings. During the year Jews read a portion of the Torah each week and on Simchat Torah they read the last verses of Deuteronomy and the first verses of Genesis, demonstrating that the Torah is a circle that never ends.

Although Simchat Torah is not mentioned in the Bible (it became a festival by the eleventh century CE), the completion of the readings is a time of great celebration. According to tradition, it is one of the two times of the year when Jews are commanded to drink heavily! There are processions, *hakafot*, around the synagogue carrying Torah scrolls, and plenty of high-spirited singing and dancing.

Chanukah

Chanukah, known as the Festival of Lights, is observed for eight days in the winter and commemorates the military victory of the Maccabees over the Syrian-Greeks, who ruled Israel around 2,200 years ago. *Chanukah* means 'dedication', and refers to the rededication of the Temple in Jerusalem in 165 BCE. The Festival of Lights refers to the flames kindled on each night on the *hanukkiya*, a nine-branch candelabrum. Beginning with one candle lit on the first night of Chanukah, each subsequent night has one more candle added and lit, ending with the eighth candle on the final evening. The ninth branch is reserved for the *shamash*, the servant light, which is lit first and used to kindle the other lights. Chanukah is popular with children, particularly among communities living in Christian countries. Perhaps it represents a response to Christmas, at which time a number of similar customs are celebrated with the lighting of candles and giving of presents.

Tu-bishvat

One month later, Jews celebrate **Tu-bishvat**, the New Year for Trees, which is an opportunity to reflect on the responsibility of humans as 'stewards of the world'. It is traditional to eat fruits and plant trees. The Bible extols reverence for fruit trees as symbols of God's bounty and beneficence. Special laws were formulated to protect trees in times of war and to ensure that their produce would not be picked until they were mature enough. In modern times, Tu-bishvat has enjoyed a revival as a celebration of the environment.

Purim

In the spring, Jews celebrate **Purim**, which means 'lots'. It takes place on the fourteenth day of Adar, usually in March, and commemorates the story of Esther. The Jewish girl Esther, along with her uncle Mordecai, helped save the community of Persia from the murderous intentions of Haman, wicked advisor to the king, who wanted to annihilate the Jewish people. Esther reads as a folk tale and is the only book of the Bible that does not contain the name of God.

The primary custom of Purim is to hear the reading of Esther, known as the *Megillah*, which means scroll. Purim often ends up as a communal party, since Jews by tradition are commanded to eat, drink and be merry. According to the Talmud, a person is required to drink until he cannot tell the difference between 'cursed be Haman' and 'blessed be Mordecai', though opinions differ as to exactly how drunk that is.

Pesach

Pesach, or Passover, is a family-oriented festival recalling the exodus from Egypt. In what is known as the *Haggadah* (Hebrew for 'to tell, relate'), Jews re-tell the story and thank God for redeeming them 'with an outstretched arm'. It takes place on the fifteenth day of Nisan and includes the **Seder** meal. The word '*Seder*' is derived from Aramaic, meaning 'order of service'. It is a feast that takes place on the first two nights of Passover. The most important people at the *Seder* are the children. The *Haggadah* states that in every generation each person must feel as if he personally had come out of Egypt. 'You should tell your child on that day, "When I left Egypt the Lord did miracles for me . . .".' Thus parents are commanded to tell their children the story of the Israelite Exodus from Egypt.

Elements of the *Seder* meal include:

- eating bitter herbs (because the Egyptians enslaved the Israelites and made their lives bitter);

- drinking four cups of wine (representing God's promises of redemption);
- eating unleavened bread (because the Israelites did not have time to ferment dough before they left Egypt);
- reclining to the left during parts of the service before the meal (symbolizing freedom, since Roman freemen reclined to the left);
- searching for the *afikomen* (a piece of *matzah* hidden during the *Seder* that children seek at the end of the meal).

During the meal the Seder Plate is explained to all, and especially children, because it holds all the main symbols of Passover: a roasted shank bone, representing the Temple sacrifices in biblical times; a roasted egg, representing the offerings given in the Temple; parsley, reminding Jews that Passover corresponds with the spring harvest; a dish of chopped apples, nuts, and wine, called *charoset*, which represents the mortar used by the Israelites in bondage; finally, bitter herbs, which represent the bitterness of slavery.

Shavuot

While Passover represents physical freedom from bondage, **Shavuot**, which commemorates the giving of the Torah to Moses, represents spiritual freedom from the bondage of idolatry. It is also called Feast of Weeks (*shavuot* means 'weeks'), and stands for the seven weeks between Passover and Shavuot. The giving of the Torah is far more than a historical event, and the Rabbis compare it to a wedding between God and the Children of Israel. According to tradition it was at this point that Jews agreed to become God's Chosen People and the Lord became our God.

Figure 6.2 The Ten Commandments in Hebrew and English

A well-established custom calls for all-night study of the Torah on the first night of Shavuot. There are many reasons given for the custom. My favourite is that when the Children of Israel were due to receive the Torah, they overslept. According to the Jewish mystical work, the Zohar, pious individuals therefore have to remain awake all night as an act of atonement. During the Shavuot service, Jews listen to the reading of the Ten Commandments (see Figure 6.2), which symbolize the giving of the whole Torah.

Modern Festivals

In the twentieth century, two new festivals have been added to the Jewish calendar. These are Yom ha Shoah, Holocaust Remembrance Day, observed on 27th Nisan, a few days after Pesach; and Yom Ha-atzmut, Israel Independence Day, observed ten days later.

Yom ha Shoah was first instituted in 1951 by Israel's parliament, the Knesset, to mourn the six million Jews who perished in the Holocaust. Jews in the diaspora now commemorate it as well. Yom Ha-atzmut marks the establishment of the modern State of Israel, observed on 5th Iyar, corresponding to 14 May 1948, the day Israel was declared an independent state.

The creation of two new festivals demonstrates the continuing vitality of Judaism and also illustrates that Judaism is a way of life. In this case, life – in the creation of the State of Israel – overcame death in the devastation wreaked by the Holocaust. Indeed, for many Jews the creation of the State of Israel represents the spiritual and physical resurrection of the Jewish People.

 The synagogue

The word 'synagogue' is derived from the Greek *sunagogé* (whence the Latin *synagoga* and the English word) and means a meeting or assembly, and is used in the Septuagint. As well as being a place of worship and prayer it is a place of meeting and study, as is denoted by the Hebrew name Bet Knesset, 'house of meeting'. The synagogue is perhaps best described as a community building with a social as well as a religious function: a place that houses prayer, study and education, charitable work as well as social activity.

The most important interior feature of the synagogue is the 'ark' (an acronym of the Hebrew *Aron Kodesh*), which is generally located on the side facing Jerusalem. Above the ark is located the *ner tamid*, the eternal lamp, which symbolizes the commandment to keep a light burning in the tabernacle outside the ark of the covenant.

The earliest archaeological evidence for a synagogue is dated to the third century BCE and is found in Egypt. By the first century BCE it was a widespread institution in Israel and the diaspora. In Rabbinic literature it is referred to as the 'little Temple', and some terms used in Temple services were transferred to the synagogue. For example, the Hebrew word *avodah*, 'service', referring to service in the Temple (sacrifice) was replaced by service of the heart (prayer) in the synagogue.

Most importantly, the synagogue was a democratizing institution for it brought Jewish worship within reach of every Jew, not only those who could visit the Temple in Jerusalem. Since no sacrifices could take place in a synagogue, worship did not have to be conducted by priests. And since sacrifices were replaced by prayer, the worshippers were able to participate rather than being mere spectators as they had been in the Temple.

As a house of prayer, worship takes place primarily in Hebrew, although the prayer books are generally in both Hebrew and the vernacular, or language of the country. At a Progressive synagogue the service is largely in the vernacular. Jews are expected to pray as individuals and as a family; and they are also expected to pray as a community. Tradition says that it is more beneficial to pray in a group than alone; indeed, certain prayers can only be said in the presence of a *minyan* (quorum of ten adult men, according to Orthodox Judaism). Men and women sit separately in Orthodox services but in Progressive synagogues all sit together. Men are required to cover their heads in both.

As a house of meeting, the synagogue offers a social dimension for the community, including both religious and non-religious activities. It often hosts, for example, clubs for the youth and also for the elderly, as well as social events for the congregants. The synagogue also functions as a social welfare agency, sometimes working closely with local churches to collect and dispense money and other items of aid for the poor.

 Prayer

In Hebrew the verb 'to pray', *hitpallel*, literally means 'to work on oneself', demonstrating that prayer benefits the worshipper rather than God. For Jews prayer is an act of introspection and self-transformation. It is not magic, nor is it an attempt to bend the world to our will. If anything it does the opposite: it helps us to notice the things we otherwise take for granted. And seeing things differently we may begin to act differently. Jewish prayer always begins with the praise of God, and its imagery denotes the worshipper approaching God directly.

When the Bible commands Jews to serve God 'with all your heart', the Rabbis asked, 'What is service with all your heart?' They answered: 'It is prayer.' Jews traditionally pray three times a day, corresponding to the three daily sacrifices held during Temple times. The basic unit of Jewish prayer is the blessing, which has the power to transform an everyday act into one that is an acknowledgement of God's role in the world.

Some prayers that were originally composed in biblical times are still used today, such as the *Shema* and the Ten Commandments. Other prayers, such as the *Amidah* (which means 'standing', because Jews stand during its recital), were developed in the post-biblical period. This prayer is also called the *Shemoneh Esrei* (which means '18' and refers to the 18 blessings originally contained within the prayer). It can be broken down into three categories: praising God, petitioning God and thanking God.

From biblical times the Jewish service also includes teaching. The Prophet Isaiah describes how the people gathered in the Temple courts to receive instruction as well as to pray. Nehemiah describes how Ezra recited and translated passages from the Pentateuch for the benefit of the whole community.

This practice continues today. A reading from the Written Torah and from the Prophets (known as the *Haftorah*) are central features of the synagogue service. The Torah is divided into sections, so that if one section is read each week the Torah can be covered in a year. These are read on Mondays and Thursdays in Orthodox synagogues and on *Shabbat* and some holidays in all synagogues. The Torah is paraded around the sanctuary before it is brought to rest on the podium. It is considered an honour to be called up to recite a blessing (*aliyah*) over the reading.

Jewish–Christian relations

Christianity and Judaism have a unique relationship, not least because Jesus lived and died a Jew. The first Christians were Jews, and it was centuries rather than decades later that Christianity and Judaism went their separate ways. By the completion of the Talmud (*c.* 500 CE), Judaism and Christianity had diverged and Jewish Christianity ceased to exist. Nevertheless, Christians and Jews remained (and remain today) intricately intertwined in their claim to the same Scriptures. For the most part, what Christians call Old Testament and Jews *Tanakh* is the same, although they interpret Scripture quite differently – hence the aphorism that 'Jews and Christians are divided by a common Bible.'

The main theological divide concerns Christian claims about the divinity of Jesus. Gradually the Church came to view Judaism as the preliminary and outdated people of Israel replaced by the new and true Israel (*verus Israel*). Yet many Christians in the early centuries were attracted to synagogue services. Thus church leaders (such as the fourth-century Church Father, John Chrysostom) delivered vitriolic sermons against Jews and Judaism (creating a literary genre known as *adversus iudaeos*), insisting that Jews did not understand the Old Testament.

Since Judaism was a minority in both the Islamic world and Christendom, Jews were prompted to consider why God allowed these faiths to flourish. One view was that Christianity was a form of idolatry, perhaps not in the full biblical sense but through inherited patterns of idolatrous worship. Another approach categorized Christianity in terms of the Noachide Laws, which formulated moral standards without a demand for conversion to Judaism. Another view – propagated by the eleventh-century Spanish Jewish poet Judah ha Levi and the twelfth-century scholar Maimonides – was that Christianity prepared the way for nations to worship the God of Israel and prepared the way for redemption. The thirteenth-century theologian, Menahem ha'Meiri, put forward the most positive view in medieval times when he argued that Christianity should be understood as a form of monotheism. He coined the phrase 'nations bound by the ways of religion' to enable a more fruitful interaction between Jews and Christians.

From *c.* 1100 onwards, as Christendom became more homogeneous, Jews were seen as one of the last 'different' groups. By the sixteenth century they had been expelled from most of Western Europe. Unsurprisingly, Jews viewed the Reformation as a positive development, partly because it diverted Christian attention away from Judaism and because the Protestant return to the Hebrew Bible also contributed to a rise in messianic fervour among Jews. Despite its early promise, however, the Reformation saw the Christian teaching of contempt continue. A shift in Jewish attitudes towards Christianity can be noted following the Enlightenment and Jewish Emancipation. Figures of Reform Judaism, such as the nineteenth-century leader Abraham Geiger, embraced the Jewishness of Jesus. Even some Orthodox Jews argued that Jesus embodied the essence of Judaism. It was not a huge step for Martin Buber to call Jesus his 'elder brother'.

At the same time, Jews continued to hold negative views of Christianity as a result of continuing anti-Jewish prejudice and the rise of antisemitism. The Enlightenment doctrine maintained that while society could be remade, certain persons were beyond redemption. This cast of mind provided the basis for modern racism and reached a crescendo during the Nazi period and the Shoah. The overall failure of the Churches during that period, 1933 to 1945, resulted in anger towards, and distrust of, Christianity.

The reassessment of Christian attitudes towards Judaism in modern times can be seen first in the writings of Christian scholars of the early twentieth century, such as James Parkes and Robert Travers Herford. This trend accelerated after the Shoah, and deep-seated theological change soon followed. Pope John XXIII placed consideration of the Church's 'teaching of contempt' for the Jewish people on the Second Vatican Council's agenda, which resulted in *Nostra Aetate* (1965). Its insistence that 'Jews should not be presented as rejected . . . by God' was a significant turning point for the Roman Catholic Church and has been followed by further documents. When Pope John Paul II led the Vatican to recognize the State of Israel in 1994 and made a pilgrimage to the Holy Land in 2000, he overturned centuries of teaching that tied Jewish eviction from their land to their sinful rejection of Christ. Pope John Paul II repeatedly enhanced the appreciation of Judaism and its people. Yet the Church, as representative of God and Christ on earth, was still not seen as guilty of any error or wrong.

Since 1970, mainline Protestant churches have adopted positive views of Judaism and rejected supersessionism. The Evangelical Church of the Rhineland's 1980 document was a major turning point. This asserted that Jews were permanently elected as God's people and that the Church was taken into this covenant with God through Jesus Christ the Jew.

The change in modern Jewish attitudes towards Christianity was slower in occurring, partly as a result of suspicion about Christian motives and the legacy of the 'teaching of contempt'. Nevertheless, the publication in 2000 of *Dabru Emet* ('speak truth'), a cross-denominational statement exploring the place of Christianity in Jewish terms, represents the most positive portrait of Christianity in many centuries. It proposed the following:

1 Jews and Christians worship the same God.

2 Jews and Christians seek authority from the same book.

3 Christians can respect the claim of the Jewish people upon the Land of Israel.

4 Jews and Christians accept the moral principles of the Torah.

5 Nazism was not a Christian phenomenon.

6 The humanly irreconcilable difference between Jews and Christians will not be settled until God redeems the entire world as promised in Scripture.

7 A new relationship between Jews and Christians will not weaken Jewish practice.

8 Jews and Christians must work together for justice and peace.

It is too early to evaluate the long-term impact of *Dabru Emet*. But this is an unprecedented response to Christianity in modern times and may represent a new stage in the 2,000-year history of Jewish–Christian relations.

? QUESTIONS

1 What is Judaism?

2 To what extent do Jews and Christians share the same Bible?

3 'The God of the Hebrew Bible is the God of History.' How do Jews sustain this principle in the aftermath of the Shoah?

4 What are the differences and connections between the terms, 'People of Israel', 'Land of Israel' and 'State of Israel'?

 # Glossary

Chanukah literally, 'dedication'. Refers to the rededication of the Temple in Jerusalem in 165 BCE. Chanukah, known as the Festival of Lights, is observed for eight days in the winter and commemorates the military victory of the Maccabees over the Syrian-Greeks who ruled Israel.

Halakhah Hebrew 'to walk'. Refers to Jewish law. *Halakhah* covers every aspect of life, effectively regulating Jewish individual and communal existence. Today Orthodox Jews maintain the undiminished authority of *Halakhah*, while Progressive Jews either modify it conservatively or reconstruct it on the basis of a non-fundamentalist reading of Scripture supplemented by modern considerations.

Havdalah literally, 'separation'. *Havdalah* marks the end of the Sabbath on Saturday evening with prayers, making the transition from the holy day to the secular week.

Holocaust biblical Greek translation of the Hebrew *olah*, 'whole burnt offering'. Refers to the murder between 1933–45 of nearly six million Jews under the Nazis, and millions of others including Roma, Sinti, Poles, Soviet prisoners of war, homosexuals, Jehovah's Witnesses and communists. The Holocaust is a central preoccupation of post-war Jewish–Christian relations, and three areas dominate discussion: anti-Judaism/antisemitism; Christian responses, 1933–45; and post-Holocaust responses.

kibbutz(im) literally, 'gathering'. Refers to collective agricultural settlement(s) in Israel.

Midrash Hebrew for searching, inquiring and interpreting, generally referring to a genre of rabbinic literature. Consists of an anthology of homilies, a commentary on a particular book of the Bible, and is viewed as a religious activity.

Mishnah a comprehensive compendium, primarily of rabbinic law, from the early third century CE, edited by Judah ha-Nasi; the base-text of the Talmud.

mitzvah deed commanded by *Halakhah*. Popularly refers to any good deed. *Bar/bat-mitzvah* ('son/daughter of the commandment') refers to the coming of age ceremony for males at the age of 13 and females at 12 or 13.

Pentateuch formed from two Greek words, *pente* (five) and *teuchos* (scroll), and meaning five scrolls. It designates the first five books of the Bible, known as the (written) Torah.

Pesach literally, 'sacrificial lamb' and 'passing over'. Refers to Passover, a family-oriented festival in the spring when Jews re-tell the story, known as the *Haggadah* (literally, 'to tell, relate') of the Exodus from Egypt, and thank God for redeeming them 'with an outstretched arm'.

Purim literally, 'lots'. Celebrates the story of Esther and takes place usually in March. Esther, along with her uncle Mordecai, helped save the community of Persia from the murderous intentions of Haman, the wicked advisor to the king who wanted to annihilate the Jewish people.

Rosh Hashana literally, 'head of the year'. Refers to the Jewish new year, in the autumn. Rosh Hashana is a solemn festival, requiring self-reflection, and marks the beginning of a ten-day period that ends with the observance of *Yom Kippur*, the Day of Atonement.

Seder literally, 'order'. Normally refers to the Passover meal (*seder*).

Shabbat literally, 'to cease'. Refers to resting from work in order to remember God as creator. The day is observed from Friday sunset until Saturday nightfall, day following night in the Jewish calendar.

Shavuot literally, 'weeks'. Commemorates the giving of the Torah to the Children of Israel on Mount Sinai; represents spiritual freedom from the bondage of idolatry. It is also called the Feast of Weeks and stands for the seven weeks between Passover and *Shavuot*.

Shema literally, 'hear', and is the first word of Deuteronomy 6.4, 'Hear, O Israel'. The *Shema* is the name of the most important declaration of faith; it consists of Deuteronomy 6.4–9; 11.13–21 and Numbers 15.37–41.

Shoah literally, 'total destruction'. Hebrew term used to describe the murder of Jews during the Second World War. It is used by some as an alternative to the term Holocaust (see above).

Shofar literally, a ram's horn, blown on special occasions such as Rosh Hashanah and Yom Kippur.

Sukkot literally, 'booths'. Refers to a celebration of the harvest; also called Tabernacles. A *sukkah* is built of branches and leaves, with openings to enable the light of the sun, moon and stars to be seen, and is decorated with fruits and vegetables hung from the roof and the walls. It also recalls the temporary shelters in which the Children of Israel lived while they wandered through the desert.

Talmud literally, 'learning'. Refers to the most important works of rabbinic Judaism. The Jerusalem Talmud dates from the late fourth century CE, while the Babylonian Talmud, which is more authoritative, is dated to the late fifth century. The Talmud consists of a commentary on the Mishnah and includes legal sources, ethics, biblical exegesis, homilies and stories.

Torah literally, 'teaching', 'instruction'; often translated as 'law'. Torah carries a wide variety of meanings. It can be used to describe the Five Books of Moses (Written Torah) but in its broadest sense is equated with the whole body of Jewish teaching and law (Oral Torah), explaining what the Pentateuch means and how it should be interpreted.

Tu-bishvat New Year for Trees, when it is traditional to eat fruits and plant trees. Tu-bishvat celebrates the environment and reminds Jews of their attachment to the land of Israel.

Yom Kippur literally, 'Day of Atonement'. The most solemn day in the Jewish calendar, biblically ordained as a day of fasting and abstinence and entitled 'the sabbath of sabbaths'. Yom Kippur is seen as the time for a fresh start and, unlike other fast-days, enjoys the status of a major festival.

115

Further reading

Cohn-Sherbok, D., *Holocaust Theology: A Reader* (Exeter: University of Exeter Press, 2002).

Halevi, Y. K., *At the Entrance to the Garden of Eden: A Jew's Search for God with Christians and Muslims in the Holy Land* (New York: William Morrow, 2001).

Kessler, E., *An Introduction to Jewish–Christian Relations* (Cambridge: Cambridge University Press, 2010).

Lange, N. de, *An Introduction to Judaism*, 2nd edn (Cambridge: Cambridge University Press, 2009).

Magonet, J., *A Rabbi's Bible* (London: SCM, 1991).

7

Christian thought and practice

Roger Bowen

Anyone who travels in Europe will notice at once that the largest and most beautiful buildings in any village or town are the Christian churches, especially those built hundreds of years, even a thousand years, ago. Enormous sums of money were spent on building these churches for the glory of God. Today church buildings are found on every continent, sometimes in huge numbers, in countries like Nigeria and Korea. They may be massive, modern cathedrals or, more likely, small buildings that look just like one of the nearby village houses. They may be just a space under a tree where Christians gather for worship.

Still today, on Sundays, the traveller will hear bells calling Christians to worship God in these churches, just as the Muslim is called to prayer by the muezzin and the Hindu is called by the sound of the conch shell. Africans may be called by the sound of drums or the banging on a steel pipe or car wheel. Travellers who wish to enter these churches are welcome to do so, and even to take part in the worship. The churches may look different from one another; the Christians may hold different traditions from one another, but certain essential elements remain the same in every Christian church.

Christians believe that Jesus Christ was uniquely chosen by God to reveal his love to the world. They listen to the reading of the Bible, both Old and New Testaments, with attention and respect. They sing songs, usually to musical accompaniment. They pray to God in ways that may include praise, confession of sins and asking for God's blessing upon the Church, the nation and any local or global

The Lord's Prayer

Our Father in heaven,
hallowed be your name,
your kingdom come,
your will be done,
on earth as in heaven.
Give us today our daily bread.
Forgive us our sins
as we forgive those who sin
against us.
Save us from the time of trial
and deliver us from evil.
For the kingdom, the power,
and the glory are yours
now and for ever. Amen.
(English Language Liturgical
Consultation)

needs that they recognize. They may use words taught by Jesus in The Lord's Prayer. They listen to a sermon that applies the teaching of the Bible to issues facing people in their lives today. The service may include the 'sacraments' of the Lord's Supper or Baptism (see p. 123). A few Christian groups (such as the Salvation Army and the Quakers) do not observe these sacraments.

Some churches worship in a formal way following a set order written in a prayer book. Others worship spontaneously with noise and movement. There may be dancing, special ministry for healing the sick or opportunities for people to exercise any gifts that God has given them for the benefit of the whole church.

These forms of worship are inherited from the practice of the very first Christians. They are all mentioned in the Bible and, for the most part, arise from Jewish patterns of worship that were used by Jesus and his disciples.

There are different levels of worship and fellowship. Most Christians worship on Sundays in a *congregation*, perhaps in a medium-sized building. But they also need closer fellowship in worship by meeting, perhaps at home, in *cell* groups of just a few people. And sometimes congregations and cells should come together in their hundreds for *celebration*, perhaps in a mother church or conference centre.

The world of Jesus

At the time of Jesus, Palestine was part of the Roman Empire. Some districts were ruled by Roman governors, others by local princes appointed by Rome. Most Jews longed for freedom and independence from Roman rule. They thought it shameful that the nation God had chosen as his own in order to lead the world to the knowledge of the true God now had to obey foreign rulers. They expected that one day in the future, 'The Day of the Lord', God would send his special messenger, his anointed Messiah, to restore freedom and spiritual renewal to the Jewish nation.

Rome kept her empire in subjection through the power of her army, but allowed the Jewish people a lot of autonomy. Roman rule brought many benefits to everyone. There was peace and security. Good roads linked all the main cities and there were regular shipping services across the Mediterranean Sea. One language (Greek) united ordinary people throughout the empire, even though Latin was the language of government. Many Gentiles (that is, non-Jews) were attracted to Judaism and became 'proselytes', worshipping in Jewish synagogues.

For all these reasons it was, in the words of Paul, 'the right time' to bring a new message for the people of the ancient world. People were hungry for it and it could be communicated everywhere without difficulty. This message was all about Jesus the Messiah, not only what he taught but also what he did and who he was.

Jesus

One of the best-known stories in the world is the story of the birth of Jesus at Bethlehem, in Judaea, as it is told by Matthew and Luke. His mother was the Virgin Mary, who became pregnant not by a human father but by a miraculous act of God. Mary was married to Joseph, a carpenter. The family lived in Nazareth, in Galilee.

Little is known about the early years of Jesus, but he and his parents were faithful Jews attending Temple and synagogue worship. When he was about 30 his cousin, John 'the Baptist', began preaching in Judaea, calling people to repent of their sin and baptizing them in water as a sign of cleansing and forgiveness. He said that he was just 'a voice' telling people about 'the one who was to come', Jesus. Jesus too was baptized, returned to Galilee and began his ministry of preaching, teaching and healing. Many people followed him, but he chose an inner group of 12 disciples to 'be with him'. The number 12 corresponds to the 12 tribes of Israel, and the Gospel writers saw the birth and ministry of Jesus as God's fulfilment of his promises to the Jewish people.

As Jesus and his disciples travelled from place to place, people flocked to see him. Out of compassion he cured many of sickness and demonic possession. On occasions he raised the dead, stilled a storm on the lake, turned water into wine and made a few loaves satisfy the hunger of thousands of people. These miracles are called 'signs', especially in John's Gospel, because they point to the fact that God was with Jesus in a spe-

> Jesus said:
> I am the bread of life
> I am the light of the world
> I am the good shepherd
> I am the resurrection and the life
> I am the true vine
> I am the way, the truth and the life

cial way. They made people ask the question, 'Who is this?' Christians recognize him to be God's Son, not because of his miraculous birth but because, from the beginning, he was one with God his Father. They turn to him as God and worship him as Lord, using the Jewish word for the name of God, Yahweh.

Gradually Jesus' closest disciples began to recognize him as the Messiah, the promised messenger from God. Then about halfway through his ministry he began to tell them about his approaching suffering and death. He began to experience opposition from the Jewish leaders, mainly because he insisted that caring for the poor and outcasts was more important than keeping religious traditions. That had always been what God required, as

> Jesus said: 'Come to me, all you that are weary and are carrying heavy burdens, and I will give you rest. Take my yoke upon you and learn from me; for I am gentle and humble in heart, and you will find rest for your souls.'
> (Matt. 11.28–29, NRSV)

the Hebrew prophets had taught. If people needed healing on the Sabbath (the Jews' holy day) he would heal them. He loved the company of sinful people, women, tax collectors, Samaritans – all of whom the religious leaders regarded as 'unclean'. He turned out of the Temple traders who were making money out of poor people. Neither the Pharisees (keepers of religious tradition) nor the Sadducees (keepers of the Temple worship) could tolerate his growing popularity.

There were others, like the Zealots, who hoped he would assume the role of a political King and get rid of the Roman occupiers once and for all. But this was not his aim, nor was it what he meant when he spoke of the Kingdom of God.

Finally, Jesus entered Jerusalem to a rapturous welcome from the crowds who had gathered there for the Passover festival. He was aware that this was the end. He met with his 12 disciples for a final Passover meal. He was betrayed to the authorities by one of them. The Jews accused him of blasphemy because he called himself the Son of God, but their accusation before the Roman governor was that he claimed to be 'King of the Jews' and therefore a rival to the Emperor. He was crucified on the Friday of Passover week. By sunset he was dead and buried. The cross is the sign of the Christian faith recognized all over the world.

The disciples thought it was the end. They could not believe that God would allow his chosen servant to suffer and die a shameful death. All their hopes were dashed.

The women went to anoint the body of Jesus in the tomb on the first day of the week, but found it empty. So did Peter and John. Later they discovered why. Jesus had risen from death and came to meet them, first in the room where they were gathered and then to different groups of people in several places over a period of nearly six weeks. He showed them that the prophets had predicted all these events long before. They must now take his message all over the world. He promised he would never leave them and would give them his Spirit (the Holy Spirit) to enable them to do this.

On the Day of Pentecost seven weeks after Jesus' resurrection, the Holy Spirit came upon the disciples. They were immediately transformed from a bunch of disillusioned cowards into triumphant preachers of 'Jesus and the Resurrection'. Persecution could not stop them. Even the Pharisees believed in the resurrection of the bodies of the faithful – but now Jesus had actually demonstrated this by rising from death himself, so there was nothing to be frightened of, not even death. So the story of Jesus turns into the story of his Church, which has celebrated his story ever since.

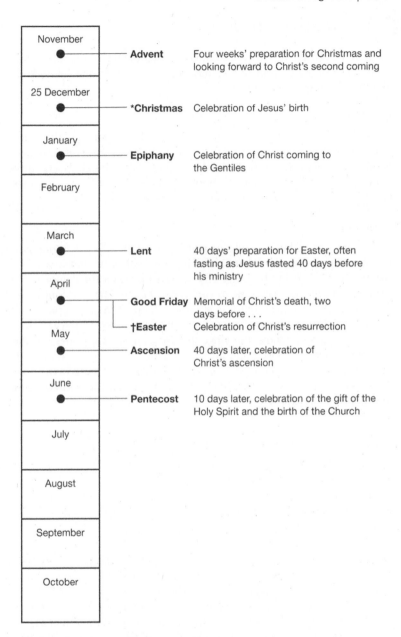

Figure 7.1 The main festivals of the Christian year
* The Orthodox Church celebrates Christmas on 6 January
† The date of Easter varies each year
Source: Adapted from Myrtle Langley, *World Religions*, Lion, 1993.

Roger Bowen

 The teaching of Jesus

Right at the outset, the Gospels summarize the teaching of Jesus: 'The time is *fulfilled*, and the *kingdom* of God has come near; *repent*, and *believe* in the good news' (Mark 1.15, NRSV).

Fulfilled

Jesus did not bring a brand new message; it was the fulfilment of the history of Israel and the promises of God through the prophets. The Old Testament, the Bible of the Jews, was the Bible of Jesus and of the Church. His favourite name for himself came from the book of Daniel, 'Son of Man', a human being on whom rests the power of God to save all God's people.

Kingdom

This is not a place but 'the rule, or reign, of God'. It is in the future. Jesus told his followers to pray that God's kingdom will come. But it is also in the present: 'if it is by the finger of God that I cast out the demons, then the kingdom of God has come to you' (Luke 11.20). The kingdom is here because the King is here, but it is at present hidden; many people do not receive it, so Christians pray for it to grow and be accepted everywhere. Jesus told many parables about the kingdom. They are simple stories but they do not give simple answers. On the contrary they are intended to make the listeners think deeply about what the rule of God should mean in their own lives. The kingdom is not the same as the Church but the Church should always be testing and reforming itself so that its values reflect those of the kingdom of Jesus' teaching.

Repent

The coming of Jesus was a critical moment for the Jews. If God is the ruler and Jesus his anointed King, people must 'turn round' and live as God intended them to, in faith and love. He gave many warnings about the judgement that would come upon them if they failed to respond.

Believe

Jesus did not expect people to be able to fulfil the moral law. Even his Sermon on the Mount (Matt. 5—7) set an impossibly high standard for human behaviour. But his primary message was not good advice but good news: that the door to God's kingdom is open to everyone, however poor or wretched they are, if they will only put their trust in God the Father as Jesus had revealed him. Then they will be members of his new family. Like Jesus, they will be the light of the world. Through the power of his Spirit living in them, they will show the world a new way of living, not for themselves but for others, with love.

Jesus supported his teaching by giving his followers two concrete, visible signs or sacraments, which the Church has used ever since. The first is Baptism in water. A new believer is taken down into the water and taken out again. This is a sign both of cleansing and of dying to the old life and rising to a new one, as Jesus did. The new Christian confesses Jesus as Lord, is united with him, receives his Spirit and is admitted into the Church. This happens just once, at the start of one's Christian life. John called it being 'born again'.

Believers observe the second sacrament regularly, perhaps every week, when they share bread and wine together as Jesus did at the last supper. The bread and wine signify his death on the cross and help us to remember it. There are different names for this sacrament – the Lord's Supper, Holy Communion, the Eucharist (Greek for 'thanksgiving'), the Mass, the breaking of bread. Both sacraments are dramatic pictures of Jesus' death and resurrection and our participation in these events. They are sacraments of the 'new covenant' (the contract God made with his people) and correspond to the chief signs of the old covenant (circumcision and the Passover).

> Jesus said:
> Go, make disciples of all nations, baptizing them them in the name of the Father and of the Son and of the Holy Spirit.
> (Matt. 28.19, NRSV)
>
> Do this in remembrance of me . . . As often as you eat this bread and drink the cup, you proclaim the Lord's death until he comes.
> (1 Cor. 11.24, 26, NRSV)

 ## The Bible

Christianity, like Judaism and Islam, is a 'religion of the book'. Its chief source of authority is the Scriptures, which it recognizes were inspired by God. This does not mean that God dictated the words. The Bible is made up of 39 books of the Old Testament, which the Church inherited from the Jews, and 27 books written by the first Christians. The books had different authors,

> The sacred writings . . . are able to instruct you for salvation through faith in Christ Jesus. All scripture is inspired by God and is useful for teaching, for reproof, for correction, and for training in righteousness.
> (2 Tim. 3.15, 16, NRSV)

and each book bears the marks of the personality, ideas and language of the human author. But the Church recognized that all were guided by the Spirit of God to write as they did. As a result, the Church put itself under the authority of these books and has been led by them ever since. It believes that the Bible is the written word of God and bears witness to the Living Word, Jesus.

The Old Testament was written for the most part in Hebrew, but writers of the New Testament often quoted from the Greek translation, called the Septuagint. The New Testament was written in *koine* Greek, the simple Greek spoken in the street, apart from a few words of Aramaic, the usual language of Jesus and his followers.

Although the Church accepts the Bible as the ultimate authority for belief and behaviour, the Bible needs to be both interpreted (What did it mean then?) and applied to modern life (What does it say to me today?). For this we need help from reason and from tradition.

Scholars have translated the Bible into all the major languages of the world and into hundreds of tribal languages. They have worked on discovering the original Greek or Hebrew text and the meaning of the words in the time and situation of the writer. In doing this they have drawn on the wisdom of the universal Church and have learned from the way Christians have interpreted the Bible over the last 2,000 years.

The New Testament
The Four Gospels
(*four accounts of Jesus' life*)
The Acts of the Apostles
(*story of the early Church*)
The Letters of Paul
(*to seven churches and three individuals*)
A Letter to the Hebrews
A Letter from James
Two letters from Peter
Three Letters from John
A Letter from Jude
The Revelation to John

It is more important to read the Bible than books about the Bible. As a first step, you might like to read *The 100-Minute Bible,* which summarizes its message in 50 readings (17 from the Old Testament and 33 from the New), each of which can be read in two minutes (see Further reading).

 The story of the Church

After the Day of Pentecost the Church spread the good news of Jesus crucified and risen among Jewish people in Judea and scattered throughout the Roman Empire. Soon, however, they found that Gentiles were showing interest in the message and even turning to Christ and receiving the gift of his Spirit. This posed a problem for the Jewish Church: could Gentiles become Christians without first becoming Jews and observing the Law that God had given? After a lot of argument the Holy Spirit led them to issue the 'Apostolic Decree', which declared that anyone could be right with God simply through faith in Jesus Christ as Lord and Saviour. They did not need to be circumcised or to observe the Jewish ceremonial law. But they were asked to observe certain food laws so as to preserve open fellowship and not cause offence to their Jewish Christian friends or division between Jewish and Gentile Christians.

This agreement paved the way for the rapid growth of the Church in every corner of the known world, in spite of persecution and even martyrdom at the hands of both Jews and the Roman authorities. Then, in 312 CE, the Emperor Constantine saw a vision of Christ and granted the Church freedom to worship and evangelize. He called 300 leaders of the Church to the Council of Nicaea in 325 to formulate doctrine, particularly the doctrine of the nature of Christ as both man and God. As a result of this Council, the Church eventually produced its major statement of faith, the Nicene Creed. It dealt with the philosophical and theological issues of that time, some of which are not relevant today. One statement that is relevant, however, is the four adjectives that describe the nature of the Church. The Church is:

- **One**: just as God is One, but three Persons within the Unity, so the Christian Church is one, even though its visible forms may be different. Christians everywhere should recognize and act upon their God-given unity – though they often fail to do so. The baptism that they share is a sign of this unity.
- **Holy**: the Church does not exist for itself but is 'holy', that is, set apart for God and to fulfil his purposes of extending his love throughout the whole world.
- **Catholic**: this word means 'universal'. The Church belongs within all the diverse cultures of the world and therefore appears in many different shapes and expressions.
- **Apostolic**: the Church is 'sent out' by Jesus, as his first followers were. It represents him and it cherishes and proclaims the apostolic faith once delivered to the saints by Jesus and his apostles.

By the fifth century, Christianity had become not only acceptable but respectable. Only Christians were given positions of leadership in the empire. This marked the beginning of 'Christendom' and the close connection between Church and state. A popular folk festival was chosen as the date for Christmas; Latin became the language of the Western Church; priests wore clothing worn by state officials (and many still do); the Church was organized along civic patterns and its buildings were prestigious architectural triumphs.

Gradually divisions grew up between the Church in the East, based on Constantinople (now Istanbul), and the Church in the West, based on Rome. After many years of disagreement, in 1054 the Pope in Rome, who claimed to be God's appointed leader of the universal Church in succession to St Peter, excommunicated the Patriarch of Constantinople – who then did the same to the Pope. As a result, the 'Great Schism' has divided East from West ever since.

The Eastern Church became known as 'Orthodox'. There are different branches of it as far south as Ethiopia and as far east as India: the Russian branch is the biggest (100 million); the Ethiopian (15 million) is one of the oldest; the Coptic in Egypt has 8 million members. For the most part, the branches are in fellowship with one another but have different leaders and use a variety of languages.

Orthodox churches are now to be found throughout the world. They have proved attractive to many Protestant Christians because of their ancient historical roots and the centrality of the presence of Christ in their worship. Their mission to the world focuses on the worshipping Church as the Body of Christ. They have not been troubled by the controversies of the Western Church, and they have been leaders in the ecumenical movement for Church unity.

The Catholic Church has one leader – the Pope, elected by the College of Cardinals – and has traditionally used the Latin language. During the Middle Ages the Popes were involved in arguments and violent struggles. They launched the Crusades in order to defeat the Muslims and recapture Jerusalem for Christendom. But at times the Crusaders even fought against their fellow Christians of the Eastern Church. At this time the Church had become thoroughly corrupt and superstitious, even 'selling' God's forgiveness to those who paid enough money.

There were always spiritually minded people who tried to reform the Church. Some tried from within, like Francis of Assisi, Dominic and Ignatius of Loyola. These men belonged to the monastic movement that has been a feature of the Church since the second century. The first monks were ascetics who withdrew into the desert to pray and fast in solitude. Later monastic orders specialized in social service or missionary work. Others, like John Hus and John Wycliffe, led movements outside the Church, often based on rediscovering the Bible in the language of the people.

In the fifteenth century there was a 'revival of culture and learning' – the Renaissance. Its leaders rediscovered the classical writings of Greek and Latin and promoted new art and literature. They criticized the Church for its backwardness, ignorance and corruption, but were not primarily interested in spiritual renewal. However, the Renaissance paved the way for Protestant reformers – Luther, Calvin, Zwingli and many others – to understand the message of the Bible and to proclaim it. Hitherto in the Western Church the Bible had been in Latin, which only priests and scholars could understand. The English scholar William Tyndale saw that people would remain ignorant unless 'the Scriptures were plainly laid before their eyes in their mother tongue'. As a result people could read and accept the good news of Jesus for themselves, without being dependent on a priest of the Church. The 'priesthood of all believers' meant that anyone could worship God freely – which was clearly the intention of Jesus himself. Many of the reformers were condemned and executed. Protestants split into many

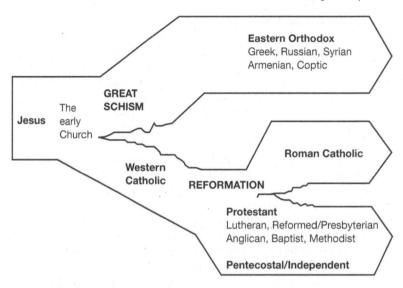

Figure 7.2 The main streams of Christianity
Source: Adapted from Myrtle Langley, *World Religions*, Lion, 1993.

different groups, often along national lines – Lutherans in Germany, Anglicans in Britain. Today these denominations are spread all over the world. For the most part they are in fellowship with one another. They even enjoy much fellowship and cooperation with Roman Catholics and Orthodox, but are still not officially allowed by these Churches to share Holy Communion with them.

Roman Catholics in the sixteenth century and Protestants in the eighteenth began to take seriously the commission given by Jesus to his disciples to evangelize the world. (In fact groups of Celtic and Nestorian monks had been doing this since the fourth and seventh centuries.) Missionaries were sent out by Catholic orders and by Protestant voluntary societies to plant new churches in Latin America, Asia and Africa. They respected and learned from the cultures and people to whom they went. Later, it was inevitable that some missionaries (but by no means all) seemed to be working hand in hand with colonial powers and imposed on their converts their own forms of Christian doctrine, ethics and worship. It was all they knew but it did not always fit well with local culture. Nevertheless their labours bore abundant fruit. Today the Churches in Africa and Latin America are immeasurably bigger and stronger than their parent Churches in Europe, so much so that more missionaries now travel in the opposite direction, to evangelize the secular, irreligious people of the North.

This is the way the Church has always grown – serially, not progressively. As it gains ground in one place it loses it in another. The first Christians were Jewish, but not for long: the faith took root among the Gentiles and soon the Church was more Greek than Jewish. The Church was threatened by the heathen barbarians from northern Europe as they began to conquer Rome and Italy – but very soon those barbarians had themselves been converted to Christ. Then Islam in the seventh century conquered the 'Christian' lands of Turkey and North Africa. Over the past 200 years the Church in the North has become weak, only to find new strength among peoples of the South. In 1900, some 70 per cent of the world's Christians were European; now Africa holds 25 per cent of the world's Christians and Latin America another 25 per cent.

It is difficult to measure numbers of Christians because there are many different criteria, but it is estimated that one-third of the world's population is Christian. Christianity has grown rapidly in sub-Saharan Africa, where the majority in almost every country is Christian. On any one Sunday there are more Anglicans in church in Nigeria than in the British Isles, North America and Australasia put together. In China, Christians number anything from 90 to 140 million (yet only one church was open as recently as the time of Chairman Mao). Korea was 1 per cent Christian in 1900; in 2000 South Korea was 49 per cent Christian. North and South America have large Christian majorities: 45 per cent of all Roman Catholics live in Latin America.

At the beginning of the twentieth century Pentecostal churches began to emerge in the USA. Pentecostals now number 50 million in Latin America, outgrowing all others. Pentecostalism has always been more of a 'movement' among Christians than a denomination. Their keynote is Baptism in the Spirit and the power of the Spirit in giving many 'charismatic' gifts to Christians. Gifts of 'tongues' and of healing are often emphasized, and there are many others. But movements of this kind have been present in the Church in every age since New Testament times, and now they can be found in every denomination as well as in specifically Pentecostal ones. They are particularly strong among people of African descent, but the 'black-led' churches always welcome worshippers of all ethnic groups.

In Africa we must take special note of the AICs – African Instituted Churches. These have grown spontaneously over the last 100 years, usually so as to offer people an indigenous option over against the mission-established churches that had often failed to take account of African tradition, culture and psychological needs. AICs vary a great deal but typically honour their clan ancestors, have ministries of healing and exorcism and can in some cases appear to be more pagan than Christian. But it is not possible to understand either Africa or the Church in Africa without seriously engaging with these movements that are sweeping the whole continent. The mainstream denominations recognize that they must adopt Pentecostal or AIC practices if they are to appeal to the youth of today.

The teaching of Christianity

About God

Like Jews and Muslims, Christians believe in the one God (called Yahweh in Hebrew and Allah in Arabic) who created the world. But unlike Jews and Muslims they believe that the one God has revealed himself as three 'persons'; that is, the Trinity, described as Father, Son and Holy Spirit. The one God was fully involved in creating, sustaining and saving the world, but sometimes one 'person' seems to take the lead. So the Father may be seen as primarily the Creator, the Son as the Redeemer and the Holy Spirit as the Sanctifier. But this is only a human attempt to understand God who is beyond our understanding. Indeed, it is necessary to emphasize that the word 'Trinity' is never used in the Bible, and Father/Son does not imply any physical generation but only an eternally intimate relationship.

As explained above, the teaching of Christianity comes from Christ and from the Old Testament that he used and the New Testament that speaks of him.

- **The Incarnation** means that God became a human being in Jesus. Jesus did not cease to be truly God, but he 'emptied himself' of much of his divine glory and power. He was without sin, and fulfilled the will of God perfectly.
- **The Atonement** means that Jesus took on himself the sin of human beings when he died as a sacrifice for sin on the cross. This is sometimes called 'redemption' – he paid the price of sin; or sometimes 'reconciliation', which means being at peace with God.
- **The Resurrection** means that God raised Jesus from death. The Church celebrates this central event of the faith not only every year at Easter but on the first day of every week. It shows that God can and does overcome not only sin but the very worst things that happen in the world, even when there seems to be no hope.
- **The Holy Spirit** was given to the whole Church after the departure of Jesus. The Spirit continues the work of Jesus – often through the Church but sometimes in spite of the organized Church that has, because of human sin, often acted against the will of God. But the Spirit gives his gifts to individual Christians and to small groups who have been faithful to the calling of Jesus when the majority have sought wealth or power for themselves. At times the Spirit may work in people or events outside the Christian community – and Christians need to be aware of this possibility.
- **The Second Coming** was promised by Jesus. He will come not in weakness but in the power and glory of God to complete his work of putting everything right. Many of the writers of the New Testament

thought this would happen in their lifetime but in fact we know nothing about when, where or how it will happen. But Jesus said it would be accompanied by God's righteous judgement. At that time people's eternal destinies will be determined and God will put to rights the disorders in his world.

About human beings

Humans were created by God 'in his image' and were given authority to care for the rest of creation. The stories at the beginning of the Bible show how the first humans misused this privilege and turned away from God. This is called 'sin', which has characterized human life ever since. It means that the image of God in humans is not lost but it is defaced. Sin always results in sins, that is, sinful acts. Sinful human beings are rightly condemned by God and under his judgement. But because God is not only perfectly just but also perfectly loving, he has taken steps to put this situation right. He has done this through the life and death of his Son.

Through his messengers God has always called people everywhere to repent and to believe (see p. 122). Since the coming of Christ, faith must be in him; he is 'the way' back to God.

When people trust in Christ and what he has done, they are 'justified', that is, set right with God. They are at peace with him and are set free to live their lives for him, not for themselves. As they become witnesses to his grace and love they have a new purpose in life. This is what God created them for at the beginning. This is how the Spirit of Christ empowers them to follow his example of self-giving love.

Many Christians say they are 'saved' now. In one sense this is true, but according to the Bible, Christians look forward to salvation in the future. All Christians, not just special ones, are called 'saints' in the Bible. This means they are set apart or 'sanctified', that is, growing to be more like Christ, a process that will not be completed in this life. After death Christians will be 'with Christ' according to Paul and 'like Christ' according to John. At the final judgement the bodies of Christians will be raised, as Christ was raised, and they will be with him for ever. Paul said that the risen body will be a spiritual rather than a physical body, whatever that means. Writers in the Bible found it difficult to describe these things because they are quite outside human experience. Neither they nor we have the language or the intellect to picture them.

About ethics

Unlike Islam and Judaism, Christianity does not have a fixed system of law. It has inherited from Judaism the Ten Commandments that are binding on Christians. It also frequently quotes Jesus' summary of the law:

The first [commandment] is, 'Hear, O Israel: the Lord our God, the Lord is one; you shall love the Lord your God with all your heart, and with all your soul, and with all your mind, and with all your strength.' The second is this, 'You shall love your neighbour as yourself.' There is no other commandment greater than these.   (Mark 12.29–31, NRSV)

Christians are expected to follow the first commandment by worshipping God regularly with other Christians, praying and reading the Bible privately and loving their fellow Christians, especially by caring for their pastoral needs. They follow the second by serving their fellow human beings in every way possible. Christians have set up schools and hospitals to teach and heal just as Jesus did on earth. They share their wealth with the poor. Christian teams work in development and nation-building both locally and internationally. Christians pioneered the abolition of slavery and of child labour and continue to work for their abolition. Christian leaders like Martin Luther King in the United States and Desmond Tutu in South Africa led non-violent campaigns against the injustice and violence of racial discrimination. Mother Teresa and her 'sisters' cherished destitute children in India. Christians follow the example of Jesus in giving women and children full and equal respect. They recognize their God-given responsibility to cultivate the soil and care for the whole of creation; therefore they promote responsible lifestyles, care for the environment and call for fair trade across the world. Some of this ministry is done by quietly helping those in need. But Christians also ask, 'Why are they in need?' – and this involves them in campaigning for justice and demanding political action to change things.

> Jesus said:
> 'The Spirit of the Lord is upon me,
> because he has anointed me
> to bring good news to the poor.
> He has sent me to proclaim
> to the captives freedom
> and recovery of sight to the blind
> to send out the oppressed in freedom,
> to proclaim the year of the Lord's favour.'
> (Luke 4.18–19, adapted from NRSV)

They do not do this in order to win God's favour. They already enjoy God's favour because of what Jesus has done. The reason for doing God's will is simply because they want to thank him for his love and grace. Ethics is gratitude. At the same time the Church cannot boast of its prowess in achieving the ideals set before it. Because of individual and corporate sin it constantly fails to achieve even its own modest standards. It falls far below the expectation of Jesus: 'You are the salt of the earth . . . You are the light of the world . . . Be perfect, as your heavenly Father is perfect.'

Christian spirituality is the root of Christian behaviour. Many Catholics base their spirituality on the sacraments; the Orthodox on the use of icons (sacred paintings that point to spiritual truths); Protestants on the Bible; Pentecostals on the Bible and their experience of charismatic gifts.

Christianity and Islam

These two faiths have much in common. Both are missionary faiths, that is, they are obliged to spread their message throughout the world and to win converts. This often brings them into competition with one another. Therefore Christians and Muslims need to understand how they are similar and how they differ.

Both belong to the same Abrahamic family and share concepts of faith and submission to God. Both faiths are monotheistic, believing there is only one God. Both view Jesus as prophet, Messiah, born of a virgin and worker of miracles. Both are historical faiths, that is, their faith is shaped by the history of their founder. Both appeal to a holy book as their ultimate authority. Both observe a special day of worship every week. They share many ethical values in connection with personal and family life. Neither belong to any ethnic group but claim the allegiance of all peoples equally without discrimination. Both are 'holistic' faiths, that is, the faith directs every department of life, not just religious life.

Muslims, however, cannot accept the Christian doctrine of the Trinity nor of Christ as Son of God, nor that he died on the cross. Christians too may expect to suffer as Christ did. Muslims and Christians often have a different attitude to politics and the state: while in the foundation texts of Christianity there is a separation between faith and politics, in Islam, politics form an inseparable part of the religion. In the Bible sin and sacrifice are prominent themes; Islam emphasizes human weakness and divine compassion. For Muslims the Qur'an is a divine book written in Arabic and revealed word for word to Muhammad, and its *interpretation* is subject to criticism, whereas the Bible, though divinely inspired, was written by human authors and is subject to literary criticism. The application of the teaching of the Qur'an is constant but contains some elements that could be adjusted to suit time and place. Christians turn the Bible into local languages and even adapt its message to local cultures and contexts, with the result the Church may look different among different peoples of the world. When Christians fail to adapt they often cause needless misunderstanding both with Muslims and with other cultures. It is helpful to recognize that for Christians it is Christ who is divine but for Muslims it is the Qur'an.

 # The future of Christianity

It is impossible to predict the future without studying the past and learning from it. As we noted above, the Christian faith has always been flexible and able to adapt to local cultures. Its outward forms are therefore always changing, even though there are always people who want it to remain in the form they are accustomed to. But if it does not adapt it is not true to itself. If it is to remain the same it must change.

We can identify four major setbacks in the twentieth century. The first was the genocide of 1915, when one and a half million Armenians (the world's oldest national church dating back to 301 CE) were killed by Ottoman Muslims, and many of the remainder fled, especially to Australia and North America. Second, the Marxist regimes in the USSR and China closed 99 per cent of Christian churches and forbade the propagation of the faith. Third, Hitler's regime in Germany in the 1940s did not openly suppress the Church but demanded that it join the Nazis in promoting an exclusive German culture based on 'blood and soil' and marginalizing all other cultures, especially the Jewish. This split the Church and robbed it of the essence of the gospel. Finally, the 1960s saw the beginning of the secular resistance to Christianity in the West (and even the rise of aggressive atheism), which has led to a sharp decline in church membership.

There are, however, positive indications of renewal, chiefly outside the traditional culture of Western Europe. The emergence of Pentecostalism and the AICs (see p. 128) is seen in many black-led European churches, for example Kingsway in London (where the annual offerings amount to £7 million) and The Embassy of God in the Ukraine (with 20,000 adult members, 90 per cent of whom are European). The chief pastor in both churches is a Nigerian immigrant. Protestant Christianity has experienced major revivals in Malaysia and Indonesia, and most dramatically in Korea, China, Russia and Latin America (see p. 128).

Statistics show that Christianity is the fastest-growing faith in the world. But statistics are not enough. Questions must be asked about the ethical quality of the faith being promoted. Pentecostals can sound as though their good news is chiefly about material prosperity. AICs can at times make unacceptable compromises with traditional customs and superstitions. These may be echoed in the brutality of the Lord's Resistance Army in North Uganda, in the abduction and murder of albinos in Tanzania and Burundi and in the abuse of 'demonic' children in West Africa and even London.

In 1948 the ecumenical movement led to the creation of the World Council of Churches. It is significant as a concrete expression of the Christian desire for unity but it has largely failed to be the voice of world Christianity. The biggest and the fastest-growing Churches are not much involved in it because they feel it has not held firmly to the biblical foundations of the faith. Yet at the informal level Christians are often not troubled by denominational differences. Churches have united successfully in regions such as the Indian subcontinent. Christians are ready to converge, to adapt, to worship together in an open market of many Christian options – especially in a world where faith is challenged by secularization, materialism, individualism, neo-paganism and political rivalry.

Violent conflict between Christianity and other faiths has received much publicity at the start of the twenty-first century, particularly in Northern Nigeria, Sudan and India. Yet Christians and Muslims have lived harmoniously and respectfully together for centuries, even in the same families, in West Africa, the Balkans, the Middle East. But the rise of fundamentalism in Islam, Hinduism and even Christianity has created tensions. It is not always recognized, however, that the underlying cause of most of these religious conflicts is the exploitation of religion by would-be politicians in their bid to gain power. In almost all these regions Christians are playing significant but unobtrusive roles in promoting understanding and peace between the faiths. It is by no means certain that purely religious conflict will grow in the future.

But challenges in plenty await the future Church. The era of Christendom when the Christian religion was led by relatively affluent, educated, authoritative men is well and truly over. Women's gifts for ministry are increasingly recognized. It is the poor who throng the Pentecostal and independent churches. They may not read much but they sing and speak and dream of immediate spiritual experiences. There are more urban people than rural. Many have lost their familiar roots and are looking for a place to feel at home. This is especially true of the millions of displaced persons escaping conflict, poverty and environmental degradation. Many end up in refugee camps in their own land, others cross borders to seek freedom abroad. Affluent countries of the North barricade their gates against the stranger but Christian churches offer welcome and companionship. The northern Churches in their turn may look to these immigrant missionaries from the South for the revival of their own faith and life.

The Churches already challenge national leaders to set up fair terms of trade between North and South and to take action to reduce greenhouse gases and promote ecologically friendly policies. They see this as an extension of Jesus' kingdom ministry for total human well-being, and are ready to do it in partnership with people of other faiths and of none.

Since the Second Vatican Council in 1964 the Roman Catholic Church has taken huge steps in the direction of greater relevance to the modern world but still has further to go. Facing both a shortage of priests and the scandals of child-abuse it will be challenged to consider the ordination of women and a non-celibate priesthood. All Churches will continually rethink their response to issues of sexuality such as homosexuality, abortion, contraception and genetic engineering.

Christians will increasingly communicate in one dominant language – English – but will often do both evangelism and theological education through the internet and mobile phones. But they must not forget the history of their own culture and of the Church, without which they can neither understand the present nor plan for the future. They may learn from their Muslim cousins the need to return frequently to the foundational documents of their own faith in the original languages of Greek and Hebrew.

? QUESTIONS

1 How far is the description of Christianity above like, or unlike, the Christianity you have observed where you live?

2 How would you explain the doctrine of the Trinity to a non-Christian friend?

3 What, in your opinion, is the most important event in Jesus' life? Do the Christians you know agree with your opinion?

4 What is a sacrament?

5 Why do you think the Pentecostal type of churches are growing so fast?

6 In what ways have churches known to you changed during your lifetime?

7 Look at the denominations listed in Figure 7.2. What are the names of the main Churches in your part of the world?

8 'Love is the fulfilment of the law,' wrote Paul. In what ways does Christian ethical behaviour as described on p. 131 show love?

Further reading

The Bible: recommended modern versions of the Bible are the Revised English Bible; the New Revised Standard Version; the Good News Bible.

Chalke, Steve, *The Lost Message of Jesus* (Grand Rapids, MI: Zondervan, 2003).

Hinton, Michael, *The 100-minute Bible* (Canterbury: 100-Minute Press, 2005).

Kim, Sebastian and Kirsteen, *Christianity as a World Religion* (London: Continuum, 2008).

McGrath, Alister, *The Future of Christianity* (Oxford: Blackwell, 2002).

Wright, Tom, *Simply Christian* (London: SPCK, 2006).

From the International Study Guide series

Jesus

Baxter, Margaret, *Jesus Christ: His Life and His Church (New Testament Intro-duction 1)*, ISG 24 (London: SPCK, 1987).

The Bible

Baxter, Margaret, *The Formation of the Christian Scriptures (New Testament Introduction 2)*, ISG 26 (London: SPCK, 1988).

See also the ISGs to individual books of the Bible.

The story of the Church

Bowen, Roger, . . . *So I Send You: A Study Guide to Mission*, ISG 34 (London: SPCK, 1996; 2007).

Foster, John (revised Frend, W. H. C.), *The First Advance (Church History 1: AD 29–500)*, ISG 5 (London: SPCK 1972; 1992).

Foster, John, *Setback and Recovery (Church History 2: AD 500–1500)*, ISG 8 (London: SPCK, 1974).

Thomson, Alan, *New Movements (Church History 3: AD 1500–1800)*, ISG 14 (London: SPCK, 1976).

Christian ethics

Taylor, Harold, *Tend My Sheep (Applied Theology 2)*, ISG 19 (London: SPCK, 1983).

8

Muslim thought and practice

Haifaa Jawad

 Introduction

This chapter presents **Islam** as a living reality that gives meaning to billions of its followers. My approach will be rooted in the spiritual and intellectual heritage of Islam, without neglecting modern modes of interpretation. Islamic tradition answers many questions asked by humankind throughout the ages, such as the purpose of creation and existence, ultimate destiny, the place of humans among other creatures and the way to deliverance in this world and hereafter. For never has there been such a complete and systematic ignorance of the reason why we are born, why we are alive and why we must die. I emphasize how Muslims understand their religion as it developed within the Islamic tradition and survived the test of time.

The birthplace of Islam is Mecca in the Arabian Peninsula. We start by looking briefly at Arabia before the advent of the faith.

 Arabia before Islam

Arabia is a vast region of desert and steppe centrally located between Africa, Asia and Europe, making it an ideal place from which to spread Islam. In Yemen and along the Gulf coastline there were urban centres with settled civilizations. Yet most Arabs, especially the Bedouin tribes, lived a nomadic life. The climate of Arabia is hot and arid with scarce rainfall. People moved at night, carefully observing the moon, stars and planets. They calculated time in months, regarding the fourth month as sacred, when fighting was prohibited. They lived on dates, cereals, camel's milk, and ate camel's meat on special occasions. The desert landscape of Arabia was dotted with oasis towns and cities, chief among them **Yathrib** (later Medina). Mecca was also a prominent and wealthy trade centre. Whether they lived nomadic or sedentary lives the Arabs preferred nomadic culture. The social unit of Arab society was based on the family; several related families formed a clan and a cluster of clans formed a tribe. The head of the tribe was a chief (or **Shaykh**) elected by members of the tribe by consensus. He advised rather than imposed his own opinion. The chiefs formed a council that acted as the mouthpiece of public opinion and implemented tribal rules. Protection was given to full members of the tribe as well as their slaves and others temporarily with the tribe. They relied for their survival on tribal solidarity, and the tribe took corporate responsibility for wrongful acts committed by its members. The fear of continuous vengeance tended to prevent individual crimes being committed in the first place.

The religion of the ancient Arabs was polytheistic. They worshipped about 360 idols, mostly housed in Mecca, especially at the central shrine, the **Kaba**. This shrine was the site of the annual pilgrimage and trade fair. Although polytheism was widespread, the Arabs were aware of the existence of the one supreme high God, the creator of the world. However, they viewed the Ultimate Reality as remote and used gods and goddesses as a means to approach the Divine. Along with polytheism there existed some forms of monotheism. There were Jewish communities in Medina, for example, and some Christians in Hijaz. There were also pre-Islamic monotheists, called **hunafa**, who were followers of the Prophet Abraham. Seventh-century Arabia witnessed a great renaissance in literature, especially poetry

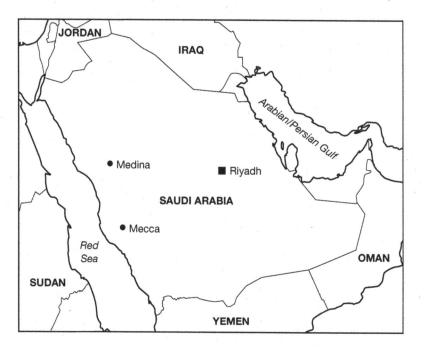

Figure 8.1 Mecca and Medina: two important sites of Islam

that was recited loud in public, so poets were highly respected. The Arabs had an ethical code that was gained through their tribal experience. Its main points were manliness, bravery in battle, loyalty to family, hospitality, patience, persistence and protecting the family honour. They also believed in a form of this-worldly fatalism. Society was socially divided into classes and there was a wide gap between the rich and the poor. It was into this materialistic society that Muhammad, future Prophet of Islam, was born.

The early life of Muhammad

Muhammad was born in Mecca around 570 CE. His father, Abdullah, belonged to the powerful Quraysh tribe but died before Muhammad was born. Following the custom of all noble Arab urban families to send their sons to the desert to be weaned, and spend their early childhood among the Bedouins, Muhammad was sent as a baby to the desert in order to imbibe the desert's fresh air, acquire pure Arabic tongue and gain the desert's bounty needed for his soul. When Muhammad was six years old his mother died, after which he was placed under the care of his grandfather, Abdul Muttalib, until he too died when Muhammad was eight. Then he joined the household of his uncle, Abu Talib, whom he loved dearly. At the age of nine he was already a contemplative person, spending much time alone in the desert and thinking of the wonders of the creation and the problems within his society. By the time he was 12 his uncle took him to Syria along with a trade caravan; at Bosra, one of the stopping points where Meccan caravans halt, Buhayrah, a Christian monk, saw him and predicted his future prophecy. When he reached the age of 20 he began to accompany his uncle in many different activities, not only trade but also wars that took place between the Quraysh and other tribes, which gave him the opportunity to learn more about different aspects of human nature. During this period he began to exhibit a purity of character and acquired a reputation for being trustworthy, honest, upright and wise, and having a sense of justice such that people in Mecca came to call him the Trusted One, or *al-Amin.*

It was this outstanding reputation of good manners and character that led a respectable merchant woman of Mecca, Khadija, to ask him to take care of her trade affairs. At the advice of his uncle he accepted the offer. His countenance, honesty and dealings impressed her so much that she proposed marriage to him; the marriage took place around 595. She was his senior by 15 years and bore him four daughters who all survived, and two sons who died in infancy. The household also included Ali ibn Abi Talib, cousin and future son-in-law, and an adopted son called Zayd ibn Haritha. The marriage with Khadija was so perfect and complete that Muhammad did not marry another wife as long as she was alive, despite her being 15 years his senior and that polygamy was a very common practice in most parts of the world at that time, including Arabia.

Muhammad as Prophet

Muhammad was happy looking after his family but discontented with the social injustices that prevailed in his community, especially the deprivation of the poor. He also felt that there was something missing in his life. Especially during the month of Ramadan (the traditional time of fasting) he used to retreat to the hills of Mecca to fast, meditate and reflect. One night during Ramadan, aged 40, he received the message of Islam through the angel Gabriel. It was an overwhelming and frightening experience. Muhammad told his wife Khadija, who supported him. She took Muhammad to see her cousin, Waraqa ibn Nawfal, an elderly Christian or monotheist. It was Waraqa who first recognized Muhammad as a prophet. For three years Muhammad preached secretly to a small circle of relatives and friends, in particular his wife Khadija, his cousin Ali, his friend Abu Bakr, a merchant from the powerful Umayyad family, Uthman ibn Affan, Talhah ibn Ubaydullah and Zubayr ibn al-Awam. There were also followers from poor backgrounds, including several women. Muhammad preached in Mecca for 12 years, during which he and his followers had to face rejection and severe persecution to the extent that some of his followers were sent to Abyssinia, where they were given refuge by the Christian king. The situation worsened when both Khadija and Muhammad's uncle, Abu Talib, died. The death of Abu Talib in particular left Muhammad exposed to his opponents in Mecca.

The persecution intensified, and Muhammad's life was in such danger that he decided to migrate to Yathrib (Medina), situated 200 miles north of Mecca. The year of this migration was 622 , which is taken as the beginning of the Islamic calendar because it was here at Medina that Muhammad established the first Islamic state with a social, political and religious order. He established a religious community (**Ummah**) that was bound by faith rather than blood or kinship. Its aim was **Tawhid** (Oneness); that is, integrating all life into a united community that would demonstrate the unity of God. There was no distinction between the holy and the profane. In Medina the ritual aspects of Islam as a religion were also revealed and implemented by the Prophet for the first time.

In 630, after many battles with the Quraysh and its allies, Muhammad peacefully took over Mecca, the seat of the *Kaba*, bringing the city into the heart of Islam. While in Mecca he declared a general amnesty for all those who opposed him, and destroyed all idols, the physical manifestation of idolatry. The purge of egotism from the heart of the believers was a matter of private choice not coercion. In his farewell sermon, Muhammad reconfirmed the Qur'anic assertion, 'that there can be no compulsion or violence in religion' and that those who were not interested in accepting the Truth were at liberty to go their own way with no let or hindrance, on condition that they would extend the same courtesy to others.

Muhammad died in 632, by which time most of Arabia was united under Islam.

The spread of Islam: the early Caliphate

When Muhammad passed away he did not leave specific instructions about his successor. Some, a minority, believed that his cousin, Ali ibn Abi Talib, should assume the leadership of the community. He had been close to Muhammad and inherited his special qualities. Others thought Ali was too young and inexperienced to take up such responsibility. After a period of discussions the majority voted for Muhammad's close friend and mystic, Abu Bakr, who ruled from 632 to 634. One of his major achievements was the reunification of the Arabian Peninsula under Islam after it had been disturbed by the so-called 'wars of apostasy'. But he also succeeded in consolidating the authority and structure of the young Muslim state. As a spiritual person he was the first to recommend the systematic practice of remembrance of God, or *dhikr* in Arabic.

Islam expanded remarkably quickly under the rule of Umar ibn al-Khattab (634–44). A man of leadership and justice, he extended the frontiers to include most neighbouring countries, among them Iran, Iraq, Syria, Egypt and Palestine. He also improved the administration, establishing a tax system, welfare system, an office for a judge, and he organized the relationship between Muslims and non-Muslims ('people of the book'). Despite his achievements of state, Umar lived a simple and austere life. He attended to the needs of the people he ruled and ensured that justice and equality applied to all. It was his custom to roam the streets of Medina asking people about their day-to-day problems so that he could take steps to rectify them. His prosperous and stable era came to an abrupt end in 644 when a Persian slave assassinated him.

Uthman ibn Affan (644–56) was elected by a council of six of the Prophet's companions. Although chroniclers report that he lacked the leadership qualities that distinguished his predecessors, he was certainly a man of integrity and generosity. Mild and pious, he emphasized kindness and moderation in human relationships. His tenure, especially the first seven years, was prosperous, and Muslims gained more land and expanded the frontiers of the state further. One of his notable achievements was commissioning the final edition of the Qur'an. Despite this, discontent among people in various provinces started to grow against him. He was accused of nepotism, giving members of his family prominent positions, even though most of the Umayyad officials were men of great abilities. Finally the discontent culminated in mutiny that led to Uthman's brutal murder in 656. His killing shocked the Muslim conscience and led to a period of strife. It was the first time that Muslims had killed Muslims.

With the assassination of Uthman, Ali, under pressure from his supporters, agreed to assume power the same year. It was the worst possible time for a man of his piety, integrity and scholarship, and he spent most of his tenure fighting protesters and opponents in Basra (Iraq), Syria and other parts of the empire. In 661 he was killed by a Kharijite (those who seceded

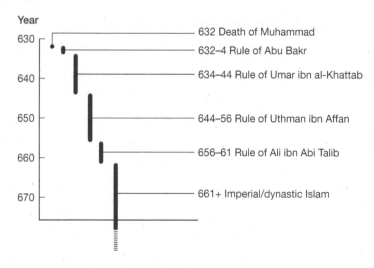

Figure 8.2 A timeline of early Islam: the early Caliphate

from Ali's camp during the battle of Siffin). With his death the period recognized by the majority of Muslims as the Rightly Guided Caliphs came to an end. Despite the tragic killing of Umar, Uthman and Ali, the era of the four Rightly Guided Caliphs is regarded as the golden era. They were early converts to Islam who personally knew Muhammad, possessed an intrinsic authority that was as much spiritual as temporal, and played important roles in defending Islam. They continue to be revered by most Muslims as wise, prudent and devout companions.

Dynastic rule and afterwards

The death of Ali brought the Islamic state into a new phase: the era of imperial Islam. The hereditary rule of the Umayyad dynasty (661–750) was established by Muawiyyah ibn Abu Sufyan, who declared himself **Caliph** and moved the capital of the Islamic state to Damascus in Syria. The dynasty produced both good and bad rulers. It succeeded in uniting the Islamic state against early civil strife and local rebels. Under Umayyad rule the Muslim Empire reached its zenith, conquering yet more territory, especially in North Africa and Spain. The dynasty set up a centralized government and followed centralized policy. The rule restricting contact between Arabs and the subjects of the empire was relaxed. Arabic became the official language of the empire, coins were produced and the famous Dome of the Rock in Jerusalem was completed in 691. It was one of the magnificent Islamic monuments that demonstrated the unique Muslim style of art. Decorated only with verses from the Qur'an it expresses the balance of *Tawhid*. Its exterior and interior dimensions replicate one another, illustrating the unity of humanity and divinity. Despite its achievements, the Umayyad dynasty continued to face resistance from the Kharijites, the **Shi'ites** (supporters of Ali), some prominent devout Muslims who were shocked by the worldly bent of the rulers, and dissent from non-Arab Muslims who resented the privileged position of the Arabs in the empire. The Umayyad lost their power in the East but re-established their influence in the West when they succeeded in creating a Muslim Empire in Spain that lasted until 1492.

The prosperous reign of the Abbasids (750–935) banked on the desire, especially among the Shi'ites, to have a member of the Prophet's family in power. Their right to the Caliphate was based on being descendants of Al-Abbas, one of Muhammad's uncles. By virtue of such descent they gained support, and managed to bring down the Umayyad dynasty. Like their predecessors, the Abbasids established hereditary rule and set up strong centralized government in Baghdad (Iraq) after eliminating the opposition.

The Persian influence became clear under their rule. They designed magnificent buildings and introduced Persian court etiquette. For example, as a symbol of the ruler's absolute power the subjects were required to bow before the Caliph and kiss the ground, something unimaginable during the times of the Prophet and the Rightly Guided Caliphs. The early part of the Abbasid rule witnessed great splendour and economic prosperity. In contrast to the Umayyad, who relied primarily on conquest, the Abbasids based their success on trade, agriculture and industry. The wealth gained allowed them to become patrons of the law, arts, architecture, literature, philosophy, medicine and translation, thus producing the most significant legacy of Abbasid rule: the Islamic civilization that contributed hugely to human civilization.

However, controlling a huge empire proved difficult to sustain. The political unity of the empire started to deteriorate, and secessionist movements appeared. Local governors and military commanders asserted their power, even though they continued to pay nominal homage to the Caliphs. Although the Abbasid rulers continued to represent legitimate government and Muslim unity, the real power passed to a series of non-Arab military dynasties in the empire. This disintegration and weakening of the empire led to a series of invasions.

In 1258, Mongol armies invaded Baghdad and ended the universal Abbasid (Arab) rule. Arabs and, by extension, Muslims, never recovered from it. The destruction of Baghdad brought havoc to the Muslim world.

In the sixteenth century the Muslim world was divided into three Muslim Empires. The Persian Safavids, with their capital at Isfahan, established **Shia** Islam as their state religion. The Mughal Empire became established in the Indian subcontinent, with its capital at Delhi. The Ottoman Empire, with its capital at Istanbul (formerly Constantinople), comprised the whole of North Africa, the Arab world and Eastern Europe. In time these empires disintegrated and lost power, the last one to be dismantled being the Ottoman Empire, after the First World War.

Islam continued to grow even after the disappearance of these empires and the emergence of the nation-state system. Islam is now a multinational, multicultural phenomenon. There is virtually no part of the earth where Islam has not penetrated, and they come from a vast range of races, nationalities and cultures. The total number of Muslims is now over one billion; they constitute the majority in the Middle East; major parts of Asia and Africa are Muslim (the world's largest Muslim country is Indonesia), while sizeable Muslim minorities can be found in the former Soviet Union, China, North and South America, Europe, Australia and New Zealand.

The foundations of Muslim religious tradition

Before we talk about the main texts that form the basis for the Islamic belief system we need to understand what the word 'Islam' means and what Islam as a faith thinks of the role of religion in society.

What is Islam?

The word 'Islam' is an Arabic word meaning submission or surrender. A Muslim is someone who surrenders or submits to the will of God and to the awareness of his Oneness. It is a submission to the Ultimate Reality, the creator, sustainer and controller of the universe, from whom all orders come and to whom all things return. **Allah** is the Arabic word for God. 'Islam' also means peace (**salaam**) – it is the peace resulting from the act of submission. Islam is nothing other than living in accordance with the will of God in order to achieve peace in this world and success in the hereafter. Furthermore, this submission and belief in Islam must come as a result of clear choice and in full knowledge and conviction – it should come after a thorough investigation rather than blind emulation. Islam also generates outward expressions of the faith in righteous actions, for the key to salvation in the Qur'an lies both in belief and in righteous deeds. Hence belief and practice should go hand in hand. Islam is also known as *al-Din*, a comprehensive term that denotes the totality of life and implies a primary orientation towards the divine as the final authority.

From the Islamic perspective, religion is not simply a part of life but the whole of it. Nothing exists outside the realm of religion. Islam stresses that there is one Eternal Truth, *Tawhid*, or Oneness of God. The Qur'an stresses that humans testified to the Oneness of God and his Lordship even before the creation of the world (Qur'an 7:172), that God is the One who neither begets nor is begotten (Qur'an 112:1–4) and that he transcends everything but is also very near and immanent (Qur'an 50:16).

The central truth in Islam is 'There is no God but God'. This affirmation is so crucial that the Qur'an says God will forgive every sin except the sin of associating some partner with him (Qur'an 4:38, 116). Religion as advocated by Islam involves the entire history of humankind. The idea that religion is based on the Oneness of God is not a new idea that came with Islam but stems from the beginning of the history of humankind. Islam, therefore, was there from the beginning. Adam was a Muslim and is called the first Prophet. He testified to the Oneness of God. With time, this concept of religion was forgotten since humans are naturally indifferent and forgetful. In order to restore this understanding of

Figure 8.3 The central statement of Islam in Arabic: 'There is no God but God and Muhammad is his messenger'
Source: Adopted from www.iris.org.nz

religion (Tawhidic), God sent messengers and Prophets to remind people of the primordial religion (**al-din al-hanif**) that lies at the heart of all messages brought about by all messengers and Prophets throughout human history. As signs of their prophethood, they were given the power to perform miracles. Muhammad's miracle was the Qur'an.

There have been a number of prophets who have established religions by different names, but Islam asserts that all these figures were essentially Muslims in the wider sense. Religions have always existed, and their existence indicates a steady loss of the primordial message and the need for it to be reaffirmed from time to time by successive revelations. In this context, Islam did not bring something new but rather came to reconfirm the primordial Truth, the truth of Oneness that was already there and will continue to be there. So Islam is a universal and primordial religion: it is a return to the main covenant between God and human beings that made them servants of God and his representatives on earth. Islam also declares itself to be the final religion in the current cycle of human history, and Muhammad is the final Prophet, or 'the Seal of all Prophets'. The reasons for such universality is that Islam expresses in a complete and perfect way the doctrine of Oneness of God (*Tawhid*) that lies at the heart of every revealed religion throughout history. This interpretation of Islam is crucial in understanding not only the religion itself but also its historical emergence. Islam is the only religion that bases itself on the Oneness of the Ultimate Reality and on the primacy of *all* humanity, not on a particular person, people or historical event, as is the case with Christianity and Judaism. As such, Muslims do not take a historical view of religion; for them religion is based on the eternal reality of God and of God's creation of humanity to obey God and reflect God's names and

145

qualities. This is the foundation of the messages of all God's prophets and is why the Prophet and the Qur'an call Muslims to protect those people of other religions who believe in the Oneness of God.

Religion in society

Islam regards religion as essential for humans. Without religion, humanity lives below its dignity. *Al-Din* means the repaying of our debt to God for giving us our life, as he creates us all. Muslims believe that they have no existence without God, from whom life issues and to whom life returns. Religion is the framework within which all human activities take place. To be human is essentially to be active and interested in religion. God's imprint is on the very substance of each individual soul. Therefore human beings cannot ignore religion just as they cannot avoid breathing. The Qur'an speaks of the creation of the human being thus: 'God breathed into him His spirit' (Qur'an 2:256).

Religion gives purpose and meaning to human life since it issues from God, the source of life itself. Therefore human life is sacred. Religion did not progress step by step during the history of humanity; rather it has always existed in various shapes and forms that contain the Eternal Truth. When the Eternal Truth was ignored or forgotten, new revelations came to restore the old order and remind humans of their duty and destiny. Religion is the source of all ethics and values because it sets the standard for human behaviour. So Islam would not appreciate any society where religion is regarded as unnecessary. Islam believes that the disappearance of religion from society brings about destruction. For the individual it leads to separation from the Ultimate Reality and consequently a loss of balance and direction. For society as a whole it means the nation is dismembered and no longer harmonious.

The Qur'an and its teachings

For Muslims the Qur'an is the revelation of God and the book within which the divine message and guidance is contained. It is also the uncreated word of God revealed to the Prophet Muhammad through the archangel Gabriel. Arabic is the language of the Qur'an and it is the sacred language of Islam integral to the Qur'anic revelation whose sounds and utterances play a crucial role in the acts of worship in Islam. This does not mean that Islam is intended solely for Arab people and that knowing Arabic is essential to be a devout Muslim. Rather, as Seyyed Hossein Nasr says:

> the formula of the Quran read in prayers and acts of worship must be in the sacred language of Arabic which alone enables one to penetrate into the content and be transformed by the Divine presence and grace (*barakah*) of the Divine Book.

According to Islam the Arabic language is sacred – the Qur'an cannot be translated into another language, even for ritual purposes, so that in this context a translation of the Qur'an is not the Qur'an but an interpretation of its meaning. Hence non-Arabic-speaking Muslims need to know at least the minimum requirements of the verses that are said in acts of worship. Nonetheless, most non-Arab Muslims tend to learn Qur'anic Arabic as part of their religious education to help them understand the Qur'an.

Muslims know exactly when the revelation to Muhammad started and when it ended. During the 33 years of prophetic mission the Qur'an was revealed through Muhammad to humankind on various occasions. The opening chapter was revealed when he was 40 years old and the last revelation when he was 63, shortly before he passed away. When Muhammad uttered the word of God his companions memorized it and wrote it down on camel bones and palm leaves. After the death of Muhammad, and between the eras of the first Caliph, Abu Bakr, and the third Caliph, Uthman, the texts of the Qur'an were assembled and systematized. Copies were made of the definitive and original version and sent to the entire Muslim world. All extant copies of the Qur'an are based on this one version, and there are no differences or revisions. It is the one text that is accepted by all Muslims and it forms the main source of Truth, guidance and enlightenment for all Muslims.

The Qur'an is divided into 114 chapters of unequal length. Each chapter is called **sura**, and each *sura* is divided into short passages or verses (*ayat*) meaning signs. The Qur'an has different names: *al-Qur'an*, meaning recitation, *al-Huda*, discernment, *umm al-Kitab*, the mother of all books, and *al-Hikmah*, wisdom. The teachings of the Qur'an focus on the nature of the Ultimate Reality, the world of nature, angels and **jinn**, sacred history and humanity. Within the context of the latter, the Qur'an talks about the moral and ethical principles by which human beings ought to live. It stresses the need for humans to follow the examples of the previous prophets, and mentions the most important ones, such as Adam, Abraham, Moses, Joseph and Jesus. It gives a detailed account of the 'people of the book', especially Jews and Christians. Indeed, Muslims believe in the previous scriptures sent to humankind, chief among them being the Torah, the Gospels and the Psalms, and they regard them as valid revealed scriptures and revere them as such.

The Qur'an talks about the devil and evil, especially Pharaoh, the archetype of human wickedness, and advises people how to live a life that is pleasing to God. The Qur'an instructs people to pray, fast, look after the needy and conduct just and humane interrelationships. It emphasizes the importance of achieving a balance between living by God's rules and worldly affairs. It warns against those who defy God's message of hellfire, and it promises paradise to those who believe and obey his message. The world will come to an end at a certain stage, and the dead will be resurrected and judged before God. Muslims believe that during the Day of Judgement

147

absolute justice will be done to all humankind. Seyyed Hossein Nasr eloquently describes the importance of the Qur'an:

> all that is Islamic, whether it be its laws, its thought, its spiritual and ethical teachings and even its artistic manifestations, have their roots in the explicit or implicit teachings of the Sacred Text. The Muslim is born with the sound of the Quran in his [her] ear . . . lives throughout . . . life surrounded by the sound of the Quran . . . he [she] dies with the sound of the Quran resounding around him [her] . . . The love of the Noble Quran and devotion to its teachings have remained central to every generation of Muslims, remain so today and will always remain so as long as Islam survives as a religion on the surface of the earth.

Sunnah and Hadith – actions and sayings of Muhammad

Muslims highly respect the Prophet Muhammad. They regard him as the perfect human and the most noble of creation. Muslims know him by different names: among them are Ahmed (the praiseworthy), *Abdul Allah* (servant of God), and *al-Amin* (the trusted one). When one of these names is mentioned, Muslims usually follow it by uttering the formula, 'May peace and blessings be upon him'. This formula originates from the Qur'an, which states, 'Allah and His angels send blessings on the Prophet: O ye that believe! Send ye blessings on him, And salute him with all respect' (Qur'an, 33:56). All noble virtues, such as humility, sincerity, sobriety, knowledge, patience, kindness, self-denial, self-respect, are found in him. The Qur'an says that he is the perfect model for humankind (Qur'an 33:21). In other words, he was an embodiment of the Qur'an. A sign of piety is to love and respect the Prophet. However, this does not exclude other prophets before him, especially those whose names are mentioned in the Qur'an. Muslims love, respect and praise them using the formula, 'Peace be upon them'. Muslims are deemed to disobey the Qur'an and the **Sunnah** if they praise the Prophet but denigrate those prophets who came before Muhammad. The Qur'an emphasizes that one cannot make a distinction among them (Qur'an 2:285; 4:150–2).

The Prophet's life, especially the 23 years of his prophetic career, have become a model for all Muslims to follow. The Prophet's acts are called *Sunnah*, while his sayings are called **Hadith**. The *Sunnah* includes all of Muhammad's actions, both physical – the way he greeted his neighbours, how he sat, ate, wore his clothes, and spiritual and moral acts – how he prayed, fasted, was kind to the needy and so on. Pious scholars, both men and women, collected the *Hadith* during the first three centuries of Islam. They ensured that all authentic *Hadith* were recorded, developing a method of research called *Hadith Criticism* to distinguish the authentic from the inauthentic. After intensive study, canonical collections of the *Hadith* emerged. The Sunnis accept the Correct Six Books. The Shia accepts the Four Books.

The *Hadith* and *Sunnah* together constitute the second source of Islamic law after the Qur'an.

The 'law' of Islam – *Sharia*

For Muslims the **Sharia** is the embodiment of moral goodness and directs the way to its achievement in human lives. *Sharia* means literally 'a path that leads to God'. It is the path that Muslims, both as individuals and as society, have to follow.

The *Sharia* is understood to mean law, but this is not an accurate definition of it. The framework of the *Sharia* provides a way to live a moral life and the sources of it are the Qur'an, the *Hadiths*, the rational personal deduction of scholars, analogy and the consensus of the community. The *Sharia* is not merely a theoretical scheme, rather a practical way of life. It aims to fulfil God's commands since in Islam God is the primary legislator for the way to live. One of its main aims is to safeguard the integrity of human society and allow humans to rise above their lower desires and tendencies. Thus it regulates all aspects of life. From a traditional Muslim perspective the main injunctions of the *Sharia* (these are *thawabits*, approved established rulings) transcend time and place and are therefore permanent. But they can be interpreted to suit any new circumstances in a particular time and place. Ultimately Muslim society has to conform to the divine injunctions in the same way Christians have to conform to the spiritual teachings of Jesus and Jews to the *Halakhah*. The Islamic law, or *Sharia*, is essential to Muslim life and identity just as Christian thinking is key to leading a Christian way of life. For Muslims God is the creator and supreme legislator. Through his law, human life is made sacred; God's law encompasses all human activities. It does not distinguish between the sacred and the profane, the religious and the secular. Even the least act carried out in accordance with the *Sharia* is regarded as sacred. Following the *Sharia* gives grace and meaning, and leads to encounter with God.

In Islam, religious actions or deeds are regarded as an external expression of the belief in God and total submission to his will. Belief and righteous actions are organically linked as key factors in the concept of Islamic salvation. Many Qur'anic verses indicate this salvation belief. One key passage is: 'Those who believe, and do deeds of righteousness, and establish regular prayers and regular charity, will have their reward with their Lord: on them shall be no fear, nor shall they grieve' (2:277).

So what are these righteous actions? Islam as a total way of life considers all deeds that a Muslim undertakes to be righteous actions. Islam does not make a distinction between so-called religious and secular deeds; hence all deeds are sacred if they are performed with the intention of pleasing God. However, there are acts of worship that are specific and particular to the faith of Islam. They are called the Five Pillars of Islam:

1 **Declaration of faith**: there is no God but God and Muhammad is the messenger of God.

2 **Prayers**: obligatory for all Muslim men and women from the age of puberty until death, and must be performed five times a day. On Fridays there are weekly congregational prayers, which include a sermon with social, political as well as spiritual importance. Apart from these canonical prayers there are other forms, such as the prayer of the heart practised usually by those who want to tread the spiritual path, *du'a'*, individual supplication and voluntary night prayers.

3 **Fasting**: an obligatory act during the month of Ramadan from the age of puberty. There are other days in the year when Muslims may choose to fast. Muslims abstain from all food, drink, smoking and sexual activity from dawn till sunset, and also avoid evil thoughts and deeds. Exceptions from fasting are made for the sick, those embarking on a journey and for women during their monthly cycle or pregnancy or while nursing a child (but they must make it up at a later time). Fasting is a time when Muslims exercise great self-discipline and practise the virtues of humility, patience, persistence and compassion, especially towards the poor and needy.

4 **Almsgiving**: this means purifying what God has given you and sharing it with the less fortunate. It is obligatory for those with wealth at their disposal, and involves an annual payment of two and a half per cent of one's net worth to the public treasury. Traditionally this charitable money was used to build and maintain public institutions such as schools, hospitals, shelters for the needy and mosques. In addition there is another kind of almsgiving, called *sadaqah*, but this is not obligatory.

5 **Hajj or Pilgrimage to Mecca**: this journey is obligatory at least once in a lifetime for people with the financial and physical ability to undertake it. It takes place during the early part of the twelfth month of the Islamic calendar. There is a lesser pilgrimage, *Umrah*, that can be undertaken at any time of the year.

Theological, philosophical and mystical movements

Like Christianity, Islam has developed different theological and philosophical movements that deal with the main principles of faith.

Theology

Theological arguments are called **kalam** in Arabic, or 'speech'. They developed mainly to defend the faith against non-Muslim counter-arguments, especially during the expansion of Islam when Muslims encountered people of other faith backgrounds. They dealt with issues such as free will, predestination, the nature of God, his attributes and the nature of the Qur'an. Although theological disputation became widespread, especially during the classical era of Islam, theology never assumed the prominence it has had in Christianity. The *Sharia* is of greater importance than *kalam* for Islam. The majority of ordinary Muslims do not know much of *kalam* but have some degree of knowledge of the *Sharia*. An ordinary Muslim can practise the faith without knowledge of *kalam*, but it would be impossible to do so without knowing at least the basic principles of the *Sharia*. Hence came the emphasis on the importance of studying the *Sharia* due to its practical benefit for people.

The main theological schools to emerge were the Mutazila and the Asharia. The Mutazila arose as a formal school during the Abbasid rule of the Islamic Empire, with its capital in Baghdad. The word 'Mutazila' is Arabic for those who stand aside or aloof. They were influenced by Greek philosophical thought that emphasized the importance of reason. They used rational deduction in their Qur'anic interpretation and theological reflection, and regarded both reason and revelation as complementary sources of guidance from God. This school played a prominent role in the theological debates that occurred during the Abbasid Caliphate of Mamun (813–33). He was persuaded to adopt the school's position and impose it on the Muslim community. After his death the fortune of the school declined and eventually lost its prominence in Islamic society. The Asharia School emerged as a reaction to the Mutazila's excessive use of logic and reason in their theological interpretation. The school derives its name from its founder, Abu al-Hasan Al-Ashari (d. 935). He was initially a Mutazilite but left them to form a school that emphasized revelation over reason in Qur'anic interpretation and theological discussion. The school attracted many followers, chief among them the **Sufi** saint al-Ghazali, and it became the dominant school of *kalam*.

Philosophy

Islamic philosophy developed alongside theology, but unlike the theologians, who focused on the Qur'an and on comprehending Muslim creed, philosophers put emphasis on the role of reason and the Greek intellectual heritage. They believed that rational inquiry offered sufficient ways to understand the nature of reality. They relied on observation and logical reasoning rather than Qur'anic references. Nevertheless, in their focus on the Reality, the Islamic concept of *Tawhid* (Oneness) was always their underlying theme. Among the greatest Muslim philosophers known to the West are al-Farabi, al-Kindi, Ibn Sina (known in the West as Avicenna), Suhrawardi and Mulla Sadra. Muslim philosophers proved too academic for the majority of the ordinary faithful, hence their impact on them is limited.

Mysticism

Sufism, or Islamic mysticism, is rooted in the Qur'an and the life of the Prophet and his companions. Sufis stress the unveiling or direct vision of God through sincere devotion to the Qur'an and the *Sunnah* of the Prophet, without excessive use of rational or imaginative powers. The Sufis very often cite the Qur'anic verse that indicated their path in approaching the Ultimate Reality: 'Be wary of God, and God will teach you.' For them the prerequisite for approaching God is the perfection of faith and practice through sincerity. Most Sufis had training in either theology or philosophy or both, so they were fully aware of their approaches and techniques. Sufi writings were concrete and direct, not abstract, which explains why Sufism has had great appeal throughout Islamic history and civilization. The Sufis employed imagery, symbolism, storytelling and poetry to express their views, and as such were able to speak to everyone. Famous among the Sufis were Hasan al-Basri, Junad of Baghdad, al-Ghazali, ibn-Arabi al-Rumi and the famous female Sufi, Rabia' of Basra.

Sects in Islam: Sunnis and Shi'ites

There are two sects within Islam: Sunnism and Shi'ism. Sunnis constitutes about 87 per cent of Muslims, Shi'ites about 13 per cent. The Sunni majority within Islam does not form a sect in the real sense of the term, but for our purposes we will use the term as if it did. Currently the majority of Shi'ites are of Iranian origin, although there are some notable Shia minorities of Arab and Indo-Pakistani origin. There are no major theological differences between the Sunnis and Shi'ites. Both sects believe in the Oneness of God and Muhammad as the messenger of God, the uncreated Qur'an, the angels of God, the books of God, all Prophets before Muhammad and the hereafter. They also believe and perform the Five Pillars of Islam. There is nothing that could lead to the destruction of the unity of the religion. Islam exhibits more homogeneity and less doctrinal diversity than other world religions. Having said this, there are some differences between the two sects. First, there are political differences related to the successor of the Prophet as leader of the Muslim community. The Shi'ites insist that the leader of the Muslim Community should have been Muhammad's son-in-law and cousin, Ali, and his descendants through his wife Fatima. They base this view on the understanding that the Prophet Muhammad had designated Ali as his sole successor and therefore rejected the rule of the three Rightly Guided Caliphs. In contrast the Sunnis do not believe that the Prophet designated any person, so they accept the rule of the four Caliphs as equally valid. The second distinction concerns the status and role of the successor. For the Shi'ites the successor (called **Imam**) is infallible and has the sole right to interpret the divine revelation. For Sunnis the successor has to be just and knowledgeable in religion, be able to maintain the *Sharia* and protect the lands, but he is an ordinary fallible person. The majority of Shi'ites, who accept that there have been 12 Imams, are concentrated mainly in Iran, southern Iraq, southern Lebanon and some parts of Pakistan. Another Shia group includes the Zaydis in Yemen, who are regarded as the closest form of Shi'ism to Sunni Islam. Although they favoured Ali, they accept the rule of the four Companions of Muhammad. Other smaller Shia sects include the Ismailis (or 'Seveners', who believe there to be seven Imams, the seventh being Muhammad ibn Ismail in the eighth century), the Bahais and the Babis. However, the majority of Muslims regard these groups as heterodox.

Ethics

In Islam the Qur'an not only asks Muslims to have faith in the Ultimate Reality but also to practise ethical actions. In order to gain legitimacy these moral deeds have to be done by obeying God and his messenger Muhammad, who is regarded by Muslims as the ultimate example of all ethical conduct. Muslims all over the world yearn to emulate the Prophet. In Islam moral principles are not abstract ideas. They are contained in the Qur'an and *Hadith*, and are made concrete through the *Sharia*. Based on the Qur'an and *Hadith*, the divine law exhorts Muslims to respect their parents, to be kind and compassionate to their neighbours, to be just, honest, charitable and to keep their word at all times. Even those Muslims who are not fully committed to practising the principles of Islam very often draw their ethical beliefs from the *Sharia*. Islam does allow for a prominent role to be played by the individual conscience in this context – the *Sharia* lays the foundations but Muslims must apply the ethical teachings according to their conscience in the circumstances. Seyyed Hossein Nasr explains this point in this eloquent way:

> The norms are determined by the *Sharī'ah* for certain basic actions while in each type of human activity room is left for [humans] to apply the Islamic ethical teachings according to the dictates of [their] conscience. There is, therefore, nothing mechanical or blindfolded in Islamic ethics as some have claimed.

 Politics

In contrast to the Christian West, which has separated religion from public life as a result of the Reformation, Industrial Revolution and subsequent intellectual developments of the seventeenth and eighteenth centuries, Islam has never divorced religion from politics. Political rule in the Muslim world, in whatever form, has always been tempered by religious elements. Even when the modern secular nation-state system was introduced, Islam was intertwined with politics. The Qur'an does not specify a particular political system to be followed forever, but it issued certain rules and injunctions to be used as guidance for political rule. These state, first, that the ruler of the universe is God and that all powers in the final analysis belong to him. Second, the Prophet, as founder of the first Islamic state, sets a standard for later generations and hence the principles of rule should be based on his model. Third, any political rule arises through mutual consultation and aims to achieve Islam's ultimate goal of justice. To prevent political rule from becoming authoritarian, Islam insists on the principle that the ruler is accountable to the ruled.

 Women

When Islam emerged it addressed the position of women in society and made it clear that women, like men, have rights and duties. It elevated that status of women by acknowledging them to be equally as worthy of human dignity as men. Islam dealt with women's rights on two levels: spiritual as well as social. At the spiritual level, before God, men and women are absolutely equal in all essential rights and duties. They are equally rewarded or punished for their good or bad deeds. The Qur'an says: 'Their Lord answers them, saying: "I will deny no man or woman among you the reward of their labours. You are the offspring of one another."'

At the social or cosmic level their relationship is interdependent; each needs the other to achieve harmonious, respectable and prosperous life. To rehabilitate the status of women in society, Islam denounced the old myth of Eve as temptress and source of evil – the source of original sin and fall of humankind. According to the Qur'an, the woman is not responsible for Adam's first mistake. Right from the beginning, Islam stressed that women should be offered every opportunity to develop their natural abilities so that they might participate effectively in the growth of society. Islam also emphasized that women should be allowed to achieve the highest ranks of progress, intellectually and spiritually. To this end Islam has granted women broad social, political and economic rights, education and training rights and work opportunities. To protect these rights from being abused by men, Islam has provided firm legal safeguards. The legal status of women within the context of family ties has also been defined, emphasizing respect to mothers, sisters, wives and daughters. However, in time these rights were steadily eroded and replaced by patriarchal rules and customs. Therefore in many Muslim countries today women are faced with various forms of social, political, economic and religious oppression.

Jihad

Jihad is an Arabic word meaning 'to strive, struggle or exert efforts'. The word has an implicit meaning that emphasizes a commendable objective.

In a religious ambience it indicates a resistance against evil thoughts and tendencies within oneself. It can also mean to struggle for the sake of Islam, such as by improving the moral status of Muslim peoples through tongue or pen or by attempting to guide unbelievers to Islam. Physical *Jihad* is allowed in Islam under strict conditions and in defence of oneself or one's homeland. The initiation of aggressive acts against others, especially non-combatants, is strictly forbidden no matter what grievances Muslims might have towards the other side.

Hence greater *Jihad*, which stresses the purification of the soul, has always taken precedence over anything else and has guided traditional Muslims in times of adversity. Even when they were forced to fight aggression, the struggle was always conducted according to a divine framework of moral injunctions relevant to the circumstances. *Jihad* has to be *in* God and not just *for* God in order to be legitimate and gain the blessing of the Ultimate Reality. The means should justify the divine end, whether the realm is warfare, social or personal effort or an individual's struggle of the intellect or spirit. This understanding is in total contrast to the current so-called Jihadists' approach, which has disfigured the Islamic principles of the spirit of *Jihad*. Using radical and vile means is contrary to the traditional spirit of *Jihad*. Any murder of innocent people is totally alien to Islam and Islamic tradition.

Islam and the West

In our contemporary world there is a good deal of concern about there being a 'clash' between Islam and the West. Of course, neither entity has a single viewpoint. Nevertheless it is useful to use these broad terms in an attempt to understand an issue that affects the whole globe. It has to be said that Islam and the Christian West have common theological roots, shared views on the sacredness of life, respect for moral issues, reverence for the laws of God and so forth. Yet confrontation, contempt, ignorance and stereotyping, rather than respect and mutual understanding, have characterized their relationship. Rivalries, conflicts and misunderstanding on both sides have accentuated their differences and blurred the shared vision between Islam and the Judeo-Christian heritage.

Historically, especially during the Crusades, the Church rejected Islam as a heresy and launched both theological and military attacks that caused mistrust, death and destruction. Those events are still alive in contemporary memories. Renaissance authors exhibited in their writings a strong contempt for Islam and Islamic heritage that cannot be found in any medieval writings on the same subject. Also during this period the Christian West parted from other traditions, including Islam, and followed a path that would lead to its adoption of a secular, modern and Euro-centric world-view. This caused the modern West to view the Muslim world with disdain during the colonial period, and it has continued to do so up to the present time, whether economically, technologically or culturally. The current material inequality between the two sides means that the West dictates the agenda of many Muslim countries and assesses them on the basis of their acceptance of Western secular norms. This is a recipe for more antagonism and confrontation rather than mutual respect and peaceful co-existence. Relationships between Muslims and Christians may differ in other parts of the world but they are usually influenced by the contemporary global situation described here. It is in this context, and in the light of the current threat of fundamentalism and terrorism (from all sides), that people of good faith – both Muslim and Christian – must work very hard to bring about agreement, respect and understanding between the two communities.

? QUESTIONS

1 What is the meaning of the word Islam? How is this meaning apparent in the faith of Muslims?

2 Do Islam and Christianity have different origins?

3 What does Islam say about women?

Glossary

al-din al-hanif primordial religion
Allah God
Caliph early leader of Islamic state
Hadith sayings of the Prophet Muhammad
Hajj pilgrimage
Imam infallible successor in Shi'ism; in Sunni Islam the term is used for the leader of prayer or sometimes early great scholars
Islam literally, submission, surrender to God
Jihad literally, strive or struggle
jinn sprits, could be evil or good
Kaba central shrine of Mecca, the house of God for Muslims
kalam literally, speech; theological argument
Qur'an Muslims' holy book; contains the word of God, as revealed to Muhammad
salaam peace; it is also one of the names of God in Islam
Sharia literally, 'a path that leads to God'
Shaykh tribal chief
Shia/Shi'ites Islamic sect who take Ali, the Prophet's cousin, as their progenitor

Sufi Muslim mystic
Sunnah actions of the Prophet Muhammad
sura chapter of the Qur'an
Tawhid Oneness of God; *Tawhid*, the verbal noun stemming from the verb *wahhada*, literally means to affirm one, to declare one and ultimately to realize one; in accordance with this there is only one revelation; the revelation has different facets in order to meet the needs of different communities but it is one in essence
Ummah the Muslim Community
Yathrib pre-Islamic name for the city of Medina

 Further reading

Abdalat, H., *Islam in Focus* (Indianapolis: American Trust Publications, 1975).

Du Pasquier, Roger (trans. Winter, Tim), *Unveiling Islam* (Cambridge: Islamic Texts Society, 2006).

Eaton, G., *Islam and the Destiny of Man* (Cambridge: Islamic Texts Society, 1994).

Esposito, J. L., *Islam: The Straight Path* (Oxford: Oxford University Press, 1988).

Lings, Martin, *Muhammad: His Life Based On the Earliest Sources* (Cambridge: Islamic Texts Society, 1983).

Murata, S. and Chittick, W., *The Vision of Islam* (London: Tauris, 1996).

Nasr, S. H., *Ideals and Reality in Islam* (London: Allen & Unwin, 1985).

Nasr, S. H., *A Young Muslim's Guide to the Modern World* (Cambridge: Islamic Texts Society, 1993).

Nasr, S. H., *The Heart of Islam: Enduring Values for Humanity* (San Francisco: HarperCollins, 2004).

9

Sikh thought and practice

Shashi Bala

 Introduction: the religious and cultural background

The founder of the Sikh religion, Guru Nanak (1469–1539), lived in Punjab, north-west India, at a time when there was virtual disintegration not only of social and political values but also of moral and spiritual ones. People were obsessed with the observance of petty ceremonies, rituals and dogmas. A range of diverse beliefs and practices had simply melded together. Many followed fatalistic superstitions and indulged in the fashion for worshipping idols, nature and inanimate objects. In its fascination for ritualism, the religious atmosphere had become devoid of any higher spirituality, and obscured any true religious beliefs.

Being aware of this decline, Guru Nanak spoke out against religious paraphernalia that enhances the human ego and deprives him or her of higher spiritual truths. He condemned the formal ways of worship conducted by the orthodox priestly classes of Islam and Hinduism. The most popular faiths at the time were the three major Hindu Sects: Shaivism (devotees of Shiva), Vaishnavism (devotees of Vishnu) and Shaktism (devotees of the Mother Goddess). Priests and lay persons who presumed themselves to be contemplative and virtuous were patently ignorant of the true ways of life, and indeed indulged in the most vice-like of sins: avarice, lust and arrogance. This moral degradation was also visible at the political level in the helplessness and fear felt by the priestly caste before the oppressive rulers, whose petty interests would have to be safeguarded.

 The Rise of Sikhism: Guru Nanak and the other Gurus

Guru Nanak was born in Talwandi (a village now known as Nankana Sahib) in Pakistan, and belonged to the Hindu Bedi clan. According to popular legend, Guru Nanak had divine knowledge from his birth and received further divine revelation in the River Bein, near Sultanpur, in 1499. After that he started his peregrination all over India and in 1522 settled at Kartarpur, where he stayed for 17 years. Guru Nanak's three important precepts were, first, contemplation of the One God (*nam-japna*); second, earning one's livelihood (*kirat karna*); and third, sharing one's earnings with others (*vand chhakna*). He repudiated the orthodox practices of both the Hindu and Muslim communities and stressed instead truthful living. In a bid to undermine the caste system he insisted on having a communal kitchen. He also built the first **dharamsal**, or chapel of the Sikhs, at Kartarpur.

Guru Angad (1504–52) was appointed by Nanak as the second Guru, with the administrative charge of organizing Nanak's mission and disciples. He expanded the institution of the *langer*, or free kitchen. Amar Das (1479–1574) succeeded as third Guru at the age of 72. To strengthen and propagate the Sikh faith he established 22 provinces throughout the Punjab. The fourth Guru, Ram Das (1534–81), popularly known as Jetha, was son-in-law to the third Guru and served as head of the community for seven years. He laid the foundation of the city of Amritsar and Ramdaspura, and introduced reforms, particularly of the marriage ceremony. A long hymn in four parts, which he composed, is recited at weddings.

The son of Ram Das, Arjan Dev (1563–1606), became the fifth Guru in 1581, ahead of his elder brother Prithi Chand, who resented the system and instead joined the Mughal officials. Guru Arjan Dev was the first martyr in Sikh history, having suffered torture before sacrificing himself. He laid the foundation of Sikh theocracy by compiling the holy scripture, **Guru Granth Sahib**, in 1604. He completed the Holy Water Tank at Amritsar and shifted his headquarters there. The city of Amristar became the holy centre of Sikhism. During Guru Arjan's tenure, two important events happened – Prince Khusro's shelter with the Guru, and the marriage proposal of the Guru's son to the daughter of the Diwan of Lahore. These events led to various complications that contributed to the Sikhs organizing themselves for the first time along military lines.

In turn, the son of Guru Arjan Dev became the sixth leader, Guru Hargobind (1595–1644). He witnessed the martyrdom of his father and offered armed resistance to the Mughal Empire. He was the first Sikh Guru to wear two swords, one representing *shakti* (power), the other *bhakti* (devotion), thus combining in him royalty and renunciation.

Guru Har Rai (1630–61), the seventh Guru, was the grandson of Guru Hargobind. He became Guru at the age of 14 and passed away at the age of 30. Guru Harkrishan (1656–64), the eighth Guru and second son of Guru Har Rai, was ordained Guru at the age of five but passed away at just eight years of age. Guru Teg Bahadur (1621–75) was the son of Guru Hargobind and became ninth Guru at the time of Aurangzeb, a Mughal emperor who ordered forcible conversions of Hindus to Islam. To save the Kashmiri Pandits, Guru Teg Bahadur sacrificed his life and was beheaded in 1675.

His son, Gobind Singh (1666–1708), became the tenth Guru. Fond of literary and artistic activities – he had 52 eminent poets working with him – he incorporated his father's hymns into the holy *Granth Book* and inaugurated the **Guru Granth Sahib** as a living Guru, the ultimate teacher of the Sikhs. He confronted the Mughal Empire under Aurangzeb, and despite losing all his sons in a series of battles still refused to embrace the Islamic faith. In 1699 Guru Gobind Singh gave a new order to the Sikh faith when he created the **Khalsa** ('Pure' religious community), whose members undertook to arm themselves and serve the **Panth** (Sikh community as a whole) militarily if need be.

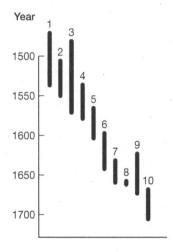

1 Nanak (1469–1539)

2 Angad (1504–52)

3 Amar Das (1479–1574)

4 Ram Das (1534–81)

5 Arjan Dev (1563–1606)

6 Hargobind (1595–1644)

7 Har Rai (1630–61)

8 Harkrishan (1656–64)

9 Teg Bahadur (1621–75)

10 Gobind Singh (1666–1708)

Figure 9.1   The ten Gurus: a timeline

Khalsa

The first five Gurus guaranteed the distinct identity of the Sikh community by creating a cohesive infrastructure. Guru Hargobind, Sixth Master, added a new dimension by wearing two swords, symbolic of the integration of spiritual and temporal authority, in order to defend against attacks from the Mughal army. The spirit of this integration was continued by Guru Gobind Singh when he created the *Khalsa*. He expounded the basic tenets of the Sikh faith, then challenged the audience to give over their lives to *dharma*. Five men offered themselves and were called the 'five beloved ones'. A ceremony took place in which the five beloved ones were baptized in the order of the *Khalsa* using *amrit* (nectar) made from water and sugar crystals prepared in an iron bowl and reverently stirred with a two-edged sword.

The Guru conferred on his followers the corporate identity of the *Khalsa* expressed through five emblems, which are popularly referred to as 'the five

160

Ks'. Together they form an indispensable part of the *Khalsa*, symbolizing the wearers' saintliness (*bhakti*). The first three Ks are *keshas* (hair), *kangha* (comb), *kachha* (short breeches), the latter two being the allied symbols of saintliness, symbolizing the virtue of cleanliness and continence. As symbols of strength the Guru gave them the next two Ks: *kirpan* (sword) and *kara* (bracelet), both made of pure steel, the latter serving as a symbol of restraint, to ensure that the sword hand is used only for righteous and defensive purposes. The new philosophy of the *Khalsa* represented a distinct deviation from the prevalent Indian and Semitic traditions. While initiating the first five beloved ones, the Guru himself was in turn initiated by them. This act marked a great revolutionary step in the history of religious philosophy. In abolishing the role of the personal guru, Guru Gobind Singh conferred a collective 'guruship' on the whole body of disciples. In doing this he gave shape to the *Khalsa* community which, from then onwards, would take the *Guru Granth Sahib* as their guide.

The institution of guruship had three aspects:

1 *Nirguna*, Impersonal Supreme Being;
2 *Guru-sabad*, words of the Guru, as incorporated in the *Guru Granth Sahib*;
3 *Sarguna* (Personal divinity) in the *Khalsa*.

This order of the *Khalsa* provided a practical example of how temporal authority should be integrated with the spiritual: spiritual sovereignty was bestowed on the *Guru Granth Sahib* and temporal sovereignty was bestowed on the *Khalsa* order through the five beloved ones.

 Scripture: *Guru Granth Sahib*

The original scripture, known as *Adi Granth*, was compiled by the fifth Guru, Arjan Dev, at Amritsar in 1604. Its fuller title, *Guru Granth Sahib*, was confirmed and ceremonially conferred on the scripture by the last Guru, Guru Gobind Singh, in 1708. The holy scripture consists of compositions made by the first five Gurus and the ninth Guru, as well as 349 hymns of their followers, known as **bhagats**. The criteria for selecting the compositions of the *bhagats* were *Nirguna* (impersonal absolute without attributes), religiosity and conformity to the basic tenets of the *Guru Granth Sahib*. Though these *bhagats* belonged to various regions with different backgrounds, yet their main doctrinal themes conform to the spirit of the scripture. Nonetheless, the reflections of their religious background remain.

Hence the ecumenical spirit of the *Guru Granth Sahib* is indicated by the inclusion of the compositions of the *bhagats*, the acknowledgement of their spiritual status and preservation of their identities. Another example of this spirit of cosmopolitanism is the provision in the scripture of an interfaith platform for discussion about religious matters as they arise in their individual cultures.

The message of the Gurus, as embedded in the *Guru Granth Sahib*, is spiritual, ethical and social. From birth to death, the role of the human as a working person, whatever his or her place in society, is to live a practical life and to gain cosmic consciousness. The holy scripture is installed in every **gurdwara** (Sikh place of worship) and certain ceremonial practices are observed in the morning and evening to revere the holy *Granth* as Guru.

The basic tenets of Sikh philosophy are:

- belief in One God; belief in the teachings of the ten Gurus;
- belief in *Guru Granth Sahib*;
- belief in the necessity of *amrit* and the *khande di pahul* (initiation ceremony).

The main pillars of Sikh thought are daily contemplation and prayer, hard work and the sharing of wealth with others.

 Teachings

God, self and divine will

Sikhism believes in the monotheistic concept of One God, who is Transcendent and Immanent; Impersonal (*Nirguna*) and Personal (*Sarguna*). The uniqueness of God is manifest in different ways. He is the only God. This absolute supremacy of God is apparent in the denial of the doctrine of incarnation or the concept of *trimurti* (the three gods of Brahma, Vishnu and Shivu) and idol-worship prevalent in Hindu society. God is defined as Creator, Sustainer and Destroyer, having all the metaphysical attributes, such as omnipotence, infinity and eternity. He is also described as Sovereign, Ineffable, Fearless and Benevolent. Though the stress in the holy scripture is on the unique, incomprehensible aspect of God as an unapproachable entity devoid of caste or creed, he is yet portrayed in his *Sarguna* aspect as dwelling in the innermost depths of man's heart. God is ever-present yet is concealed, detached and illimitable.

Figure 9.2 Ek Onkar ('There is only one God'): the first two words in the *Guru Granth Sahib*
Source: Adopted from infoaboutsikhs.com

As for the soul's relation to God, the *Guru Granth Sahib* says: 'the Lord abides in the soul and the soul in the Lord.' The aim of a human's life is to rediscover the real nature of the self. It is in no way different from God but indulgence in mundane aspirations reinforce the ego and strengthen the false notion of separateness. Although the ego is considered the greatest malady, its cure also lies within it, if one can discover its true nature. The stress lies on the transcendence of man from self-centeredness to God-centeredness, and the identification of his finite consciousness with cosmic consciousness. By discovering the true nature of the soul, one understands the real nature of God. The path recommended to reach this goal is the practice of truth, *bhakti* (devotion), the sublimation of one's ego, a life of detachment, contemplation of the divine name, all with the help of Guru and divine grace.

In the Sikh religion the concept of divine will as an imperative has a specific metaphysical significance. Divine will is all-pervasive and immanent, ineffable and inscrutable. It manifests itself in different ways that are incomprehensible to the human mind. Creation and the sustenance of the universe are in accordance with divine will. Self-transcendence is to be attained by submitting to the divine will. This submission does not mean bondage or determinism, but is indeed real freedom or real knowledge of one's innermost self. By realizing the divine will, one merges in truth, attains pleasure, conquers the mind, becomes detached and fearless. And in so doing one cultivates all the qualities that bring about the spiritual and moral enlightenment of humanity.

Divine grace and salvation

God cannot be understood with intelligence but can be attained through grace. Some humans are destined to receive grace (*bakhshish*) while others are condemned to whirl about transmigration in accordance with the deeds of their past actions. Though a mystery, grace is an overwhelming experience that can be earned by way of prayer and devotion.

The Sikh religion repudiates Indian speculations about a future life and stresses instead that heaven and hell are mental states to be experienced here and now. The immortality of the soul is also conceived in the sense of realizing eternal values in the temporal world. While the Hindu notions of traditional ethics about *karma*, transmigration and release are not taken in the same sense, the idea of the inevitability of retribution or reward for one's actions is accepted in a modified form. Our deeds lead us towards God or away from God. Therefore *karma* and rebirth are closely related to the moral life of men and women. The mystery of the cause of humanity's bondage and ultimate goal of life are explicitly dealt with in Sikh scripture. Birth and death happen because of desires. Those who contemplate the divine word remain detached from worldly entanglements and can achieve emancipation from them. It is stated that human life has passed through innumerable existences, the number being 840,000, which neither increases nor decreases. Birth and death form a continual cycle. In every birth, a human will perform actions in accordance with the accumulation of his or her past deeds.

Real perfection lies in restoring the original self through identification with the impersonal consciousness, which is the foundation of the psychophysical complex, not only of the individual but of the whole world. By surrendering to the divine will through contemplation of the word (*sabad*) of Guru, people lose their egocentricity and attain what is termed 'cosmic consciousness'. The actions and thoughts of a person who has attained this state are unmotivated and free from restrictions. The enlightened person can thus help in the further progress of the world by becoming an instrument of divine light. Such people perform actions in an altruistic spirit and participate in the working of God for the fulfilment of a worldly purpose.

 # Ethics

According to Sikh ethics, attainment of spiritual fulfilment is not possible without leading a virtuous life. The latter involves a continuous striving for perfection. The practice of universal moral norms – wisdom, courage, contentment, justice, humility, truthfulness, endurance – is desirable not only to cultivate inner harmony but also to promote good interpersonal relations at the cosmic level. It is believed that the external paraphernalia of religion, even acts of charity, are worthless if devoid of the divine name. These activities only enhance man's ego, thus creating a barrier between the person and God.

 # Sikh institutions

The importance of human conduct is clearly evident in the foundation of the three cardinal precepts of Sikhism: honest labour, contemplation of the divine name and sharing with others. These precepts are simultaneously functional at the individual and social levels. The Sikh religious institutions of *gurdwara*, *Guru*, **sangat**, **langar** and *dharamsal* all encourage the concept of community worship and provide a model for an egalitarian society.

Gurdwara

Gurdwara is a central institution of the Sikh community. The term was first used by Guru Hargobind, meaning 'home or abode' of the Guru, where the *Guru Granth Sahib* is installed. The congregational worship and *Guru Granth Sahib* are essential features of the Sikh community life. A theological and political status has been attached to the *gurdwara*, especially the Golden Temple at Amritsar, since the time of Guru Hargobind. He installed the Akal

Takht (throne of the Guru) adjacent to the Golden Temple as an example of the integration of spiritual and temporal authority. Other *gurdwaras* were built to meet social and religious needs. Historical *gurdwaras*, for example, mark important occasions in Sikh history, such as Sis Ganj in Delhi, where Guru Teg Bahadur was martyred. There are five *gurdwaras* that have special sanctity, known as *takhats* (thrones of the Guru). These include the Akal Takht at the Golden Temple, the supreme seat whence important edicts concerning the community are issued; Patna Sahib, the birth place of Guru Gobind Singh; Anandpur Sahib, where the *Khalsa Panth* originated; Nander Sahib, where Guru Gobind Singh became one with the Infinite, relinquishing his body; and Damdama Sahib.

The central *gurdwara* for Sikhs all over the world is the Golden Temple at Amritsar, built on the site where Guru Nanak is said to have meditated. Every *gurdwara* is open to all, irrespective of caste, creed or status. All who enter must remove their shoes, wash their hands and feet and cover their head as tokens of respect for the Guru. Everybody can participate in the **kirtan** and *ardas* (devotion and prayer) and can make offerings (*prasad*) and eat cooked food in the community kitchen (*langar*). All the community ceremonies, festivals and *gurpurbs* (anniversaries) are celebrated in the *gurdwaras*.

Guru, the divine preceptor

The word Guru literally means 'one who removes darkness' or 'enlightener'. According to Guru Nanak, the first and foremost Guru is God Himself, meaning the Word of God. After the death of Guru Nanak no doubt this tradition continued through successive Gurus, but Guru Gobind Singh, the tenth Guru, formally invested its authority in the *Guru Granth Sahib*. For the spiritual disciple the most imperative need is to contemplate the *sabad* (word) of Guru and to lead his life in accordance with those teachings.

Sangat: holy congregation

Sangat, literally meaning 'holy congregation', is an institution with far-reaching social implications. It inculcates the feeling of brotherhood, promoting equality and providing opportunities to serve others. Historically this institution has played a vital role as a forum for discussion of common concerns and in planning and expediting programmes of social improvement.

Dharamsal: place to practise righteousness

Dharamsal literally means a place for the practice of *dharma*, or righteousness. It is a place to hold congregations regularly for the recitation and contemplation of *bani*. These *dharamsals* were also intended to provide accommodation and food for wayfarers.

Langar: free community kitchen

The *langar* is a unique Sikh institution established to put into practice the basic tenets of Sikhism, namely, honest labour and sharing with others. This institution of the community kitchen has social implications in that it should provide equally for all and sundry, without any discrimination of caste or creed.

 # Community life

The disciplines

The Sikh community is bound strictly by instructions laid down by the Gurus for the observance of ceremonies and modes of worship. Besides *kirtan* (devotion), another significant feature of congregational worship is *katha* (discourse) and lectures organized on special occasions. Lectures are given on the lives of the Gurus and events in Sikh history, especially during *gurpurb* (anniversary) celebrations. Sikh missionary schools and colleges, religious libraries and special museums have also been established, as have hospitals in the name of the Gurus.

The unique tenets of the Sikh polity are *sangat* (holy congregation), *Guru Granth* and *Khalsa Panth* (plural executive), the *Gurmatta* (collective will of the people), and the *Sarbat Khalsa* (democratic and egalitarian polity).

To maintain community discipline and make collective decisions, an executive council of five chosen ones represents the community in all important matters. Those who fail to keep the discipline have to undergo penance. This would normally be a physical act of some nature, such as washing utensils, cleaning the floor and so on, which the penitent must accept without question. Liturgical texts from the holy scripture are meant for daily recitation by the individual members of the *Khalsa*, and the *Sukhmani* and *Asa di Var* are recited and sung collectively every morning in the *gurdwaras*.

Ceremonies, rituals and festivals

The main festivals celebrated by the Sikh community are Baisakhi, Diwali and Holla Mohalla. Guru Arjan Dev ordained the celebration of Baisakhi at Harmandir, as opposed to the Hindu practice at Haridwar. This festival is a socio-political and religious occasion, important for the Sikh community as it is associated with the origination of the *Khalsa* by Guru Gobind Singh. The festival of Diwali was celebrated first by Baba Buddha to commemorate Guru Hargobind's release from the imprisonment of the Mughals in the Gwalior Fort. The Sikh community celebrates three important anniversaries (*gurpurbs*): Guru Nanak's birthday, Guru Gobind Singh's birthday, the martyrdom of Guru Arjan Dev and also the birthday of Guru Granth Parkash Divas, the founder of Sikhism.

Women in Sikhism

If we analyse the contributions of Sikh women to the development of the religious life and spirituality there is no doubt that they form the foundation of Sikh life. Prominent women belonged largely to the Guru's family, as mother, daughter, wife or sister. Their contribution has been made in various ways, such as looking after domestic affairs during the missionary tours of the Gurus; assisting them in the implementations of their ideals; accompanying the Gurus during their preaching; helping the Gurus in making an impartial choice of successor; carrying out works of social welfare; offering sacrifices for the Guru-husband, their sons and grandsons, for the cause of the *Panth*; and serving as beacon lights to the *Panth*.

 # Socio-religious movements

In the course of history, certain religious movements emerged from within the folds of Sikhism. Many have now either disappeared or separated from the parent body. The latter includes some missionary movements that still consider themselves as Sikh but have tended to deviate from Sikh orthodoxy. For instance, the Nirankari movement, founded by Baba Dayal (1783–1854), rejected idolatry and stressed worship of the Formless God and became popular as an indigenous agent of reformation. The Nirankaris differ from mainstream Sikhs in worshipping more Gurus than the ten official Gurus; they also disapprove of the militant *Khalsa*. The nineteenth-century Namdhari movement placed greater emphasis on the contemplation of the divine name. Its followers are known as *kukas* (shouters) because in a moment of ecstasy they dance and cry out. They are also distinguished by their different mode of living and belief in a living Guru.

Figure 9.3 The Sikh emblem: the Khanda. The double-edged sword in the middle symbolizes divine justice, freedom and authority; the Chakra (circle) signifies 'Ek Onkar', the continuity and oneness of God; the curved swords flanking the Chakra represent the spiritual and political leadership of the Gurus

Source: Adopted from www.sunion.warwick.ac.uk

Conclusion

To recap, the Sikh religion, one of the major world faiths, is a revelatory prophetic religion which, despite passing through various critical phases, has flourished due to its distinctive spiritual and ethical ideals. Its moral integrity is reinforced by significant historical events, such as the martyrdom of Guru Arjan Dev and Guru Teg Bahadhur, the sacrifices of the four sons of Guru Gobind Singh and of other Sikhs. Its holy scripture, *Guru Granth Sahib*, is not confined to the boundaries of space and time. Rather it encompasses the whole of humanity. It can provide solace and bliss through its cosmopolitan spirit, interfaith dialogue, concern for spiritual transformation, and it is the source of perennial solutions to the emerging problems of human life.

 ## QUESTIONS

1 How would you define the cosmopolitan spirit of the *Guru Granth Sahib*?

2 Define the major universal teachings of Sikh religion.

3 Define the uniqueness of Sikh institutions.

 # Glossary

bhagats followers of the Gurus whose writings are included in holy scripture
dharamsal place to practise righteousness
gurdwara place of worship
Guru Granth Sahib holy scripture of the Sikhs and the Eleventh Guru
Khalsa Sikh religious community
kirtan devotion
langar communal kitchen
Panth Sikh community
sangat holy congregation

 # Further reading

Bala, Shashi, 'Women and Worship: The Sikh Perspective', in Thottakare, Augustine (ed.), *Women and Worship: Perspectives from the World Religions* (Bangalore: Dharmaram Publications, 2000).

Banerjee, I. B., *Evolution of the Khalsa*, Vol. 1 (Calcutta: A. K. Mukherjee, 1979).

Cole, W. Owen and Sambhi, P. S., *The Sikhs: Their Religious Beliefs and Practices* (New Dehli, Vikas, 1978).

Gupta, H. R., *Studies in Later Mughal History of the Punjab* (Lahore: Minerva Book Shop, 1994).

Kaur, Madanjit, *The Golden Temple: Past and Present* (Amritsar: GNDU, 1986).

Singh, Ishar, *Nanakism – A New World Order: Temporal and Spiritual* (New Delhi: Ranjit Publishing House, 1976).

Singh, Kapur (eds Singh, Piar and Kaur, Madanjit), *Parasaraprasana* (Amritsar: GNDU, 1989).

Singh, Teja and Singh, Ganda, *A Short History of the Sikhs* (Calcutta: Orient Longmans, 1950).

Conclusion

Santanu K. Patro

If I were asked what is the single most important aspect of life that the human race has preserved from time immemorial, my answer without any doubt would be religion. Religious belief and practice have survived under the most adverse conditions, through the evolution of many faiths over thousands of years and the constant challenges of new thinking. To conclude this book I take a broad look at the relations between religion, culture and society, expanding the themes of the Introduction. I suggest that religion has an important part to play in the contemporary world and that this is enhanced when people of all faiths understand each other and work together.

Interaction between religion and local culture

Religious traditions have survived primarily for two reasons. First, the community of believers who put their faith into practice understand it as a transforming encounter with the spiritual – the meaning of this transformation, or liberation, is understood at a local level and depends primarily on political, social and economic needs. The second reason is religion's ability to adapt to a particular context – one of the key aspects of world religions is that they are able to reinterpret their features to fit into 'hostile' terrain. Judaism and Hinduism, for example, managed to do this though they are both territorial in nature like the primal religious traditions. In other words, many religions are becoming more 'mission-oriented' in their endeavour to make themselves universal. Today Hinduism is influencing the West by its inclusive philosophy and integrating certain religious teachings, such as yoga, into science and technology. It also influences the New Age movements with its alternative spirituality, such as naturalism and vegetarianism.

In today's world, migration and missionary endeavour have brought incoming religions into contact with the traditional faiths embedded in a region. Such a pluralistic presence of faiths has not made religion any less significant, nor has one become superior to the other. Religions have survived side by side. Even primal religions, considered to be the oldest form of religious tradition, still thrive in a modern industrial setting. When migrating from their country of origin to another, people take their beliefs and practices with them. As a result the world's religions are found in most countries. In particular the nations of Europe and North America are being challenged by faiths and ideologies from Asia.

The chapters of this book have demonstrated that religious traditions shape history, culture and society. By culture I mean our behaviour, identity and ethnicity. For example, when Christianity came to the tribes of north-east India, the tribes overwhelmingly responded to the gospel. Today the population in states such as Mizoram and Nagaland is 90 per cent Christian. Christian institutions attempted to remove all the traditional religious features of the tribes and introduced Western culture in the form of music, dress and worship. Yet there are small minorities who wanted to revive their own religious traditions. These indigenous groups adopted some of the Christian practices in their temples and shrines, institutionalized the worship and reformulated their liturgy and doctrine in line with Christianity. So they introduced the form of a world religion into their primal tradition in order to survive. Christianity today is influencing tribal traditions and lifestyles in that part of the world. There is a two-way change operating: a religion may bring about many positive and constructive changes to the existing social structure, and it frequently alters the cultural norms and values of the country; but the religion is also altered by local cultural norms.

Have you observed this two-way cultural influence when religious traditions meet each other?

Most of the primal religions of Asia and Africa have survived alongside the major religions of the world. Countries such as China, Japan, North Korea and Siberian Russia continue to have their own traditional religions, which are inextricably linked to the geography of their lands. Most cultures in which primal religion has been practised have effectively adapted, even today, to the emerging socio-cultural-scientific world-views. Religions adapt to different cultures, people and time. For example, although Europe and parts of Africa may be called Christian, there are many things that are distinct to their culture. While Europe's Christianity has matured itself under the influence of Empiricism, the Christianity of Africa continues to evolve in the context of traditional religious beliefs and practices. Shamanistic and magical world-views continue to interact with world religions in Africa. Furthermore in the West the values and practices of pre-Christian society are re-emerging. Some of the national festivals and celebrations have pre-Christian roots. For example, Halloween – All Hallows Eve – in the USA has little to do with Christian faith but has its roots in primal traditions. Likewise Europe received many of its ancient traditions after interaction with local culture.

In what ways are the thoughts and practices of your religious tradition influenced by earlier traditions?

✳ Religions and society

After reading the chapters on each of the religious traditions written by authors who practise their faith actively and take their particular religion seriously, both in personal and corporate life, one may reflect on how religion, in general terms, continues to influence society in a positive way. By society I mean our networks and institutions, health and education systems and the like. Religious communities already work with a sense of spiritual experience to help those who are in need, and address global issues that affect our earth. Christian missionaries in the eighteenth and nineteenth centuries brought a form of health care and education to Africa and Asia that encouraged the creation of new egalitarian societies. Islam, Buddhism and Hinduism have all been seen to be more active in 'missionary activities' in the West in the twentieth century, in particular by providing an alternative spirituality to the West, which suffers from a 'poverty of spirituality'. Society, however secular it might be, can recognize that religions may play important societal roles. For example, in Germany less than 20 per cent of the population attend church yet more than 80 per cent pay their taxes to the Church. One reason for this is that the Church is viewed as a major player in addressing the problems of human society, such as poverty, hunger, environmental issues, social justice and so on in the countries of the South. Christianity as a modern religion has denounced many of the evils that have been counterproductive for the community. Likewise Swami Vivekananda and Annie Besant introduced a new way of thinking for Hindus in India and redefined Hinduism for the Western mindset. They rejected the caste system and added a social dimension to Hindu spirituality. Religion, in a sense, has provided a social dimension to the community, thereby making it socially relevant to the faith community.

> In what ways do you see your religious tradition and others around you contributing to wider society?

Providing a social dimension is not the only way to make religions relevant to the community. The idea of the supernatural or the transcendental is universally acknowledged. The power of the beyond is recognized by many, and such a power remains unfathomable, even to the scientific mind. Some understand God as a being who creates, sustains and destroys, others simply acknowledge the superior power that regulates the order of the universe. According to Eastern religion that power is the ethical order, and however we conceive of God, God is in control of the universe. Recent controversies in the West may give the impression that science and religion are incompatible. Yet many scientists recognize that science has not answered conclusively on religious issues because it is asking different questions. Its questions about *how* the universe came into being, for example, may have appeared to challenge elements of the belief system, but science cannot properly answer the *why* questions. It does not give answers about the meaning of our existence. Exploring the relationship with the transcendental reaches beyond the realm of rational knowledge.

 ## Encounter with God

In Eastern religious systems there is a dominant world-view that is known as *rita*, the universal and ethical principle that regulates the order of the universe. Nothing is possible without *rita*. Sun, moons, stars, rain all do their duties in order to sustain the universe. If one of these elements fails to perform its prescribed duty then the whole order of the universe is affected. Hindus would say that the advent of global warming is due to changes made in the universal order. Changes to the seasons, the rise in temperature, depletion of the ozone layer, all occur because the system of *rita* is not fulfilled. Religion, being holistic, relates to both the sacred and the secular and therefore addresses many of the pressing issues the world is facing. Religious beliefs and practices not only help the faith community to understand its social role and functions, they also attempt to answer some of the key social issues as they relate to, for example, ecology, the economy, caste and violence. Furthermore, the fact that religion influences every sphere of life encourages the religious community to intensify its faith in God.

> Think about how you encounter God. Do you think other people encounter God in different ways? If so, how?
>
> Do you find your own faith strengthened by understanding other religious traditions? If so how?

 ## Peace through dialogue

As an attempt to know God, religion has many facets that help the community to live in harmony with neighbour, nature and the environment – all elements of God's creation. Many in the faith community use their faith to promote peace in the world. In the last few decades religious leaders and scholars have come together to promote a deeper understanding of each other through dialogue in order to achieve great peace. For example, some religious leaders belonging to the Abrahamic faiths – Judaism, Christianity and Islam – have discussed together some of the pressing issues they face in their own geopolitical context, conscious of the Palestinian cause and international terrorism. Dialogue helps people of different faiths to live together. The co-existence of people with different faiths and the development of a pluralistic understanding have become a necessity in today's modern urban society. Interfaith dialogue in a pluralistic society provides an opportunity to remove many of the misgivings held about other people's religions, and helps to promote harmonious living.

Interfaith dialogue must address two pertinent issues. First it must take place more and more in the 'base community', moving away from scholarly debate into the daily interaction between people of all faiths, as well as no faith. While dialogue remains solely in an academic forum it helps scholars to appreciate each other but it rarely influences the majority to live together positively in a pluralistic context. Second, dialogue must have a strong social dimension, tackling issues of poverty and hunger, ecological problems, violence and religious fundamentalism, terrorism, caste and ethnicity.

So far interfaith dialogue has usually remained an intellectual endeavour addressing issues of God, doctrine and faith as a theological or philosophical exercise. Unless religious communities come together and share the problems the world is facing, our contribution towards bringing about peace, justice and equality here on earth will be limited. Some parts of rural India support many faiths that have lived together for centuries. These base communities always shared their religious festivals and celebrated them together as a social function. But in recent times, due to the impact of modernization, the teachings have assumed exclusive characteristics. Faiths have become privatized and distinguished from other belief systems. As a result there is a growing phenomenon of intolerance. Claims of exclusivity (which means those who do not adhere to the professed system are damned) and attempts at indoctrination (which means persuading people to believe certain things) are becoming more common. Therefore any discussion on the theology of God, for example, does not result in promoting co-existence since nobody wants to compromise their own understanding of God. To address this intolerance and to promote harmony, many continue to celebrate different religious festivals and participate in various religious functions. I would say this is dialogue in practice. Faith communities must work together at a local level and it is important that this should happen throughout the world. Unless the global community is sensitive to religious feelings it may become merely a political entity. This will not help eradicate the problems that society faces today. For example, hatred, violence and terrorism are not religious tenets, though religious fanaticism may lead people to commit such atrocities. One can use religion to legitimize terrorism. Parochial interpretations of scriptures and traditions and 'hate language' are rooted in the politics of violence. Promoting inclusive community living is a step towards removing the misunderstanding and prejudice that beleaguers peoples of different faiths.

Can you think of ways in which your faith encourages you to promote peace? Do you work with people of other religious traditions to achieve this?

The political perception that democracy and secularism can provide an alternative solution to the crisis that exists in parts of Africa and Asia is not convincing. Many of today's democracies suffer from a lack of democratization at grass-roots level. Unless there is adequate and rightful political participation by the masses it will not be possible to break the deadlock. On that score religion must be taken seriously as contributing to the well-being of many at a grass-roots level. We must, however, recognize the danger of the world becoming divided along religious lines by the sectarian and the parochial, often guided by narrowly conceived world-views of religion. When religious people take up arms based on literal interpretations of religious teachings, there is always likely to be bloodshed. History will remind us of the terror produced in the name of religion over the centuries. Religions together need to address many pressing issues. Instead of judging the values of other religions it is important that they stay focused on issues that concern the global earth. The ecological crisis, war and weapons of mass destruction, HIV & AIDS, poverty and hunger are some of the pressing issues. It is possible for us to tackle the problems if faith communities engage themselves in helping to build new communities that are inclusive of race, gender and ethnicity.

I suggest here that the truly godly way to act in the face of human divisions and violence is to work for peace with people of other faiths. So it is more important to act in a loving way than to concern ourselves with right belief and practice. Do you agree?

 Religious communities

Religious leaders influence their faith communities and invoke the name of God. Such invocations must serve the purpose of blessing and building up others rather than cursing and nurturing hatred of those who are not part of us. I believe it is the collective responsibility of faith communities to strive for a just and harmonious world. Faith communities, irrespective of their tradition, must attempt to build an inclusive community where everyone is welcome. Such a world-view celebrates God's appreciation of plurality and diversity. The world is in danger of becoming fragmented and destroyed due to the crisis it is facing on all fronts. Humans are responsible as the stewards of God's world.

How can religious communities be inclusive and appreciate diversity? Is it possible?

In the contemporary world, the institutionalizing of religion and exclusivity of its controlling hierarchy are challenged by the more egalitarian and community-oriented religious teachings. This mutually dependent form of religious community is easily accessible and addresses immediate needs. Above all it helps faith communities work to creating a better world. Thus for them religion opens up new avenues and challenges for the common good. If we are to bring about lasting transformation of religious communities it is necessary to be critical of existing religious institutions, their hierarchies and political structure. Often it is a long and complicated process to bring about any change in religious traditions, but faith always gives hope for the future. It is hope, the essence of life, that makes people pursue religion and experience God differently.

> Do you agree that religious communities should aim to create a better world? In what ways do you think this can be done?
> What does 'egalitarian' mean? Is this something religious communities should aim for? Why?

 # Action

I have urged readers to understand other religions through living encounters with people of different faiths, appreciating faith communities and individual believers. In so doing I believe we will understand our own religious faith more deeply and inclusively. We will also challenge any prejudices that we might be carrying and overcome barriers of misunderstanding.

I have also encouraged readers to search for ways in which religions can offer solutions to some of the pressing issues our earth is facing – international terrorism, religious fundamentalism, gender discrimination, ecological crisis, war and so on. While the first question is about community effort at a local level, this second question calls for a world perspective and some self-diagnosis, looking at the faults of our own faith and the contribution it can make.

Finally, I have suggested that it is desirable to create an inclusive community that transcends all forms of identity, whether race, caste or class, for the greater good. In a globalized world, common understanding and common care for all is vital. For this to happen, religious communities would need to focus on their common causes.

To conclude, one must say that religion is alive and very much relevant to our time. It renews our life and gives us hope and aspirations. It enables us to confront the world of unresolved problems. If only religions could become more vibrant and proactive in addressing some of the key issues facing our earth and society, and bring spirituality down to earth, I would be optimistic for a better future.

Index

Abu Bakr 141
Africa: Christianity in 171
African Instituted Churches (AICs)
   128, 133
Āgamas 45, 82–3
Al-Ashari, Abu al-Hasan 151
Ali ibn Abi Talib 141
almsgiving 150
Amar Das, Guru 159
ancestors 25
Angad, Guru: and Islam 159
anicca 66
Animism 19
anthropology of religion 12–13
anti-Judaism 98
anti-reductionism 16–17
antisemitism 98–101
Apostolic Decree 124
Arabia: before Islam 137–9
Arjan Dev, Guru 159, 166
Asharia School 151
atman: in Buddhism 66; in Hinduism
   47, 53
Atonement 129

Besant, Annie 172
Bhagavat Gita 46
Bhakti movement 56–7
Bible, the 123–4; and monotheism
   92–4; *see also* New Testament; Old
   Testament
Brahman: in Buddhism 65; in
   Hinduism 46–7, 52, 53–4
Buddhism 6, 7, 8; *atman* 66; devotion
   and prayers 72–3; ethical path
   76–7; Five Precepts 66–7; Four
   Noble Truths 67–8; God in 71–2;
   karma 68; missionary activity 172;
   modern developments 74–5; *nirvana*
   70–1; Noble Eightfold Path 68; and
other religions 73–4; and politics
   75; reality in 66; *samsara* 69–70;
   schools of thought 71–2;
   teachings 65; women in 63; *see
   also* Mahayana Buddhist tradition;
   Theravada Buddhist tradition; Zen
   Buddhism

caste system 49–50, 172
Catholic Church 126, 127, 131, 134
Celtic Christianity 38
Chanukah 105, 106–7
Christianity 6, 7, 8–9; in Africa 171;
   ethics 130–1; in Europe 169; future
   of 132–5; God in 127–8; human
   beings in 130; in India 171; and
   Islam 132, 155–6; and Judaism
   111–13; missionary activity 172;
   non-Western 31, 34–6; and other
   faiths 134; peace through dialogue
   173; in primal traditions 37; *see also*
   Celtic Christianity
Church, the 124–8
comparative religion 12
Constantine, Emperor 125
cosmic religions 21, 23
Creation, the 10
culture: and religion 4, 170–1

Dabru Emet 113
Dalai Lama 75–6
dharamsal 165
dharma 42
dukkha 66

Earth Mother 24, 25
earth, the 24
eidetic vision 16
Embassy of God, The 133
epoche 16

ND - #0046 - 270325 - C0 - 216/138/13 - PB - 9780281062508 - Gloss Lamination